THE
CONSPIRACY
TO
SILENCE
THE
SON
OF
GOD

TAL BROOKE
GENERAL EDITOR

HARVEST HOUSE PUBLISHERS
Eugene, Oregon 97402

Cover by Left Coast Design, Portland, Oregon

THE CONSPIRACY TO SILENCE THE SON OF GOD

Copyright © 1998 by Tal Brooke
Published by Harvest House Publishers
Eugene, Oregon 97402

Library of Congress Cataloging-in-Publication Data

Brooke, Tal—
        The conspiracy to silence the son of God. / Tal Brooke, general editor.
        p.   cm.
        Includes bibliographical references.
        ISBN 1–56507–819-5
        1. Jesus Christ—History of doctrines—20th century.   I. Brooke, Tal.
    BT198.F336   1998   97–29013
    232.9—dc21   CIP

        98 99 00 01 02 03 04 05 / BC / 10 9 8 7 6 5 4 3 2 1

Contents

The Conspiracy to Silence the Son of God

Tal Brooke

There has been a conspiracy to silence the Son of God from the moment He declared His message and walked through the streets of Jerusalem almost 2000 years ago. That opposition led to His crucifixion, clear and simple. He predicted it and it happened. It was an event that was anything but random. It was cleverly plotted, orchestrated, and foreseen prophetically.

Christ then predicted that this same opposition—the conspiracy to ultimately and finally silence the Son of God by removing all evidence of Him from the Earth—would mount through history, especially targeting those who bore His name. It would reach unprecedented proportions right before His return, when public opposition would be at the boiling point. His people who refused to be silenced by renouncing their beliefs publicly, as in the days of the Roman Emperor Domitian, would be forcibly silenced to the point of death. This too is predicted. It is a period of history that still lies ahead in our uncertain future.

The Mysteries of Opposition

In some very real ways—and as you will learn in this book—this opposition proves Jesus is the Son of God and the only one worth following. It also shows that the direction of history sought by the opposition will lead them into a trap of cosmic proportions. It will be anything but a dull or unexciting time to be alive. Whatever side of the divide you stand on, pro or con, the patterns of history—its details—should deeply concern you. They should jar you and open your eyes.

The final outcome, Christ's return, is hugely positive for the entire universe. It is far less so for those who have dedicated their lives to destroying Him and His people. His people *cannot* be destroyed; they are citizens of eternity who live "in Him" in a way far more profound than any rival New Age mystical paradigm. It is a mystery that especially confounds the self-proclaimed wise of this Earth, those who oppose Him and the message He brings to their ears. Harder than any diamond, it unmasks who they really are, stripping their grandiosity in the noonday sun of truth. So they seek to wipe out the messenger and His message. But it is an opposition whose span is temporal, that will pass like a dying flame.

Opposition to the Son of God, His message, and His people has mounted alarmingly in our own era. It could take 20 years, 100 years, or more for this opposition to reach the critical global level. (Christians have already been executed in the former Soviet Union, communist China, and other places.) The controlled hostility of the moment in the West could escalate almost anytime into open opposition. There really isn't much standing in the way to prevent this from happening. Public consensus—at one time the major barrier—has shifted dramatically, and rather than standing in the way, could actually turn into an explosive wave that could crash down on Christians.

There are layers of reasons for this. Some of them you will never know about. Many you perhaps already know about. And others you will learn about in this book. It is a long-standing opposition that is ancient, natural, *and* supernatural. Some of the intelligence behind the opposition is almost beyond comprehension, even in the small details of the day-to-day arena, in one continuous thread from the ancient world to the present.

Over the last 2000 years, this opposition to Christ and His message has waxed and waned. During the centuries that the West unhesitatingly identified its foundation as biblical, based on absolutes created by an infinite and holy God who designed the universe with moral, spiritual, and physical laws, the opposition remained in the closet. It was forced to remain low-key, gloved, and cunning. After all, the public was churchgoing and loyal to their God, embracing His revealed wisdom in the great issues of life. These were the very masses the opposition knew had to one day be turned. Yet almost none among the opposition dared come out into the spotlight to wage war on Christ directly—at least not during a period that lasted hundreds of years right up to the Edwardian era. Now things are different, very different. And the masses have turned, basing their lives on other things and going to and fro in pleasure and confusion.

Those who opposed Christ and His message, especially when Christendom was a force to be reckoned with, knew that the world had to be slowly bent. By a process of gradualism and assimilation, changes were introduced. Civilized society needed a gentler slope in this long-range culture war. Certain "daring" philosophers, scientists, and literary figures were needed, and appeared right on cue, like actors appearing on a stage. They accrued growing acclaim. Inevitably the "open-minded" who embraced change were the intelligentsia and the wealthy.

Charles Darwin would be embraced for his theories that argued away the need for a God to explain life and existence. Karl Marx could now find the right opening to advance evolutionary socialism (known as communism). Somewhere on this progressive ladder, a D. H. Lawrence might become a *cause célèbre* for "daring to speak out honestly" about sexual desires and sensual extravagances—what men's lower natures naturally craved. This paved the way for public resentment over the fact that "religious" taboos, perhaps mere superstitions, kept people hemmed in and held them back from the "full experience of life." Sigmund Freud would then add fuel to this fire, explaining that passions had to be released and explored, not repressed.

Moral barriers that once restrained society were coming down. "Western Civ," as Stanford University loves to call it, eventually turned on its axis. Now the culture war was heating up.

What had been a slow and steady process of change, lasting for centuries, accelerated in this century, above all during the sixties when my generation rejected the traditional absolutes of biblical thought in exchange for new models of life and belief, all in a gut rejection of the "old." We sought "consciousness expansion" tinged with pleasure and the good life. New humanist mystical models for life and society were embraced, anticipating an "Aquarian Age" of liberation and change. It was like a big colorful psychedelic rock concert, a youth experience we thought would never end—"Strawberry Fields Forever." We knew we were in the dance of the hour and had history in our hands. But we were not the active agents of social change we thought we were. We were the ones whose buttons were being pushed, the "useful idiots" of a far larger revolution. What role did I play?

I went to India to become enlightened—after a telescoping of broad-range life experiences that seemed to compact decades—and spent two years in Mysore and Andhra Pradesh, South India. I was passionately engaged in a pursuit of cosmic consciousness and final liberation. I had been the inner-circle disciple of a magnetic figure, Sai Baba, who boldly claimed to be God and who appeared to back up this claim with signs and wonders. But he was not who he said he was. I realized all of this in a terrible revelation that took only seconds to happen but a 400-page book to explain (see *Lord of the Air*). Then something else happened to me in a South Indian hotel room—*I came to Christ.* I was apprehended by the Son of God and a radical change came over me.

The Christianity I had disdained for so long suddenly became alive in ways I could have never known. At a very tangible moment, a great presence filled my soul, and a massive weight lifted from me. *I changed.* All the barriers and caricatures I had previously erected against Christ dissolved. I realized how deeply I had been deceived.

In my earlier years I had never been exposed to genuine Christianity. My culture of the sixties, and the sophisticated atheistic home in which I grew up, in England, Europe, and the Middle East, excluded Christ by definition. The dull church on the corner with its sleepy parishioners always seemed irrelevant and doomed to extinction, mere monuments of a bygone era.

I had become involved in the occult at a prodigiously early age, always looking for my own answers to life and existence. I did not learn things by reading about them in the public library, but went out into the fields of experience. I also knew what it was like to see the universe through post-Christian, mystical eyes, fully divorced from anything Christian. It is truly another consciousness that is completely foreign to Christians who have never lived on the other side.

Since that era of the sixties, things have rapidly changed, carrying us into a multicultural age that anticipates a different world, a *unified* one. As the 2000 year mark of the anniversary of the birth of Christ approaches, opposition is heating up. One day it will equal and surpass that seen in the early church. What forms has this opposition against Christ and the Christian faith taken? An extraordinary variety.

A Think Tank Experiment in the Laboratory of History

It is time to view history through a different lens. I will use a telescoping conspiratorial approach, from a devil's advocate position, because it is dramatic and powerful and helps make the point.

Let us pretend—so that we can take a fresh look at what is happening—that we are members of an enormous think tank of hereditary initiates and geniuses whose sole purpose is to rid the world of Christ, Christians, and the Christian faith. Our goal is to erase Christ from history, burning the books and evidence of Christianity, so that the greater masses living in the world will never be tainted by its message. (Indeed, perhaps our group would like to be the messiah for the masses.) Let us assume that our means to this end will be ruthless and variegated with almost boundless resources as time goes on.

In our think tank experiment there will be times we will merely prescribe what we think is needed—not presuming we can manipulate all the events of history but merely presenting ideal catalysts (like the French Revolution) that would serve our long-range purpose. The aim is a post-Christian world order under our influence and control.

As in the heat of real war, when people and property are being swept up in destruction, we will do anything—repeat, *anything*—to achieve our end. If it's "the geniuses against the idiots," it is only a matter of time for this conquest to be complete, that is, unless the hand of God or some genuine revival like the Great Awakening intervenes. If the contest is one of human cunning alone, it is an open-and-shut case. In this agenda, we are certainly not hampered by any Christian concepts of conscience and honesty. We have a far wider base of resources against a group whose hands are ethically tied and who tend to be very naïve about evil.

Attacking from the Inside

If we followed the model of the virus or leaven—*invasion under camouflage*—we would change Christendom from within. We would enter and infect the host, changing the genetic structure—in this case affecting the faithful transmission of its beliefs over time—the same way a virus changes a cell's DNA. We would become members of the church under protective camouflage. As we introduced subtle heresies, we would hope that the sleeping masses of true believers would never wake from their slumber long enough to take seriously ancient biblical admonitions against this very thing (such as, "beware of wolves in sheep's clothing who enter to devour the flock," or, "if anyone comes to you teaching a different gospel...").

One potent route of infection would be for us to enter the schools of theology and philosophy of the great universities and change the message of the Faith. Starting at the very top of the church hierarchy, we would enter its seat of learning. We would have to be resourceful and patient, since this process is likely to take well over a century. Those from amongst us who slowly altered the historical message in the heart of academe would be given such protective labels as "courageous," "open-minded," or "visionary." They and their most brilliant disciples would be published and quoted widely by prestigious presses and journals. We would reward these scholars (men like Julius Wellhausen, Paul Tillich, and Rudolf Bultmann) with wide acclaim so that following them would be the "in thing" among the academically ambitious (operating within a peer group with built-in conformity and fear of confrontation).

The wealthy from among our ranks would endow huge sums of money to prestigious schools for professorial chairs, thus advancing the efforts of our key scholars. This would begin to monopolize the doorway of accepted knowledge, especially when they become deans and presidents of school after school. A coalition of deans and presidents would be formidable. It would be book-burning by consensus, away from public scrutiny.

Elite scholars of our choosing would occasionally address the public, using the prestige of their academic degrees to overwhelm the credulous masses, confusing them with high-sounding arguments they weren't equipped to unravel. The few in academe who saw this and had the conviction to protest would be silenced and marginalized by various means (refusing them tenure, humiliating and embarrassing them by scandalous allegations, the media, and so forth). Once departments were under siege, only the *right* faculty would be hired, cutting off the traditionalists at the source.

Once academic theology was infected, graduates could infiltrate the broader churches and denominations to preach ever more novel messages (the social gospel, process theology, liberation theology, gay theology, New Age theology, and the like). Such messages would evolve constantly, but always be protected under some high-sounding spiritual corrective ("love everybody," "don't judge anything," and so forth). The traditional message would be replaced by a new belief system almost seamlessly, with hardly a soul noticing. This task would be especially easy in the broader older denominations where doctrinal deviations could ride upon tradition and lofty ceremony almost unnoticed.

When the national mood became sufficiently tenderized, we would accelerate this process of theological deconstruction by using such groups as the Jesus Seminar as battering rams to break into public awareness. Regardless of how small such groups were, they would still gain national attention on the covers of *Time* and *Newsweek*. A once sacrosanct creed would now be in shambles before the public. The boundaries of Christian behavior would involve little more than token public displays of lame affection, grinning simpletons who embraced all things. We would have a large impotent mass of people with empty convictions that would collapse under the weight of a feather duster.

Millions of church members would be no different morally or spiritually from the rest of secular society. Polluted morally, their spiritual blindness would harden them into an unbelief almost beyond penetration. The way would be open for clergy whose perversions are among the most defiled to ascend the pulpits of the land.

Wearing giant crosses and flowing colorful robes, the new clergy would institute things like "transsexual appreciation week," and "sexual diversity" workshops with films and even demonstrations within a new kind of "loving" church body whose collective judgment and discernment was permanently disabled. Our goal in this social experiment would be to create parishioners so dull that even goddess-worshiping sex in the sanctuary would one day be tolerated as an acceptable form of worship (*loving the goddess of permissive wisdom, Sophia*).

This future church would be composed of men and women fully indistinguishable, one gray androgynous mass of "persons." The final product would be an outrageous caricature of the church's earliest beginnings, when it was bold, pure, and on fire. If the early church was willing to die for their Lord, our final congregation would be willing to giggle and hug and show all varieties of "love" in His name as long as there is no public disapproval.

We would have a creed indistinguishable from the very beliefs of society at large. Our goal would be reached when the Faith that we slowly developed was merged—by its very indistinguishability—with all other faiths across the globe. This global religion, people would realize, was for the higher good of the human race.[1]

Attacking from the Outside

Rewind history once again. Let's move the arena of opposition against Christ and His church to the outside into an unbelieving world.

This next creative exercise for our think tank would be to trace out ways one could marginalize and destroy Christianity, starting at least three centuries back, taking it from the time it reigned as the worldview of the civilized West to the present world at the close of the millennium. Forget about practicality for a minute. Just dream of situations and events that would do the trick. The means to this end could be arrived at later. Just outline what it would take.

We would realize that one exemplary model of change took place 200 years ago when France's social order collapsed almost overnight during the French Revolution. In this master strategy, centuries of tradition were turned upside-down as the long-standing rule of church and monarchy were broken. It took cunning revolutionaries to pull it off—including the Grand Orient Masonic lodges across Europe, with a host of aristocratic discontents and various financiers.

This explosive revolution would set off other coming revolutions. The next social revolution could be precipitated through guaranteeing the masses true equality above the wealthy classes and "oppressors" by promising them food and housing in exchange for personal freedoms. They would bite this carrot and become the new serfs.

New post-Christian social systems—whether communism or socialism—would provide little or no room for Christ and His church. The rhetoric of anti-Christianity would remain safely political and social, all for the common good. In one land mass, after the revolution, this would be accomplished by purging an entire "class," the bourgeoisie (in truth, the Christian middle-class). A "pogrom" of 60 million (mostly Christian farmers) would sweep the land in a greater reign of terror than had ever gripped France in its revolution.

That same land mass of people would continue in abject poverty no matter what system of governance came along. In fact, after 50 years of communism these tired masses would become so accustomed to dictatorial rule that their self-sufficiency and spirits could not rally to face their newfound freedoms under "democracy." They would instead be ripe for the worst elements of Western depravity to enter through the doors of this new "democracy." Here would be a block of people who had been vanquished for a long time. But what about the last holdout, America?

The New Order Visits America

What about Christian America sitting safely away from the shadows of Europe's revolutions of socialism and secularism? How could this "Christian" land be deconstructed?

One means would be to turn the dial so that cherished inalienable rights of a constitutional republic slowly devolved into government-granted "liberties" and privileges that could later be revoked. The key: centralized government. Democracy would replace the republic. In turn this "democracy" would change into a centralized federal power, perhaps a fascist police state. And those once great freedoms of responsible citizens would devolve into public license and a host of depravities and excesses passing in the name of "freedoms." They would be nothing like the original concept of God-given rights of the sovereign individual spoken of in the Bill of Rights.

The welfare system would weaken the family. The courts of the land would slowly legislate away Christian freedoms using a "church/state" argument while mandating diversity agendas. Freedom of speech would be squelched using "hate crime" legislation. Add to this escalating race problems, changing demographics through unbridled immigration, drugs, and divorce. Give America the sixties revolution, as its best and brightest chased the dream of a New World Order, and change would be irreversible.

The private citizen would be assaulted from all sides. Public education would "open minds" to the grandeur of humanism. Later on, diversity training, sensitivity training, multicultural consciousness raising, and gender workshops would really "open minds" to a collective worldview that was fully hostile to the Christian worldview. Gender-bending and gay rights would arrive. The youth would look to short-term pleasures, not to meaning or purpose. Rather, this youth would look really different, even with its guy/gal earrings, colored hair, and unisex attire. What a success story for social engineers.

Somewhere in all this they would lose the heart and character to ever stand up to the increasingly ungloved iron fist of the state. They would be shadow figures compared to their ancestors who established America so they could have the freedom to love God and live in America's bounty, virtuous and strong.

The themes of public entertainment—books, television, and movies—would only flow in one direction. To be "in" they would have to be post-Christian in outlook. Only certain themes would be allowed. They would constantly pry apart the Christian consensus—via historical accusations, modern scandals, debunking of heroes, and guilt by association—while showing other "better" alternative beliefs.

Books and films about slavery are one example that would always reveal the real culprit—Christian civilization—that victimized women, blacks, and minority groups. White men would be portrayed as unchangeable bigots no matter what. Empowered and angry women would be the new stereotype, replacing the feminine and contented homemakers of yesteryear.

The family would die a slow death. Lesbian alternatives and gay consciousness-raising would be everywhere. And this is where the youth, knowing nothing else, would hop aboard and end the family system forever. State *in vitro* fertilization would be next on the horizon with social engineers filling the role of parents. That would create a generation that would never hear of Christ. To them, He would be fully erased. Realistically, this probably would not take place before a New World Order had locked in place.

Invisible Waves of Influence

What about the "Christianity" seen in the millions of American living rooms as it comes across the airwaves? What "gospel" would they see during these critical transitional times?

As the multitudes channel-surfed, they would come across preachers who were vulgar, insincere, and manipulative, pressing for donations in return for healings. "Just touch the TV screen," one twitching face would implore in an unnatural voice, "and I will send you this prayer cloth that I blessed at the Sea of Galilee." Countless people would be turned off permanently to so-called Christianity. (Such broadcasts are even more effective in creating a public caricature than Andrew Lloyd Weber's *Jesus Christ Superstar*, *Godspell*, or Hollywood's *The Last Temptation of Christ*.)

On another channel an hour later, Smopper Bob the Evangelist (recently caught in a hotel room in a shocking act yet to be reenacted on a TV primetime special) would slide across the stage in a metallic polyester leisure suit while putting on the

barnyard growl, shaking with sweat for "JEEZZZUSSSSAAAH."
He would be howling into the mike guttural slang in King James
English as gravelly and cacophonous as a chicken yard during an
earthquake. Morphemes and phonemes would come out at ten
per second in a drawl as thick as molasses and with as much content as an idiot without Novocain wailing away in a dentist's chair.

Three channels away, a primetime program—let's call it "Sat-
urday Night Live"—would have an ongoing caricature of the same
evangelist. Yet the real thing would be even more outrageous than
the comedy team doing the caricature. Anyone watching television
would have a lifetime overdose of "Christians" that would make
them immune to all genuine attempts to reach them. It would be
ideal for persecution, creating an ever-widening gulf between
Christians and a politically correct, savvy, and secular public far
more open to New Age alternatives.

An already alienated youth culture would get the cue to
avoid "Christians" at all costs—"don't even be seen associating
with them." Rather, such losers should be taken out of society as
quickly as possible. New Age leaders would be saying exactly
this—"Take out these people, they're toxic. The Harmonic Convergence, the Quantum Leap, can't happen as long as they're
around to impede the flow of history."

On a primetime channel three clicks away from Smopper
Bob (known for blasting people in the head with his hands as
they fall down and roll on the ground under "old-time Holy
Ghost power"—which the youth have learned to imitate hilari-
ously in high school hallways and soda fountains), an articulate
Ivy League graduate with movie-star looks would tell them, with
winsome smiles of sincerity, about an experience of *oneness* that
is the source of all religions—an embracing cosmic love. He
would show how man as a collective was the true divinity on
Earth. That we were free of old stereotypes of sin and judgment.
That this outmoded judgmental view was the source of the
ugliest bigotries and hatreds, the source of all attitudes that separated peoples, races, and nations.

On another channel would come news of a miracle-working
Godman who held the secrets to planetary love and unity, daz-
zling viewers with impressive footage. The religious figure would

address millions. He would materialize solid objects. He would be one of many cosmic Christs and world teachers who had come on the earth-plane to liberate the earth and make it ready for the coming paradigm shift into a new civilization.

Meanwhile, New Age fairs, world initiatives, UN celebrations, massive peace rallies, rock concerts—all with billions of attendees collectively—would inundate post-Christian society and push the envelope of change.

According to the most accurate projections of our think tank, Christianity would be totally erased with this combination. A hostile public would be on-hand to finish the job if the state lapsed in its job of excising this "Christian" cancer from the "planetary body."

The End and the Beginning

The only force greater than a seemingly omnipotent New World Order in the full thrust of carrying out the ancient conspiracy to silence the Son of God—now decimating the world's Christian population and vaporizing all evidences that Christ ever walked the earth—would be His return to stop history in mid-electron orbit. The giant beast of the global machine would freeze in terror.

His return is certain. Let us now proceed ahead and see how the opposition has been maneuvering in the shadows of history as of late to silence the Son of God with deft strategies, hidden agendas, and spiritual teachers—some even working great signs and wonders and proclaiming to be God.

One naked truth stands out across history—that the name of Christ is often either praised or cursed the instant it is uttered. This is unique with only one other name, the name of God. When men curse in a gut reaction (apart from the long list of obscenities), they utter either the name of God or Jesus Christ—not Buddha, Krishna, Moses, Mahatma Gandhi, or any other messiah figure. None of these other names draws blood in the mouth. And that in itself is a dead giveaway. Those who do not believe in Christ will still utter His name as a profanity as though unconsciously recognizing that He is vested with powers they do not want to acknowledge or consider. It is an emotion that parallels the angry child cursing his father.

What is it that is hiding behind this concerted opposition to the name of Christ? Does it not, in a subtle way, acknowledge the mystery of who He is? "His name is above all names," we are told in Scripture (Philippians 2:9-11). How did He respond to the Pharisees almost two millennia ago regarding His true identity? He flatly asserted, "Before Abraham was, I AM" (John 8:58). Then *they* responded. They picked up stones to kill Him because they knew perfectly well that He was claiming Messiahship—equality with God.

Christ's claims have not changed. If He is who He says He is, He cannot be blotted out. He cannot be manipulated. He stands at the door of eternity and *will* be encountered by one and all no matter what. When we encounter Christ, it is we who change and not Him. *Not* to consider Him is the height of folly and blindness. Our understanding and relationship with Him has eternal consequences, as this chapter—indeed, this book—shows.

1

JESUS AND THE
DEN OF THIEVES

Tal Brooke

Those of us who have encountered Him
know that Jesus Christ is at the center of history and stands at
the end of history. I learned that fact in a hotel room in South
India over 20 years ago. Like it or not, the nations of the
earth, perhaps with one exception, set their calendars to the
birth of Christ. Newspapers, government documents, birth
certificates, and the dates on passports are so dated. Even in
India, a Hindu nation, the *Hindustan Times* is dated by the
Christian calendar. A titanic event must have happened 2000
years ago for this to be a fact—for the calendars of the earth
to be set by this one event, the birth of Christ. These calendars
are set to the life of no other man, not Plato, not Caesar
Augustus or Alexander the Great, not Leonardo da Vinci, Sir
Isaac Newton, or Mozart, not Confucius or Buddha.

The proclamation of Christ is embedded in the high
architecture of Europe, in its greatest classical music and art,
and in the guiding declarations of the greatest universities in
the world. This fact speaks of a providential act of God. In
time, however, this presence will erode in a great falling away
to take place over an unspecified period of time. Such a
process of apostasy has accelerated in our own lifetime. This
"great falling away" from the faith is predicted to be a key sign

signaling Christ's return—a moment that many have tried but failed to predict.

The Wall of Division

When Christ walked the earth almost 2000 years ago He would enter a public place and people became instantly divided. Their reaction to Him was explosive and instantaneous. The sheer magnitude of truth confronting them demanded a response; they saw a blinding light that not only offered hope, but at the same time revealed the terrible lies, private sins, and contradictions within them. Their response to truth determined where they stood on the great divide. It was almost impossible for those in His presence to sit on the fence, looking directly into the Light, while remaining indifferent. They had come into the presence of the Son of God. And there was no time for diplomacy, equivocation, or compromise.

Polarized, they fell into two camps (sometimes they crossed sides later, either "falling away" or "falling under conviction"). It is what happens when the lone self encounters the Holy. They either loved Him, acknowledging that He was the truth incarnate, the long-awaited Messiah who offered salvation. Or they conspired to remove His presence from the earth, to extirpate every word He said, and every act and miracle He performed. They were offended by the Holy and would conspire to destroy it, if such a thing could be done. Those first doubters set the stage for other doubters down through the centuries. They tried to unmake Him through myths and rationalizations.

Those who rejected Christ demonized Him—calling Him evil rather than confess the evil that resided within the recesses of their own souls—claiming that He performed His miracles "by the power of Beelzebub" (Matthew 12:24). This was one of the first myths devised to explain Christ's ability to work miracles. Yet Christ warned these accusers that in attributing His divine acts to Satan, they were blaspheming the Holy Spirit and bringing perdition upon themselves (verse 31). They could not live with the fact that He was the Son of God. With each confrontation the Pharisees hardened in their stance. His messianic advent and proclamation flew in the face of their sacrosanct and elaborate traditions—"the traditions of men" formulated during the Babylonian exile and which were a departure from the Torah. The gospel was an offense to their ears and sense of self-importance, especially since it pinpointed their sinfulness and distance from a holy God.

Jesus' opposers wanted to expunge Him and His message from the earth in any way they could. When they could not remove His presence by force, they resorted to cunning and deceit to rob Him of His truth and identity. Among the earlier myths they created was an explanation for the resurrection: the body had been *stolen* while the Roman guards looked the other way or slept—a dereliction of duty for which Roman guards received the death penalty from their own garrison (Matthew 28:13).

After the resurrection appearances, the next myth proposed by Christ's opponents was that He had been herbally sedated while on the cross, only appearing to be dead, even after the spear was thrust into His side. The myth states that He somehow recovered within days after His brutal crucifixion to present Himself to His followers as resurrected. His opponents still had to explain the willing martyrdom of the apostles, who were willing to die violently rather than deny Him. Would they do this for someone who had faked His own death? Would these disciples really undergo agonizing crucifixion themselves for a deception they had helped to rig, going to their deaths for a lie? Does that tally psychologically with their timidity and fear after the crucifixion during that period before the resurrection? Does it make sense that they would become emboldened for a lie they helped create?

Besides these questions, there was another obstacle for the opponents of Jesus—and it has remained a historical embarrassment. Why couldn't the scribes and Pharisees either prove that Christ faked His resurrection or come up with the actual body, and settle the matter by dragging it into the marketplace for all to see? Christianity would have died on the spot if they had produced the body. But they didn't.

Like today's most successful and unscrupulous lawyers, who bend and twist facts, the opponents of Christ have continually redefined and changed His identity, His message, and the events of His life with cleverly crafted tales, interpretations, and myths—the very thing the Bible warned would happen (see 2 Corinthians 11:4). Once neutralized, the offense of His presence is gone—at least for the moment.

The Offense

The polarization continues to this very day with great numbers offended by the man and His message. Hence the obsession throughout history to create or excavate other Christs and other gospels. In the early church there was the Christ of the Docetists, Montanists, Arians, and various early Gnostics (see chart on page 23). Newer versions of these earlier heretical models can be seen in the Christ of the Mormons and the Jehovah's Witnesses. Redefining Christ by altering the record and the revelation is an easy way to dispose of the real one, yet still appear spiritual.

To change Christ is to replace Him, and thereby dispose of Him. It is to plunder and rob on the deepest level possible. There have never been so many myths in all of history surrounding one figure—from the ancient Gnostics of the first century to the metaphysical *Course in Miracles* in the twentieth century. Fallen man has consistently displayed an all-consuming need to change Him. This perverted need keeps appearing in passionate waves, era after era, like a bright floodlight emphasizing the sheer importance of an issue, a significant signal in itself.

Alongside the myths, invented interpretations, and tales there is another phenomenon—the counterfeit Christs,

Docetism: A heresy concerning the person of Jesus Christ. The word derives from the Greek *dokeo,* meaning "to seem" or "to appear." According to Docetism, the eternal Son of God did not really become human or suffer on the cross; He only *appeared* to do so. This heresy arose in a Hellenistic milieu and was based on a dualism which held that the material world is either unreal or positively evil.

Montanism: A Christian apocalyptic movement that arose in the second century preaching the imminent end of the world, austere morality, and severe penitential discipline. It took its name from Montanus, a Phrygian, who, shortly after his baptism as a Christian (A.D. 156), claimed to have received a revelation from the Holy Spirit to the effect that he—a representative prophet of the Spirit—would lead the Christian church into its final stage.

Arianism: A fourth-century Christian heresy named for Arius (c. 250-336), a priest in Alexandria. Arius denied the full deity of the preexistent Son of God who became incarnate in Jesus Christ. See the chapter by Ron Rhodes on the Jesus of the Watchtower Society.

Gnosticism: A dualistic system of thought that appeared in the first three centuries of Christianity. Good and evil, light and darkness, truth and falsehood, spirit and matter were viewed as opposing one another in human experience as being and non-being. The created universe and human experience were characterized by a radical disjunction between the spiritual, which was real, and the physical, which was illusory. Sparks of deity were seen as entrapped in human bodies in the physical world. These could be freed only by saving knowledge that was revealed to the spiritual elite by a transcendent messenger from the spirit world, variously identified as Seth (one of the sons of Adam), Jesus, or some other figure. Renunciation of physical desires and strict asceticism, combined with mystical rites of initiation and purification, were thought to liberate the immortal souls of believers from the prison of physical existence. Reunion with divine reality was accomplished after a journey of the soul through intricate systems of hostile powers. See both chapters by Peter Jones.

avatars, and saviors who appear in person, such as Sai Baba, Meher Baba, Yogananda, Ramakrishna, and Muktananda. Some of them are not always seen but are rumored to be on the earth and hidden away, such as Babaji or Maitreya. Invariably, the opponents of Christ find it useful to get on this bandwagon, trumpeting various new messiahs.

Think of the devotion that so many well educated, sophisticated, and affluent Westerners—who would not give Christ any response above a smirk or a knowing chuckle—poured on Rajneesh, the Indian guru of tantric sex, pleasure, and anarchy. He was the God they wanted, and no other, even after he was deported from Oregon back to India, minus his 90 Rolls Royces. He never healed a soul or showed an ounce of love. His "calling cards" were a parody compared to the real Christ of history. Yet it was Rajneesh whom these masses wanted—the man in saffron robes who spent their money, lied to them, then died. Their perversity of choice, in the very god they wanted, showed their contempt for real truth and goodness. They sought the god of their own desires. And when he passed away, most of them went searching after other gods and other spiritualities in today's diverse religious marketplace.

There are ample warnings in the New Testament about "other Christs" coming in His name and claiming to be Him. Matthew 24:24, for example, warns of exactly that—"For there shall arise false Christs, and false prophets, and shall show great signs and wonders; insomuch that, if it were possible, they shall deceive the very elect" (KJV).

This was the verse I read from an old worn-out Bible given to me by two missionaries from atop a hill overlooking Puttaparthi in Andhra Pradesh, South India. I had spent two years under a man who appeared to work miracles (even reported in *Newsweek**) and who claimed to be God incarnate. Once I read this verse in Matthew, it stung me to the quick. I knew

* 26 November 1969.

that the man in India whom I had followed was one of these predicted "other Christs," indeed, an anti-Christ—and he remains so to this very day, as millions believe he is the world savior and messiah—the Kalki Avatar. He is one among many claiming to be Christ (or Christ's mouthpiece) in this and other centuries. From Ramakrishna to Chinmayanda, they came, claimed to be God in the flesh, then died and were buried. Yet the world keeps looking on expectantly.

Altering the Christ of Scripture

The reigning mood among the cultural establishment continues to be that society in general must still tip its hat in Christ's direction, acknowledging that His legacy remains as a force to be reckoned with. Those who don't like Him the way He is still have the option of redefining Him. If nothing else, this will continue to erode the church and the Christian presence till His mention brings no more than a sneer or a blank stare from the youth of some future world.

Until then, something must still be done with Christ and Christianity. The "spiritually conscious" continue to have an obsessive preoccupation with Christ and with fitting Him into their schema as though their consciences cannot rest until they have included Him in some way. The conventional wisdom of a cultural period is always a powerful incentive to redefine Christ. For Him to be acceptable during the Romantic era, certain things had to be changed.* It has become more so with Modernist preconceptions and theories. Theology found new ways to make Christ "relevant." For a while it was the "social gospel."

---

* In the late eighteenth and nineteenth centuries the Romantics, spearheaded by influential writers and artists, revolted against classicism and philosophical rationalism with its emphasis on reason. They idealized man's return to nature while believing in his innate goodness. If man was innately good, and therefore not tainted by sin, he did not need a Savior (from sin before a holy God). Thus Christ's central role as Savior was jettisoned so that He could now be cast into various other roles—teacher, higher master, even the "Christ consciousness" of the various occult groups that emerged in the late 1800s.

These days, people are calling for a broad-minded, non-judgmental Christ who is politically correct. Somehow He must be rescued from history or simply rediscovered. He must be a Christ who sanctions all paths as leading to God, who is not exclusive or judgmental, who in fact teaches the ancient mystery religions of the divine within, that spark of divinity within all men waiting to be awakened.

It must be a Christ who will syncretize well with Buddha, Krishna, the Imam Mahdi, and perhaps some future Jewish Messiah. This Christ will be seen as a type of the New Man, a perfect Master among other perfect Masters, who is leading the way for the whole human race to enter into the secrets of enlightenment. He is seen as an exemplar at the head of the pack.

Intellectual Thieves

Certain things need to be done, however, to bring about this other Christ. In one approach, the New Testament must be doubted, then edited and deconstructed. More and more of its passages must be expunged. Academic criticism provides this mode of attack and has done so vigorously since the start of the nineteenth century. One begins from a position of absolute doubt—doubting the books and parchments, the writers and their motives. One throws it all away and defies the canon to prove itself first. Dates are doubted, methods of copying are doubted, and so on. Here we have the German and continental schools of biblical criticism: redactive, historical, and form criticisms.* Academic criticism turns out to be a most effective means of frontal assault on the historic Christian faith. It is one way to get Christ to the makeup artist and erase the prophetic and judgmental aspects of His nature that so grates against the present mindset.

---

* *Redaction criticism* seeks to identify the sources which the biblical writer used and the editorial work that was done on them. *Historical criticism* aims to determine what actually occurred. *Form criticism* seeks to "get behind" the written sources to determine what was actually said and done. It seeks to identify and evaluate layers of material that were added to the tradition during the period of oral transmission.

For instance, German higher criticism created the perfect atmosphere for liberal scholar Julius Wellhausen to announce that Moses did not write the Pentateuch alone.[1] In fact, Wellhausen repeatedly declared that Moses never said and recorded all the material attributed to him in the books of Deuteronomy, Leviticus, and the rest of the Pentateuch. Such books, he believed, came from a contribution of multiple authors over five centuries to whom he gave the initials J,E,P, and D. Wellhausen's Documentary hypothesis put him on the academic and historical scoreboard (though he only perfected an idea invented by earlier doubters such as Jean Astruc). The academy jumped at the idea, even though this hypothesis was held together with the scantiest of evidence.

Finally, higher criticism in its various forms crossed the Atlantic from Marburg and Tübingen in Germany to the Ivy League in America. And it has been emptying churches and the hearts of believers ever since. When conservative scholars disproved Wellhausen's hypothesis, it barely got a mention. By then, the academy was following liberation theology or process theology or some other concoction, of which there have been many. And who can undo the emptying of churches during the first half of this century because of this one theory? It helped change the spiritual landscape of America, partly because theologians on this side of the Atlantic embraced it with open arms. It also widened the doctrinal highway for the post-Christian era, along with the many other theories before and after that have done similar damage.

On one level, changing the canon is a problem of hermeneutics and exegesis.* In the case of the Bible, if you can editorially cancel out certain words and phrases, or invent

---

* *Hermeneutics* is the broad discipline that explores the philosophical parameters and rules for interpreting meaning, intent, and what can be known and/or deduced from a communicated sequence.

Exegesis involves interpreting the biblical text, not as just "hanging in space," but with regard to word meanings, grammatical context, historical context, and the background of the passage as related to the era and its linguistic rules—including connotative and denotative meanings of words.

new contexts surrounding certain statements, you can skew the entire meaning of a major passage. Literal realities can be conveniently thrust into a symbolical context. (Existential theologian Paul Tillich did this all the time.) Then you can look for "Jungian" meanings behind ordinary events as these moments in history are doubted and now attributed to "symbolism."

Today, divinity schools, graduate departments of religion, and seminaries have taken the cue from the academic posture of fashionable skepticism and used this as a way to reshape Christ to fit current fashion with a tolerant, left-leaning, socially conscious, inclusive Christ. Once conformity-minded students take the cue that this is the only acceptable position among their fellow students and academic peers, it is a rare individual who will dare to step out of line. They have come up with an emasculated Jesus to appease feminists, gays, and other special interest groups who sit in judgment on the New Testament Christ.

This Christ of academia is such a conciliator that he loses ground at every strategy meeting in which he is discussed. These days he is a champion of the lesbian/gay caucus and radical feminists. He is even a champion of homosexual Eros—as long as it involves "responsible," "caring," and "safe" sex among "persons of alternate sexual preferences." This pallid invention of the academy is ready to fall right into line with the mystery-Christ of the New Age movement.

It is a rare faculty member who will risk tenure to stand against this wave. Each faculty member can grin knowingly, these doctors of knowledge, as they add the emperor's new clothes to their already considerable collection of vestments and tassels. They can still walk in ponderous academic lines with furrowed brows, trading on their reputation for intellectual profundity, while passing on the mantle to those whom they choose. Individuals, especially brilliant "individualists," who differ with their liberal agenda are instantly branded as "intolerant" and "narrow-minded." Through the conformity of the academy, Christ has been remade in a few generations, starting in the most prestigious universities. It has been a remarkable strategy indeed—one of ponderous faces and furrowed brows, ambition, peer pressure, personal agendas combined with moral cowardice among the few who know better.

Churches exposed to these unbelieving pastors become poisoned wells, as members lose their faith and drop away. The churches shrink in membership, and what were once great stone edifices become empty tombs. This has happened throughout America and Europe.

Most recently, the methodology of doubt has been raised to new levels. The Jesus Seminar has been boldly shredding the New Testament at such a rapid rate that it has earned the full adoration of the media, who have decided to "discover" it and put it on the map of respectability (featured on the covers of *Time, US News and World Report,* and *Newsweek,* at Easter, with lead articles). In the method of doubt, Christ is first reduced, then redefined. He becomes *so* reduced, as in the Jesus Seminar, that His opinion no longer amounts to anything. He is certainly no longer either Messiah or Son of God. By this corrosive skepticism, biblical revelation is eaten away, bit by bit. Of course there are dire warnings in the Bible about doing exactly that. The Bible predicts that this is what many false teachers will do—take away from the passages of divine revelation. It is the method of subtraction ("the leaven of the Sadducees").*

Stealing by Addition

There is another equally effective method of changing Christ, and that is by *adding* to the biblical account and teachings

---

* The Sadducees were known in their day for denying key teachings of Scripture—miracles and the future resurrection, for example—which in itself is a form of subtraction from the canon. Incredibly, the next to last verse of the Bible ends with a dire warning concerning those who would subtract from Scripture: "And if any man shall take away from the words of the book of this prophecy, God shall take away his part out of the book of life, and out of the holy city, and from the things which are written in this book" (Revelation 22:19 KJV).

("the leaven of the Pharisees"). These extrabiblical revelations can appear in grandly staged events or quiet discoveries.

Previously hidden writings might be discovered after having been buried for hundreds or thousands of years, revealing a different Christ from the powerful figure depicted in the New Testament. Such is the Gospel of Thomas, suddenly unearthed to join the four Gospels that have been the pillars of the New Testament. So too with other apocryphal writings written anonymously or under pseudonyms. This has been true of any number of Gnostic writings. Even the Jesus Seminar has been trying to canonize the Gospel of Thomas. No one seems to consider that heretics have been writing their own unauthorized versions of Christ for 20 centuries. Finding one of these documents is no great achievement, nor does being found make that document a coequal with the canon of Scripture.

Beyond the process of unearthing old material, added revelations can come through contemporaries who claim that their new revelations surpass the traditional canon of the New Testament. There have been a number of New Age Christs appearing by this method, mostly by channelers, from psychic Edgar Cayce to Helen Schucman, who recorded the New Age *Course in Miracles* dictated to her by an inner voice claiming to be "the Christ."

Channelers and psychics commonly communicate with some "Cosmic Christ" and divulge his new teachings to the world at large. This is because the world is now "evolved enough" to handle the deeper teachings. Those who encounter a being of light in a near-death experience, such as Betty Eadie, can "reveal" some universal creed of spiritual evolution as coming from him. In her latest book Eadie opens the doorway for reincarnation, after her multimillion-copy initial bestseller, *Embraced by the Light,* put her in the public eye. At first she appeared "Christian." Now she is showing her true colors by emphasizing her American Indian heritage. Her "Christ," in the form of a "being of light," is now talking about reincarnation and soul evolution. And the ride is not over for the millions hooked on the revelations of this bestselling author.

Changing Christ for Global Peace

When false teachers redefine Christ, whether using the methods of doubt and subtraction or addition and new revelations, there must also be new systems of interpretation for going into the New Testament and ferreting out the new and different Christ. New meanings must be given to ancient words and phrases. For instance, when Christ told Nicodemus, "You must be born again" (John 3:7), the new hidden understanding is that He was speaking of reincarnation. But only certain "advanced" teachers will know these hidden meanings. Gradualist skewing of word meanings can enable a new interpretation of words whose intentions in the original were clearly different.

This happened to the early church when the Gnostics came on the scene and spiritualized things in new ways. This was why the early church needed to have church councils, such as the Council of Nicea, so that the great doctrines would not be corrupted through time.

Contemporary Gnostics such as Matthew Fox announce that these higher teachings have been hidden and suppressed by the church; that they were quashed at the ancient councils, such as Nicea and Constantinople; that the church was engaged in a cover-up operation of obscuring the very "mystery-Christianity" that would have so perfectly fit, like a piece to a puzzle, with the other world religions, especially Buddhism and Hinduism; that this suppressed mystery-Christianity would have helped provide the groundwork for a universal faith based on the universal nature of God, the brotherhood of man, and the divine basis for all life. Instead, they claim, the historic church has become a divisive obstacle that is intolerant of other paths. It obstructs the smooth flow of this effort at world unity. Long before Matthew Fox, this was the message of Teilhard de Chardin, who taught at the halfway mark of this century that it was time for a universal creed and a new revised Christ. Why? Because planetary needs demanded it. Christianity must bend its narrow way for the new collective cause of man.

Other mystics and globalists have climbed aboard Teilhard's vision. A universal nonoffensive creed, they believe, will be a major element in ensuring that the world will be unified. It must be brought about and anything divisive must be quashed. Christ is to be rediscovered as the Avatar, Gnostic Redeemer, Incarnation of the Godhead, and mystery figure who fits the pages of the world creeds. As far as historical Christianity is concerned, however, it must be observed that this mystery-Christ is far from the Jesus who hurled accusations at the Sanhedrin, overturned the tables of the money changers, and bodily rose from the dead. The mystery-Christos is light years removed from Jesus Christ, born in Bethlehem, who healed lepers, spoke pointedly about sin and moral condemnation, fed thousands miraculously, and claimed to be the unique son of God, without peer, who existed before time began, and who foretold His own return to judge the world.

Today's New Age Christ is altogether different from the New Testament Christ. He emerges from countless peripheral sources except the canon of the New Testament. From this sealed canon he cannot emerge, for the early manuscripts and autographs don't breathe a word about him.

As the mystical "true" believer will tell you, the only real evil now is doubt—especially doubting this new Cosmic Christ—which prevents the miracle from happening. Something must be done with the doubters, for they are spoiling the harmony that the world is about to experience.

These doubters are the orthodox Christians who do not recognize the new gospel coming from today's other Christs. They are still "hung up" over their carefully transmitted 2000-year-old canon that has survived the centuries intact. They claim it has already worked the miracle of grace upon their lives and does not need changing. For they have encountered Christ *personally*, and when they read the New Testament, that is indeed the one being described whom they have encountered. Through the New Testament they have encountered the true historical person of Jesus Christ. And this biblical Christ in no way resembles the new cosmic and politically correct Christs coming on the scene through the Jesus Seminar, Matthew Fox, or Betty Eadie, among many others. We will continue to be confronted with counterfeit Christs and false gospels followed by waves of eager acolytes. We will see these deceptions increasing until the end of the age.

Everyone is given a choice. There is the politically correct Christ who has been invented by the den of thieves whose message changes moment by moment, suiting the needs of various eras and various people. Then there is the Christ we encounter in the timeless Word of the New Testament, preserved by God's providence and decree through the centuries. He is of a different magnitude. The sincere follower is called to discern the genuine Christ, having already been forewarned of counterfeits coming in His name (Matthew 24:4,5).

Scripture tells us that the earmarks of the followers of the genuine Christ will be an abiding love of the truth, a sober awareness of the constant reality of deception, and a persevering knowledge and devotion to the true, historical, biblical Christ and the faith once for all given to the saints. Those who are truly His have this knowledge not only from the biblical canon, but also by meeting Him as their Lord and Savior. These are the redeemed of the ages, the living stones of the true church. And neither death, tribulation, nor anything on earth or in the heavens can wrest them from the grip of the Son of God (John 10:28).

He is yet to return to the earth. But when He does, He will split history and eternity, and all upon the earth will know without question who the real Christ is. The myriad of counterfeit Christs will dissolve into the mists of history, as every knee shall bow and every tongue confess that Jesus Christ is Lord (Philippians 2:10,11). Until this day, we must discern the true from the false with every means God has given us.

OVERVIEW

The momentum of change is upon us. An international *Who's Who* of statesmen, intellectuals, and financial leaders met on June 15, 1995, at the UN's 50th anniversary in San Francisco. At the key ceremony, it was revealed that Mikhail Gorbachev, the former head of the Soviet Union, had the backing of world leaders to set up a United Nations sister organization in San Francisco called the United Religions (UR). Modeled on the UN, it would have a 500-member assembly, a 36-member executive council, and a General Secretary. Multi-faith peacemaker teams would be dispatched around the world by the UR to trouble spots, just like the UN.

What is going on? Gorbachev and other leaders realize that a world federation cannot be fully realized without a world religion in place. Why? Religious differences comprise the final barrier among ethnic populations that stand in the way of the real goal—a one world order. The political, military, and economic pillars of these world states cannot hold up a world order without the fourth pillar of a global religion standing beneath the fourth corner, lest the structure collapse. It is that simple.

Is it any mystery, then, that perhaps the most powerful force to move across the church in 2000 years is now trying to prepare the way for such a global religion? In this chapter you will see the groundwork behind this goal and why the groundbreaking philosopher, Teilhard de Chardin, is also the John the Baptist from the West of a coming world religion.

2

PREPARING FOR A GLOBAL RELIGION
THROUGH THE SUBVERSION OF CHRISTIANITY

Tal Brooke

The Planetary Mass at San Francisco's immense Grace Cathedral claimed to be an early preview and invocation of the coming global millennium due to intersect history at the year 2000 Earth-time. This sacrament was seen as a pinpoint of light that would help catalyze the Earth's ignition of consciousness. Similar devotionals would fuse to form a spiritual sunburst, inaugurating the long-awaited New Age. From the Earth's multitudes more were looking with expectancy toward this threshold of human history at the magical point of A.D. 2000.

The high priestly celebrant and innovator of the Planetary Mass is Matthew Fox, the renegade New Age Catholic priest who had been silenced and recently excommunicated by the Church of Rome. Now it was time for mainline Protestantism, open-minded and liberal, to welcome the heretical Catholic priest into its ranks with open arms.

On the other side of America, New York City's Cathedral of Saint John the Divine—another massive historical monument to a once robust and orthodox Protestantism—had been having similar global celebrations and ecumenical convocations. Going back to 1981 it celebrated the *Missa Gaia,* or Earth Mass, commissioned by its dean, the Very Reverend

Morton, and performed by Paul Winter in honor of mystical ecological consciousness.

Since the 1960s New York's oldest and grandest Episcopal cathedral had grown new innards that obscured its once uncluttered and expansive sanctuary of stained glass windows and unobstructed pillars. Now exhibition hall style add-ons, which were included in the name of "holism," vivisected the great cathedral like a New Age fair. There were sectors of the cathedral that resembled New York subways—with mystical graffiti and posters—all creating a sense of confusion and chaos. It is what happens when anomalies are grafted to beautifully ornate architectural harmonies. At the base of magisterial columns were sectors dedicated to various special interest platforms—feminists and devotees of the goddess, environmental groups, Gaians (who see the Earth as divine), areas for "gay-lesbian-bisexual" issues, and areas for Native Americans, Eastern mystics, New Age leaders, and gurus.

The great Cathedral of Saint John the Divine had been widened, by constant doctrinal roadwork, from its once narrow path into a spiritual superhighway containing enough lanes to hold all the world's religions. The multitudes could commune regardless of belief, as long as they were not part of the narrow way of orthodox New Testament belief. This cathedral was preparing the way for the cosmic millennium. And exclusive Christianity was not invited to the altar.

In another part of New York City, the United Nations building loomed in the air of Manhattan like a vast secular cathedral. It was on the eve of its fiftieth anniversary and was looking toward the year 2000 with expectation. After all, its whole purpose was global in every aspect—governmental, economic, military, social, medical, scientific, educational, cultural, and religious. From the UN General Assembly, the World Court, World Bank, World Health Organization, to its own UN forces and flag, it had everything in miniature to develop into a full-fledged world government—*a United Nations with teeth*—if the nation-states would concede their sovereignty. Until then it was just a symbol and vehicle for world goodwill. Yet, even if the UN acted as midwife for another form of world rule, it would have still served its purpose. Global unity was the quantum evolutionary leap of civilization that Teilhard de Chardin foresaw and wrote about with expectation, even coming by the end of this century.

The United Nations had its own spiritual sanctuary, a meditation room. It was constructed as a hologram depicting, by its very design, the unity of the major religions of the world. Not a pretty sight, to be sure, but a utilitarian statement of sleek functionality. It was under the watchful eye of Sri Chinmoy, who also served as the chaplain of the United Nations. He guided and spoke to thousands. This UN chaplain was not a Christian—the once reigning faith of the host nation where his cathedral skyscraper stood—but an Indian yogi whose face resembled a death mask, eyes half-closed, staring into the cosmic void. And indeed, no one could be more fitting as high priest of the UN than this Indian guru, who claimed to be in a state of perpetual cosmic consciousness while embodying the divinity of man. In this *brave new world,* man is the final measure of truth. It is a dream come true for mystics who have prepared the way.

Meanwhile, in the aging cathedrals of Christendom, cosmic sacraments such as the Planetary Mass were seen as gateways through which all the world's faiths could converge. They were the Western gesture toward syncretism—spiritual disarmament—involving a total abandonment of history, tradition, and religious sovereignty. It was a capitulation for the sake of peace, world peace—but willingly, with eyes open, and running to the invading army to lay down its weapons and possessions at the feet of these gateways.

The challenge was to harmonize the holy books of the Earth into one unitary voice while brushing aside the diverse faiths and fundamentalisms of the Old World Order. Disarmament was necessary. And this took visionaries who could see far and wide. They had to be dizzyingly optimistic about mankind and world government and very trusting about the whole process.

The participants who filled the two largest and oldest Episcopal cathedrals in New York City and San Francisco beheld a new faith rising from out of the Earth. It came in time to meet a world at the geopolitical crossroads of the long-heralded New World Order. It would be a time when nation-states entered the dusty back shelves of world history as a new world was born. Most of its prophets felt this could only come about by an evolutionary leap in consciousness. There was a whole new vocabulary for this transition—*planetary convergence, Omega point, paradigm shift, transformation, the coming of the cosmic Christ, New Age*. And true believers could be spotted from out of the multitude by their infectious, manic, perhaps nirvanic, optimism, as they sped gleefully toward the millennium without a fear or a doubt in the world.

Teilhard de Chardin: The Father of Spiritual Globalism

Teilhard de Chardin (1881-1955) is almost without question the leading candidate in the West for spiritual father of the rising spiritual and political globalism now taking the world by storm. He formulated the dominant conceptual framework in the West for a planetary religion and social order. In the early part of this century, Teilhard outlined and predicted a coming "convergence of religions" (his own term) to rise in tandem with political globalism. Each force would accelerate the other. It is a vision that has fired the imaginations of a wide swath of people now in leadership positions (including those who have misunderstood or modified Teilhard's views).

Teilhard described himself as a mystic and evolutionary scientist. What he fully expected was an evolutionary leap in consciousness to come upon the human race, possibly at the year 2000. He felt that the spiritual and political unification of the Earth was the next great leap to come and that it was vital for the survival of mankind. He said,

The Age of nations has passed. Now, unless we wish to perish we must shake off our old prejudices and build the earth. . . . Life cannot henceforth advance on our planet (and nothing will prevent its advancing—not even its inner servitudes) except by breaking down the partitions which still divide human activity and entrusting itself unhesitatingly to faith in the future.[1]

Naturally, he saw the United Nations as a key vessel for this process.

Teilhard constructed a broad theological bridge between East and West, pioneering today's global sacraments, interfaith celebrations, and other planetary consciousness-raising events. Fifty years ago, Teilhard foresaw today's Planetary Mass, but termed it the "Mass on the Earth," long before Matthew Fox came up with his version.

Mystical Guidance from a Rival Star

What propelled Teilhard de Chardin down this long road? By his own testimony, it was mystical experiences—which began in his early childhood and continued throughout his life. He would stand in deserts and wastelands, always alone, usually in the wilds, and sense a mystical unity with the cosmos. Was there a guiding hand behind these experiences? And where was it taking him? He disclosed the fact that an enigmatic force was guiding him that emanated from some "rival star":

Ever since my childhood an enigmatic force had been impelling me, apparently in conflict with the "Supernatural," toward some Ultra-human; and in trying to pin it down I had become accustomed to regard it as emanating not from God but from some rival Star. All I had to do, then, was to bring that Star into conjunction with God and dependence on Him.[2]

Whatever emanated "not from God but from some rival Star" knocked at the door of Teilhard's mind and inspired him, and through him, knocked on limitless doors right up to the doors of the United Nations and the European Parliament. Such is the strategic power of an idea, inspired from beyond, when it seems to arrive at the right critical juncture in history. It can have enormous impact on the course of history, as with Karl Marx's *Communist Manifesto*. With lesser inspirations, such as *The Celestine Prophecy*, the direction of a culture can be prodded. However, the source of such ideas and revelations is yet another concern.

Fellow Catholic and well-known scholar, R. C. Zaehner, an Oxford University orientalist, saw Teilhard's ecumenical bridge-building toward a global religion as a betrayal of the Church of Rome. To Zaehner it was a heady enterprise that was dangerous, blind, if not naive, especially in its seeking religious unity with the pagan East. Zaehner also questioned the mystical inspiration for this dangerous course:

> His whole vision of a world converging irreversibly on a cosmic "center of centers" is based . . . on his prolonged participation in "cosmic consciousness" which he had experienced from boyhood but which only became acute in the mire and misery of the First World War.[3]

Teilhard's mystical experiences were his ultimate authority for understanding everything. Early in the century he read Richard Bucke's *Cosmic Consciousness,* undoubtedly to compare his unitive bliss-states with others. Down through the years he read Romain Rolland, the disciple of Ramakrishna, Aurobindo, Vivekananda, Radhakrishnan, as well as Western mystics such as Meister Eckhart. In fact, Teilhard's mystical experiences were more important for him than his loyalty to the doctrines of the Catholic church, under which he was a Jesuit priest, or to the scientific establishment, under which he was a PhD paleontologist. His special formula was to combine evolutionary theory and science with his own mystical experiences and then reinterpret church doctrine through this "cosmic" filter. The final product of this process was a hybridized mystical Christianity that met Eastern pantheism more than halfway. Today we would call it New Age Christianity.

Teilhard de Chardin also saw that the Catholic church was a vehicle-in-waiting suitable for occupation by this larger cosmic mystical faith. Fellow Catholic Zaehner observes that Teilhard "saw in the Roman Catholic Church the only human institution on and around which humanity as a whole could possibly converge upon itself."[4] The Romish structure could then become the world church of mystical unity. To Teilhard, the need for planetary survival justified this pragmatic takeover. To the Catholic hierarchy, Teilhard's vision had all the makings of a mutiny. It was too much change, too quickly, coming from yet another independent mind within the Jesuit Order.

Formulating a Planetary Faith

In late 1938, in Peking, Teilhard finished one of his landmark works, *The Phenomenon of Man*, which explored his vision of the "Omega point" and the evolution of consciousness, themes he would return to again and again. Somewhere near his bedside table must have been the writings of G.W.F. Hegel. Teilhard notes:

> The universe is a collector and conservator, not of mechanical energy, but of persons. All round us, one by one, like a continual exhalation, "souls" break away, carrying upwards their incommunicable load of consciousness. One by one, yet not in isolation. Since, for each of them, by the very nature of Omega, there can only be one possible point of definitive immersion—that point at which, under the synthesizing action of the personalizing union, the noosphere (furling its elements upon themselves as it too furls upon itself) will reach collectively its point of convergence—at the "end of the world."[5]

Teilhard's evolutionary fusion of consciousness is partially reminiscent of the "Day of Brahman," described in ancient

Indian Vedanta, when souls return to merge into the God-head. But there are also great dissimilarities. Teilhard prefers to use the concept of evolution rather than reincarnation. And his version of pantheistic union allows for the survival of the individual self in the great fusion of souls at the Omega point. In Teilhard's cosmic union with God, unlike pure monism, there is no dissolution of individual consciousness (the drop returning to the ocean, ending all distinction). Indeed, he fought against the idea of Vedantic monism in which the self, the *atma,* dissolves irretrievably into the ocean of being, the *paramatma.* He was at great odds with this Eastern view. He also opposed the Indian view of the world as being an illusion or *maya.* Rather, Teilhard looked toward the transformation of matter through consciousness to higher levels. This too was part of his evolutionary schema.

With regard to transforming matter through conscious-ness, Teilhard was not far removed from the revolutionary ideas of Sri Aurobindo Ghose, his Indian contemporary and counterpart, who was building the bridge of global spirituality from the East to the West. Aurobindo, the Oxford educated political revolutionary and mystic, sought to move Indian pan-theism away from its standard passivity and withdrawal from life, with its low view of the world, into catalyzing the direction of civilization. Aurobindo wanted to apply India's mysticism to the course of the world, making India a player among the nations and not a vassal (through its usual non-involvement). Like Teilhard, Aurobindo was global and futuristic in his thinking, ultimately seeking the union between East and West for planetary holism. Today, Aurobindo's estate in South India, Auroville, has pioneered international communal living and global consciousness-raising. Auroville has Western luminaries visiting it from all over the world, including some of the leading lights of the United Nations, in continual cul-tural cross-pollination.

Throughout the long decades of exile that Teilhard spent in China and other parts of Asia (the church hierarchy kept sending him away), his writings grew into a corpus—a mystical summa theologica—with new terms like *noosphere, Omega point, Mass on the Earth, convergence,* and *confluence.* They were ideas that were so revolutionary—indeed, heretical—that an absolute seal of silence was put around them, never to be published in his lifetime. The Church of Rome, during his lifetime, allowed only his writings within the very narrow field of paleontology to be published, and anything beyond that was hushed. This was enforced until his death in 1955.

To Teilhard, the cross of Christ was simply "a gesture" that showed "progress through effort."[6] His view of evil paralleled the Hindu view of evil as ignorance, self-consciousness, and illusion, the other half of light on the plane of duality, also like Taoism's yin and yang:

> For him evil is the same thing as multiplicity: it is "the inevitable corollary of the creative act," for "in this perspective physical suffering and moral faults inevitably creep into the world, not by virtue of some defect in the creative act, but by the very structure of shared being (that is to say, as a statistically inevitable by-product of the unification of the multiple)."[7]

Teilhard duplicated Alice Bailey and the Theosophists in diminishing the Genesis account of the fall of man and putting it within the schema of spiritual evolution. Teilhard said: "That the Genesis story of the 'Fall' can be explained along evolutionary lines I have tried to show elsewhere."[8] Like the Theosophists, the Fall, to Teilhard, is really about the sin of self-consciousness. His way out of the problem parallels the "not-self" taught by Buddha.

> Self-consciousness developing out of group consciousness, what Genesis calls the "knowledge of good and evil," was certainly almost bound to lead to selfishness and the misuse of the knowledge acquired; and the cure for selfishness can only be selflessness.[9]

But Teilhard's diary contained something even more radical. He mentions the transformation of the Hindu god Shiva by Christ. And here he is virtually in the camp of Vedanta. Teilhard resolves good and evil by merging them, like all polar opposites, into the godhead, though he calls it "Christifying." Teilhard scholar Ursula King found a reference to Shiva in Teilhard's diary, and quotes him in her book, *Towards a New Mysticism: Teilhard de Chardin and Eastern Religions,* with her own comments:

> Among the many tentative suggestions in his diary, one of the most puzzling and least expected is the reference to the Indian god Shiva and to "Christ-Omega/Shiva" in 1948. After referring to the overpowering forces of the cosmos which can neither be tamed nor appeased, he says that " . . . It is not enough to refuse or ridicule Shiva: for *he exists.* What is necessary, is to christify him. Christ would not be complete if he did not integrate Shiva (as a component), whilst transforming him."[10]

King also found among Teilhard's cryptic diary notes and letters the idea that God had to be altered:

> It was especially the image of God which Teilhard saw in need of urgent redefinition. Modern man has not yet found the God he can adore, a God commensurate to the newly discovered dimensions of the universe. In 1950, he noted in his diary: "God is not dead—, but HE CHANGES." In a letter to a friend, he referred to "the transformation . . . of the 'God of the Gospel' into the 'God of Evolution.' "[11]

And so we get to the center of Teilhard's greatest act of theological defacement—and blasphemy: his redefinition of the very nature and being of God to suit his cosmic summa theologica. He is also paving the way for great apostasy among the undiscerning or indifferent masses in a post-Christian world. He exchanges the true Christ for a "universal Christ," and only a minority of people these days would even know the difference. It is a perfect set-up for the globalistic spirit of the age and its planetary transformation, now being proclaimed as a soon-to-come revival. Barbara Marx Hubbard has termed it, "Planetary Pentecost."

Teilhard describes his higher road to salvation:

> I can be saved only by becoming one with the universe. Thereby, too, my deepest "pantheist" aspirations are satisfied, guided, and reassured. The world around me becomes divine. And yet the flames do not consume me, nor do the floods dissolve me. For, unlike the false monisms which urge one through passivity into unconsciousness, the "pan-Christism" which I am discovering places union at the term of an arduous process of differentiation. I shall become the other only by being utterly myself. I shall attain spirit by bringing out the complete range of the forces of matter. The total Christ is consummated and may be attained only at the term of universal evolution.[12]

Christ in his schema is made possible by this universal evolution: "By disclosing a world-peak, evolution makes Christ possible, just as Christ, by giving meaning and direction to the world, makes evolution possible."[13]

What is the function of the universal Christ, who is a synthesis of Christ and the universe?

> In that case, surely the solution for which modern mankind is seeking must essentially be exactly the solution which I have come upon. I believe that this is so, and it is in this vision that my hopes are fulfilled. A general convergence of religions upon a universal Christ who fundamentally satisfies them all: that seems to me the only possible conversion of the world, and the only form in which a religion of the future can be conceived.[14]

Moving from a biblical to a "cosmic Christ," Teilhard was in harmony with Alice Bailey and the Theosophists on the Western side, and Vivekananda, Aurobindo, and other renowned Indian mystics on the Eastern side (they saw Christ as a perfect master or an avatar), long before the New Age movement came on the scene with its updated cosmic Christ. And it is this cosmic Christ—a *false* Christ—to whom the present generation of spiritual globalists look as harbinger of the planetary millennium. Whoever appears for this multitude as their messiah will not be the real Christ anymore than their "planetary revival" is a true biblical revival. The irony is, it is an apostasy—a great falling away. And it is not absolutely out of the question that this could be *the* great falling away that Christ predicted that would precede His long awaited return—or at least a preparation for it. There is no telling how long this could take. But it is a sobering thought.

The Catholic hierarchy had not completely hushed Teilhard, even though his writings were banned from publication until his death. His ideas still managed to seep out in cyclostyled format reaching "open-minded" leaders and thinkers. Teilhard was also busy at work behind the scenes within influential ecumenical circles in Europe and America, where his thoughts went out like ripples to those with a futurist turn of mind.

The Jesuit mystic had to be careful, however. If he was going to be an effective change agent within the Catholic church—thus fulfilling what he saw as his greater mandate for planetary evolution—he knew he would have to remain within the Mother Church of Rome, which to him was "the only institution on and around which humanity as a whole could possibly converge upon itself." It was the same principle as leaven, or yeast—altering the structure of dough from within. And that meant Teilhard needed the appearance of outward submission. He could not afford to be expelled or further censured. For that reason, Teilhard had to be very discreet in his ecumenical activities, such as sitting in on the smaller upper echelon meetings of the World Congress of Faiths. Indeed, he secretly drafted two pages stating the aims of the French branch of the World Congress of Faiths.

Because of his officially precarious position, Teilhard was never a publicly prominent member of the French branch of the World Congress of Faiths; yet it is known that he took an active part in many committee meetings. Among the adherents of the other faiths present on the committee were an Iranian Sufi, a Confucian, and Swami Siddheswarananda from the Ramakrishna Mission with whom Teilhard had discussions on yoga and meditation.[15]

The Planetary Bargain

It seemed that the enigmatic hand guiding Teilhard de Chardin had positioned him at the very confluence of history, not just because of the timeliness of his conceptual framework for a planetary religion, but because this idea of a planetary religion was ideal, as a synthesizing force, to bring about political and cultural globalism. (This has long been the aim of the League of Nations, the United Nations, endless roundtable groups such as the Council on Foreign Relations and the Royal Institute of International Affairs, the Trilateral Commission, the European Economic Community, and the Club of Rome.) And this gave Teilhard a whole different sphere of allies on the world stage over and above his ecumenical allegiances. The political globalists needed his religious unified field theory in order to end the era of autonomous nation-states, and, in the words of the head of the Aspen Institute, to pull off "the planetary bargain." This was where Teilhard was critically needed, because religion had been a thorn in the side of secular and political globalists. They needed a spiritual peacemaker with the intellect to bring off the grand synthesis.

Religious differences among national and ethnic groups have remained the critical factor standing in the way of global unification. Separate views of reality and unique claims to inspiration have always caused the major religions to be exclusive and independent (though some can synthesize far more easily than others). This independence is not necessarily a problem in a world containing separate nation-states who wish to live cooperatively, yet independently, as neighbors. That is the way it has been for centuries.

The concept of unique religious revelation is a hard reality. Another hard reality is that, regardless of sincerity of belief or tradition, there is only one first-place winner in the contest of absolute truth, and that is the orthodox Christian view. Thus, to change the faith for the sake of unity or peace is to compromise the truth. It is an almost impossible situation, especially among the hard-line faiths such as conservative Christianity. On the one hand, Christians know that their gospel and faith cannot be compromised without being changed, and once changed, the faith is destroyed. On the world table of chess moves, this is a perpetual stalemate, frozen in place. This will continue to make genuine Christianity increasingly unpopular.

On the other hand, global strategists outside the faith will see the unification of the planet as far more important—from their perspective—than the tiresome separatist whining by a minority of "true believers" stuck in theological minutiae. And they will eventually take a hard line. To them, the ends will justify the means, even if it means drastic solutions.

The Iron Hand of Peace

The way out of the stalemate for globalists—in order to pull off "the planetary bargain"—is to find or devise a spiritual unified field theory that resolves apparent differences among religions (and cultures). And that is what Teilhard de Chardin has offered at the altar of the Earth—though there might be "some wastage" in the event that some are not willing to go along with the "peace plan."

To pave the way for Leviathan, Teilhard's planetary faith is ideally suited to leaders and statesmen of the industrial world. It is a creed for the family of man, which fits in perfectly with the agenda of the United Nations as well as the New World Order. Robert Muller, former Assistant Secretary General of the United Nations, is a perfect example of a high ranking UN leader who is an unabashed disciple of Teilhard. Muller is dizzyingly optimistic about Teilhard's vision of the "confluence" of forces toward world government and the "convergence" of faiths into a world religion. And like Teilhard, Muller does not for a moment entertain the possibility of things ever going wrong with centralized power. Like many of his peers at the top of UN leadership, Muller embraces the idea of a strong centralized government. And no wonder, because when Muller's mentor, Teilhard, was in China during the rise of Mao Tse-tung, he enthusiastically read *Red Star Over China*, by his friend Edgar Snow, as well as the writings of Karl Marx. Teilhard saw in communist socialism the germ of world government. In fact:

> Teilhard seems to have admired any form of totalitarianism simply because it seemed to prove his theory of "convergence." Whether it was Hitler or Stalin or the early Mao Tse-tung did not seem to worry him very much.[16]

Globalists have already been monitoring the forced bussing of the cultures of the world while closely watching new resistances appear. Melting-pot nations like America and Great Britain provide a test-run for synthesis, using various methods of mass socialization based on conformity and intimidation. Rule one is that there is shrinking room for individualists, especially those with strong convictions. For the rest, new norms have been created such as unity-in-diversity, inclusiveness, and political correctness, which are pushed relentlessly on all levels of culture. The new human family is portrayed inevitably as a mandated cross-sample of ethnic quotas, especially in the omnipresent media. Television news teams, roundtable discussions and town hall meetings, quiz shows, right down to the crew members of *Star Trek*, all embody the new ethnic constellation of the human family.

Those who come out of the mold of today's rigid socialization, mostly generation-x and later, not only do not feel as strongly about their religions as their parents, but feel apologetic about their religions or anything else that might make them look prejudicial or exclusivist with their peers. They are already ripe for a New World Order, as easy to mold as soft Jell-O. No strong convictions or great strength of character will beleaguer their lives with hard choices. These are the minions that totalitarians dream about. It's the gifted individualists who may have to be crushed with a more direct approach.

Teilhard's formula for planetary convergence, by its own declaration, is a process that will change the contours of the Earth and the way we live. And once this has happened, there is no guarantee we will ever be able to reclaim the past or revisit freedoms once taken for granted. The lessons of history tell us that the stronger the totalitarian power, the more powerless is the individual in opposing or escaping it. Few in history have known the freedoms that we have, and yet we lack the sober and watchful caution of those who have lived under tyrannies and police states. (Harvard undergrads, in all their wisdom of life, mocked the warnings of Russian Nobel laureate and writer, Aleksandr Isayevich Solzhenitsyn.) We are fast becoming a decadent people ripe for the plucking, Solzhenitsyn has admonished.

Some astute Christians have been aware that a countervailing force in the world, one day seeking religious fusion, could oppose their separatist faith that stands in the way of global unity. The planetary paradigm is that the few can be sacrificed for the preservation and well-being of the many. "Surrender or be destroyed for the sake of the Earth," could one day be the choice given to separatist sects by the Leviathan of the New World Order. This was true in ancient Rome, as recorded by Tacitus and Pliny, when Christians knew that it was a lie and a betrayal of their true Lord to worship Caesar as a god. And so when they refused, they were executed. These martyrdoms have already happened.

New Age globalist Barbara Marx Hubbard has foreseen this dilemma. Some sources allege that she projects that for planetary transformation to take place, up to one quarter of the inhabitants of the Earth will have to be excised like a cancer. She doesn't say how this will be done. She merely comments on the destruction of the resistant group in the manner an evolutionist describes the extinction of a species. Marylin Ferguson and David Spangler, among other New Age leaders, have echoed similar statements about the fate of those unable or unwilling to go along with the paradigm shift of planetary transformation.

The Gathering Storm

In a technologically omnipotent world order, there will exist the full-blooded potential for bringing to pass exactly what is described, not only by some New Age strategists and globalists, but by the book of Revelation—the mass martyrdom of Christians on an unthinkable scale, surpassing the time of Nero and Domitian.

> And when he had opened the fifth seal, I saw under the altar the souls of them that were slain for the word of God, and for the testimony which they held:
> And they cried with a loud voice, saying, How long, O Lord, holy and true, dost thou not judge and avenge our blood on them that dwell on the earth? (Revelation 6:9-10 KJV)

These are the martyrs down through the ages, from the early church to those at the very end. The later group, in a bloody campaign on the Earth, are martyred in a final orgy of desperation. It is a way of removing God's presence on the Earth by getting rid of His people, who are an irritant to this future world.

At minimum, the biblical view of history is linear. History progresses from the Fall, where evil enters the world, to the end of history, when evil needs a final radical remedy. It was never God's plan that evil continue throughout all eternity. It is limited in time. During human history, the problem of sin and human rebellion are an ever-present constant that fluctuates. Christ's first advent involves the ransom sacrifice of Isaiah 53, the suffering servant, who takes upon Himself the sins of the world. His second advent is as king and judge.

Almost all Christians have understood the second coming to be one of judgment; and that presumes, not peace on earth in a spiritual golden age, but a saturation point of depravity, when, like in the time of Noah, human apostasy and evil is incorrigible. God's timetable is fulfilled at that point, and the Son of God comes to resolve human history.

One of the things that completes the final stages of this timetable is the martyrdom of God's people. To repeat, as history winds down, evil will not just go away, it will increase, *radically*. Unless someone is wearing incredibly thick rose-colored glasses, it is hard to miss the point that evil has increased almost exponentially in our own lifetimes. Of course, this time period could be yet another minor ellipse in the grand theme of history—or, we could be winding down to the real "Omega point." What we can say (and people said this during the Dark Ages) is that the signs of the end are gathering. Ironically, it is during this climate that some "Christians" have elected to say, "Don't be negative. Let's end this doomsdayer mentality." These are voices calling out peace from a deep vacuum.

The real return of Christ will bring planetary judgment, not some New Age Christ declaring the new millennium from the United Nations General Assembly or some podium in modern Jerusalem. The genuine Christ will come in fury upon a God-hating world. At the end of the world, we will get the great Judgment, not a planetary rock concert of ecumenical harmony or Teilhard de Chardin's planetary convergence.

> And then shall that wicked be revealed, whom the Lord shall consume with the spirit of his mouth, and shall destroy with the brightness of his coming. (2 Thessalonians 2:8 KJV)

Far from celebrating with the intoxicated optimism of Teilhard de Chardin, Robert Muller, and a host of cosmic millennialists, with their brash declarations of triumph about a liberated family of man, we should, as a nation, be kneeling in tears before a holy God whom we have offended with our arrogance, apostasy, and perversion. We are in desperate trouble. In God's eyes, we are blind and naked. And judgment cannot be far away. Indeed, the shadow of judgment, in the form of delusion, is rising by degrees in our midst (a sign of judgment). There are those so deluded that they conspire to oppose God by shouting Him out from heaven with their growing populations of followers.

America, in all its wisdom, has murdered its youth in the name of sexual liberation and "choice." Herod murdered a mere handful by comparison and his motives were less shallow. In this generation alone, America has killed 12 million babies (a mountain of bodies that rises far higher into the sky than any ecologically precious populations of spotted owls or snail darters, who are far more prized by today's self-righteous ecologists and humanists than babies). A rising tide of preadolescent children are awash in depravities that barely touched a small fraction of adults 40 years ago—snorting cocaine and other drugs, getting abortions, and killing one another. Legions of proud homosexuals and lesbians—the sins, judged by God, that made Sodom famous—taunt the world with gay-pride celebrations while mocking the morality of the old order. And today's politically correct secularists love this Brave New World. Secular society is becoming more brazenly anti-Christian by the day as it mocks the old standards of purity. A nation is in deep trouble when it despises goodness and mocks God's people, whether it knows this or not, because it is ultimately taunting the God of the universe. Paul describes it well:

> This know also, that in the last days perilous times shall come.
>
> For men shall be lovers of their own selves, covetous, boasters, proud, blasphemers, disobedient to parents, unthankful, unholy,
>
> Without natural affection, trucebreakers, false accusers, incontinent, fierce, despisers of those that are good,
>
> Traitors, heady, highminded, lovers of pleasures more than lovers of God;
>
> Having a form of godliness, but denying the power thereof: from such turn away. (2 Timothy 3:1-5 KJV)

Paul's words describing the last generation have applied to the world in varying degrees since the time of Rome. Yet they apply especially to a particular future epoch. At minimum, Paul's description illustrates the fact that civilization does not grow better and better through time. Quite the opposite. To reemphasize this point, we see in "the last days" a world in rebellion against God which is anything but a spiritual golden age (otherwise He would say, "In the last days men will love God, and everyone will be saved"). Meanwhile, Christians who plan to orchestrate revival in these times should get realistic and start by talking about repentance first. Only God can send real revival. Something we try to manipulate will be a hollow enterprise (even if this period is yet another grand cycle of history, a low point, with a thousand more years to go).

We are a nation fraying at the edges with our titanic national debt and our fragmenting families. We are becoming an androgynous people. And our leaders, deep in corruption and compromise, reflect the very people who elected them. We are in profound trouble. In this condition, who but an idiot or an apostate would dare dream of beating our drums down Wall Street in an ecumenical pan-religious revival to celebrate the advent of some cosmic Christ. Such a parade of clowns, dancing on the rim of destruction, will be turned to cinders by the real Christ.

> But the day of the Lord will come as a thief in the night; in which the heavens shall pass away with a great noise, and the elements shall melt with fervent heat, the earth also and the works that are therein shall be burned up.
>
> Seeing then that all these things shall be dissolved, what manner of persons ought ye to be in all holy conversation and godliness,
>
> Looking for and hasting unto the coming of the day of God, wherein the heavens being on fire shall be dissolved, and the elements shall melt with fervent heat? (2 Peter 3:10-12 KJV)

What sort of world will we have when He appears? It will have the brash defiance, willful perversity, and hedonism of Noah's world.

> But as the days of Noah were, so shall also the coming of the Son of man be.
>
> For as in the days that were before the flood they were eating and drinking, marrying and giving in marriage, until the day that Noah entered into the ark,
>
> And knew not until the flood came, and took them all away; so shall also the coming of the Son of man be. (Matthew 24:37-39 KJV)

This antediluvian world of Noah—a world God destroyed in its entirety—had the sort of evils that are predicted to reappear by the Lord's final coming. We can only guess what the particular evils in Noah's day were—Tantric witchcraft? Incest? Murder for pleasure? All of this and more? The bottom line is that God was not thrilled with the world of Noah, but destroyed it in judgment. That ancient world had the moral equivalent of AIDS that could no longer be healed or salvaged, only cut out like a cancer. At minimum, the world of Noah was completely pleasure-driven, godless, and immune to repentance. It could only go down, now beyond salvaging.

If the scriptural indicators are uniform that the second coming of the Son of God will be to a world "as it was in the days of Noah," when the Earth was judged by a great flood, then it will also be evil enough to be judged, as was Noah's world. And if we know that God warns of the very activities that we see increasing in our culture, then His return to an evil world will be, as He has predicted uniformly, to bring judgment. He will end human history as we have known it. The final images in the book of Revelation, signifying the last epoch of human history on the Earth, are the vials of God's wrath poured over the entire Earth. It is global, and not regional. And it is a horrendous sight of judgment upon the

Earth. Be certain that it is not a New Age paradigm shift or time of planetary harmony. That is the strong delusion.

Those who think they will wave banners to greet an ecstatic cosmic Christ begin to resemble a band of renegades who stand outside the huge empty military fort they have just pillaged and burned. Their delusion tells them that the bright lights in the distance are fellow pillagers coming to join in. But it is a vast returning army, not with rifles, but tanks, helicopters, and legions of soldiers.

If God's people have been martyred in the ways outlined by New Age strategists from Alice Bailey to Barbara Marx Hubbard, the returning Christ will greet the perpetrators with the relentless fire of judgment.

> And shall not God avenge His own elect, which cry day and night unto Him, though He bear long with them?
> I tell you that He will avenge them speedily. Nevertheless when the Son of man cometh, shall he find faith on the earth? (Luke 18:7-8 KJV)

Those who conceive of the planetary transformation will be surprised by the One who comes. It will not be the cosmic Christ at all, but the Son of God coming to a planet in mutiny. Delusion will then run headlong into reality, the Alpha and the Omega.

Ever since Alexis de Toqueville, visitors to America have noted the deeply religious character of its citizens. But religious faith is like nuclear power—very dangerous. It all depends on how you use it. And in this great citadel of modern Christianity a particularly noxious form of paganism has started to germinate. It has been created, in the main, by apostate believers.

For the pagan lie to succeed, it needs to look as much like the truth as it can. Hence the imperious necessity of a new hybrid—"Christian" paganism. And this is ironic. At the end of the twentieth century, the one great contribution of once Christian America is the introduction of pagan heresy into the church's Scriptures and practice. This chapter traces how this process has taken place, changing the spiritual landscape of the nation forever.

3

APOSTASY AND THE
DESCENT INTO PAGANISM

Peter Jones

T he gay black dancer eloquently high-
lighted the role of faith in his life—a powerful sense of his
spiritual belonging with all people and things. In an interview
on National Public Radio with the Jewish lesbian host of
"Fresh Air," Terry Gross, this highly articulate artist, admitting
to a very religious, Christian fundamentalist background, nevertheless stressed that his present faith had no place for Jesus
Christ or sin.

The Sharp Knife of Faith

Ever since Alexis de Toqueville, visitors to the golden
shores and fruited plains of these United States have noted
the deeply religious character of Americans. I add my testimony. As a young man, to lift the boredom from my 15
minute, thrice-weekly ride to church, from the vantage point
of the upper deck of a double-decker Liverpool city bus, I
once counted 72 pubs on the street corners we passed. When
I came to America from England in 1964, I was surprised to
see that in the New World, on every street corner, instead of
pubs there were churches. Returning to Europe in 1973, in
particular to secularized France, the absence of religion in
public life and personal relationships was just as disorienting,
for in polite conversation, the one subject never raised was

personal faith and religious commitment. Returning to the States some 18 years later, I made a shocking discovery. America was just as religious as it had always been—but America had changed religions.

Religious faith is like nuclear power and sharp knives—*very powerful* and *very dangerous*. It depends how you use them. In this sense America is the most dangerous place on the planet. Communism has faded as a real danger both to international peace and to the Christian religion. Marxism's materialism never spoke to the human need of spirituality. America was never really tempted by atheistic Marxism, even if secular humanism, via the dubious principle of the separation of church and state, has played a significant role in the slow muzzling and marginalizing of Christian expression. The New World Order has reordered many people's thinking. Christianity is not only marginalized in Christian America. According to the new, all-tolerant, pro-choice, globalist faith that is fast becoming the national religion, Christianity threatens world peace and religious harmony.

Paganism has gained the upper hand in the land that was until very recently the fortress of the Christian faith in the modern era. The change has been subtle. America has not abandoned Christianity for secular humanism, or its political expression, Marxism. America has simply adopted the fundamental tenets of religious paganism and redefined Christianity to fit the new religion. The faith of our Fathers has been turned on its head to say the very opposite of what they actually said. This is not a loss of faith, as in Europe. This is not heresy, which unduly emphasizes one doctrine to the detriment of all the others. This is *apostasy*, literally, the "standing away from" everything genuinely Christian by dressing up paganism in Christian clothing in an attempt to take over the Christian faith.

Only big lies work. For the pagan lie to succeed, it needs to look as much like the truth as it can. Hence the absolute necessity that this pagan deformation enter the church and claim its "rightful" place in the modern citadel of faith.

Neither atheists nor Muslims lead the battle against Christian orthodoxy today. The attack comes from within, from once-committed Christians who have consciously apostatsized from Christian orthodoxy. Often leaving positions of great power within the church, they have succeeded in branding orthodoxy as a marginal aberration of Christianity, and are in the process of rehabilitating their newfound spirituality as true Christianity.

Roman Catholicism:
Flying Nuns

Eighty thousand nuns have left their orders within the last 20 years. Roman Catholic journalist Donna Steichen documents that many of these, their faith destroyed by liberal criticism, have actually flown the convents and ended up in wiccan (witch) covens. She shows how the nuns are now involved in crystal reading, dream work, tarot cards, various New Age techniques, and especially forms of witchcraft.[1]

When Steichen began her research, she could not believe what she was seeing.

> At my own first exposure to witchcraft, I thought I had stumbled into a uniquely lunatic social cul-de-sac. I didn't know it was part of a movement and didn't guess how closely it was entangled with general theological dissent, broader political feminism and epidemic neo-gnosticism.[2]

Steichen documents how radical feminism, which she believes is the purveyor of this new pagan spirituality, has infiltrated the church to an extent few realize.

> Feminist women (and men) occupy prominent chairs in theology at Catholic and secular universities; they are members of seminary faculties; they hold powerful diocesan offices; they are writers and editors for Catholic journals and Catholic publishing houses that produce catechetical

materials used throughout the Catholic school system; they have access to financial resources and often official ecclesiastical support for endless conferences and workshops involving many thousands of Catholic teachers, retreat leaders, directors of religious education, etc. They are liturgists, chaplains of Catholic hospitals and sit on boards of abortion clinics.[3]

Steichen's judgment of the present state of the Roman church in America is damning: "Most of the old Catholic culture has been devoured by spiritual termites, leaving behind a structure that looks solid to the eye but crumbles at a touch."[4]

Mary Daly and Wiccan Paganism

The gold medal for flying nuns goes to Mary Daly. This role-switching woman of religion, with two earned doctorates in theology, is presently professor of theology with tenure at the Jesuit Boston College.

Having made a spectacular exit from Catholicism, and denouncing the Christian faith as fundamentally unredeemable, Daly now describes herself as an eco-feminist lesbian witch.* While Daly has moved out of Christianity (this is at least an honest thing to do), and promotes a mystical form of wiccan/lesbian paganism, her writings play a very dominant role in the thinking of many leading religious feminists who remain in the church.

Rosemary Radford Ruether and the Mother Goddess

Rosemary Radford Ruether is professor of theology at Garrett Evangelical Seminary in the Midwest. This daughter of the Catholic church has chosen to remain within the church, though at the outset of her academic career she rejected Catholic belief, saying that she found paganism more attractive than Catholicism.[5] "A lot of evil had been done in the name of Christ," she wrote, but "no crusades or pogroms had been sent in the name of Ba'al, Isis or Apollo." [6] From

---

* Eco-feminism is a blending of feminism and pagan earth worship.

within the church, Ruether has reconfigured "Christian" worship to fit with her feminist paganism. In her "Women-Church" the liturgies come very close to wiccan ceremonies, and the names of God and Jesus Christ are never mentioned. She proposes a Halloween ceremony in remembrance of the persecution of witches.[7]

At the same time, Christianity is joyfully abandoned as the essence of an outmoded worldview that produced inquisitions, witch-hunts, pogroms, executions, censorship, and concentration camps. In the brave new world of this apocalyptic vision, the Goddess is ourselves and the world. All distinctions are eliminated and everything goes as our culture as a whole evolves toward life.[8] In Ruether's new style Christianity,

> Mother Goddess is reawakening and we can begin to recover our primal birthright, the sheer intoxicating joy of being alive. We can open our eyes and see that there is nothing to be saved from . . . no God outside the world to be feared and obeyed.[9]

Ruether describes the empowerment of women that comes through pagan rituals:

> Awakening often occurs through mystical experiences in nature or with other women. . . . Awakening implies the ability to know or see what is within oneself, once the sleeping draft is refused. . . . For women, awakening is . . . a gaining of power . . . it is a grounding of selfhood in the powers of being.[10]
>
> Trust in yourself, believe in yourself. Bring that energy up, up, through your roots, into your body. Let it come in through the soles of your feet, rise up your body, all the way to your fingertips. That energy can handle whatever comes to you. All you need to do is call it up. Feel the power of that energy. Now allow that energy to spiral around your spinal column, rising . . . and then allow the energy to sprout out your head as branches. . . . Feel your connection with the other women in the circle . . . Be aware that this circle is not complete without your energy. . . .[11]

This is powerful spirituality, but *it is not Christianity*. This pagan departure from Christianity is also seen in "The Coming-out Rite for a Lesbian," which is described as a "new birth." In this "Rite" the lesbian praises the goddess, Sophia:

> It was [Dame] Wisdom who gave me true knowledge of all that is, who taught me the structure of the world and the properties of the elements, the beginning, end and middle of the times, the alternation of the solstices and the succession of the seasons, the revolution of the year and the position of the stars, the nature of animals and the instincts of wild beasts, the varieties of plants and the medicinal properties of roots, All that is hidden, all that is plain, I have come to know, Instructed by Wisdom who designed them all.[12]

The themes in this prayer—knowledge of the elements, astrology, animals, herbal medicines, and the joining of the opposites—are all found in witchcraft, where the manipulation of elements is known as the "Craft."

Ruether provides one further example of her departure from Christianity. In a vivid playing out of the rejection of the patriarchal "myth of original sin" and Eve's "victimized" place within it, Ruether and the Women-Church community celebrate the "blessing of the apple," saying:

> This is the apple of consciousness raising. Let the scales of false consciousness fall from our eyes, so that we can rightly name truth and falsehood, good and evil.[13]

Incredibly, the primal act of sin in the Garden of Eden is now elevated as the sacrament of gender liberation. The Fall is now hailed as the ascent to divinity.

Clearly we are in the presence of two opposing views of spirituality. One is true, the other is false. One is Christian, the other is apostasy from Christianity. Ruether is truly one of the guiding voices among feminist "Bible teachers" in seminaries and universities, as well as among radical women's groups in the church at large.

Matthew Fox and "Playful Worship"

This androgynous priest promotes the use of sweat lodges and American Indian prayers to the spirits. Excommunicated by the Dominicans, Fox, with this badge of honor, was welcomed without delay and ordained by the radical wing of the Episcopalian church. Fox defends sexuality—in particular, homosexuality—as playful worship.[14] "There can be no renaissance," he maintains, "without a mystical sexual awakening." He tells us that "love beds are altars. People are temples encountering temples . . . Wings of Cherubim and Seraphim beat to the groans and passions of human lovers."[15] Someone has said that when beds become altars, altars quickly become beds, as ancient pagan orgies easily illustrate. As hard as it is to believe, these notions are making a stunning comeback in contemporary American society and church. It is telling that Fox's seminars are met with sell-out crowds all across the country. (See Ron Rhodes's chapter, "The Cosmic Christ," for more on Fox's theology.)

A New Age Pope

Longtime Vatican observer and novelist Malachi Martin, in his fictional work *Windswept House* (1996), describes a situation in which the Curia is equally divided between "progressives" and "traditionalists," between those who favor abortion, women priests, homosexuality and openness to non-Christian religions, and those who oppose such an agenda. According to the story line, while numerically equal, strategically the progressives hold all the important positions of power, and so are able to bring about a major palace revolution.

In an interview Martin stated that while his work was fiction, the situation he describes is not. Certainly the prospect of a New Age pope bears reflection. What would happen to the delicate balance in international politics and social ethics if the Vatican abandoned its stand on many points of Christian orthodoxy and practice and began to put its considerable weight behind the agenda of the radicals as expressed in the World Council of Churches and in the various conferences organized by the United Nations? At the very least it would constitute one of the most spectacular expressions of apostasy in the modern era, dressed up in all the traditional robes and much of the terminology of Christianity but denying its essence.

Mainline Protestantism:
The Goddess Comes to Church

Why did 2000 mostly middle-class, middle-aged women from middle-of-the-road, mainline Christian churches end their "RE-Imagining" conference (on imaginative spirituality) by blessing the "sacramental milk and honey" in a sort of Lady's Last Supper and reciting a hymn to the goddess that bordered on lesbian pornography? Read for yourself:

Our maker Sophia, we are women in your image; with the hot blood of our wombs we give form to new life. With the courage of our convictions we pour out lifeblood for justice [a reference to abortion?];

Our Mother Sophia, we are women in your image; with the milk of our breasts we suckle the children; with the knowledge of our hearts we feed humanity;

Our sweet Sophia, we are women in your image; with nectar between our thighs we invite a lover, with birth a child: with warm body fluids we remind the world of its pleasures and sensations;

Our guide, Sophia, we are women in your image: with our moist mouths we kiss away a tear, we smile encouragement: we have the honey of wisdom in our mouths, we prophesy a full humanity to all the peoples;

We celebrate the sensual life you give us: we celebrate the sweat that pours from us during our labors: we celebrate the fingertips vibrating the skin of a love. We celebrate the tongue that licks a wound or wets our lips: we celebrate our bodiliness, our physicality, the sensations of pleasure, our oneness with earth and water.[16]

While the Bible joyfully celebrates sexuality within marriage—for instance, the Song of Solomon and Ephesians 5:22–23—there is absolutely no equivalent of this in the Hebrew or Christian Scriptures as a description of God. So the above is "imagination" with a capital "I." How can people so much in the middle be so far into the extreme? As Donna Steichen has shown, mainline Protestants "discovered" this kind of spirituality only because orthodox groups in the Presbyterian and Methodist churches blew the whistle.[17] But it has been a feature of feminist religious groups since the early eighties.[18]

Speakers at the Minneapolis RE-Imagining Conference defended sex for children, and playful sex among friends, as normative and healthy. These examples are but the tip of an enormous iceberg. The conference served to provide a sort of religious/theological justification for the sexual liberation of the sixties—and the beat goes on. Though the Presbyterian Church USA in its General Assembly of 1994 denounced RE-Imagining, a similar pagan-influenced conference in June 1994 at San Francisco's Episcopalian Grace Cathedral sounded the same note, as conferees were told to "discover and cultivate sacred Eros in all its ecstatic connections."[19]

Under the guise of Christian freedom, sin and spirituality are ritually wedded. At the RE-Imagining Conference, one of the speakers held up an apple, bit into it, and then with cheers from the audience asked, "What taboo have you broken today?"[20] The taboo was the warning against apostasy found over and over again in Scripture. Their sacramental sacrilegious bite ingested the forbidden fruit of paganism, the worship of the creature rather than the Creator. One has come to expect such excesses from theological liberalism, but surely not from Evangelicalism!

Evangelicalism—The Coming Age of American Apostasy:

Emily Culpepper and the Hindu Goddess Kali

Raised in an evangelical Baptist church in Macon, Georgia, Emily Culpepper became involved in the counter-culture movement of the sixties. Today she is an eco-feminist lesbian witch who has come into contact with a "familiar," a spirit guide from the Hindu goddess Kali that, according to Culpepper, possessed her cat.

Describing her Christian roots as "compost," Culpepper proposes the following agenda: Christianity should be seen as "a complex tissue of truths and lies"; the idea of the Incarnation is not only "implausible . . . (but) offensive" to feminists; she promotes the adoption of "an expanding personal pantheon of goddesses and other mythic images [as] a great psychic counterweight to the father gods of patriarchy."

Through her cat, Culpepper found great inspiration from Kali who is pictured as a female deity with

> red eyes, disheveled hair, blood trickling at the corners of her mouth, lips saturated with fresh blood, a dangling tongue, long sharp fangs, a gaunt, dark-skinned body. . . . Her necklace contains fifty human heads; her waistband is a girdle made of severed human arms; she is wearing two dead infants for earrings. . . . She holds a blood-smeared cleaver in her . . . left hand and a dripping severed head in the . . . left.[21]

How can such a bloodthirsty picture inspire anyone? Lest you think I am attempting to be sensational by the use of such marginal and bizarre material, please note that this essay by Culpepper was required reading for bright 16-year-olds in the Governor's School (a summer program for gifted teenagers) in Arkansas in the late eighties.[22] Apparently some state officials in the so-called "Bible Belt" believe that today's bright teenagers need such spiritual resources for a fruitful contribution as adults in tomorrow's America.

Virginia Mollenkott's Stand Against Patriarchy

The future age of bliss, called by some the Luciferic Initiation, is described by the radical feminist-lesbian pagans as the Sophianic Millennium. This is the imminent utopia where the goddess shall reign "where'er the sun doth its successive journeys run"—well, at least from sea to shining sea!

The Reverend Nancy Wilson, senior pastor of the (homosexual) Metropolitan Community Church in Los Angeles, who calls herself a "lesbian ecu-terrorist" (ecu = ecumenical), adds a kinky twist to this radical eschatology. She proposes a "queer theology" justifying all sexual choices—a theology that can lead *all* Christians (gay, lesbian, and straight) into the next Queer Millennium.[23] Virginia Mollenkott, the "evangelical," applauds her work as "stunningly important, both for our tribe [by this she means gays and lesbians] and for any other person, church or organization that seeks to be whole."[24]

Mollenkott was raised in Brethren circles, taught at Nyack Missionary College, and in 1993 was still being called an "evangelical author" by *Christianity Today*. Prior to that date Mollenkott was "born again" into a new spiritual freedom using I Ching (pagan Chinese divination), tarot cards, and the study of the New Age *Course in Miracles*.[25] She calls her experience of enlightenment both a coming "out from fundamentalism" and

> one distinct "holy instant" [a notion taken from *A Course in Miracles*, as she admits]. . . . Like my Elder Brother, Jesus, I am a sinless Self traveling through eternity and temporarily having human experiences in a body known as Virginia Ramey Mollenkott. . . . Perhaps my Self has been on earth before in other bodies, perhaps not.[26]

In this new freedom sin is eliminated. "Gone," she declares, "are traditional Christianity's emphasis on sin, guilt, and retribution; instead, we are empowered toward co-creatorship, welcomed to continual renewal on a continuous Great Non-Judgment Day."[27] Her freedom is not just spiritual; it is sexual and moral. As an openly practicing lesbian—"one of my identities is that of an evangelical lesbian feminist"[28]— with a new moral code, Mollenkott is "righteously" committed to lying and deceiving to bring down the heteropatriarchal culture.[29] (In the newspeak of feminism and homosexuality, "heteropatriarchy" is the oppressive cultural consensus which considers normative for society family values [with the father as head of the home] and male-female marriage.)

With no sin, there is no guilt for Mollenkott's lesbian activity, which, all of a sudden, has become "sensuous spirituality" (the title of one of her books). She will not condemn those who engage in "promiscuous or easy sex,"[30] nor women who have abortions.[31] "I believe that every honest attempt to relate to another human being is a good attempt, including recreational sex or sensuality, if that is all a person can achieve."[32]

With this newly-minted "evangelical" faith she can speak of "the one really foolish assumption . . . that anyone could possibly arrive at a situationless, culture-free, objective interpretation of any text, let alone a text as complex as the Bible."[33] One must wonder what happened to the evangelical notion of the sufficiency and perspicuity (clarity) of Scripture?

Mollenkott's new faith has a new eschatology. At the RE-Imagining Conference in 1993, she re-imagined the future church's message:

> We would avoid the androcentric language (Father, Son, etc.) and the dominant submission theology. . . . I can no longer worship in a theological context that depicts God as an abusive parent and Jesus as the obedient trusting child.[34]

Submission to God and the Father making the Son to be sin for us sounds like the gospel to me (Romans 8:3,4; 2 Corinthians 5:21). But in the gleaming future of pan-sexual syncretistic spirituality, the Bible, the Christian message of redemption, and the Christ of the Scriptures will not be welcomed, especially by ex-evangelicals.

The Jesus Seminar

If there is a Jesus in the new, liberated world of tomorrow, He will fit all the parameters of this new paganism. The Jesus Seminar will see to that. In what follows, it is not my goal to provide a detailed discussion of the methods, goals, and conclusions of the Jesus Seminar. Other chapters in this book adequately handle that task. My goal is simply to show, in brief fashion, the connection of the Seminar to the shift toward paganism in our culture.

Robert Funk and His Escape from Fundamentalism

A recognized New Testament scholar, Robert Funk as the founder of the Jesus Seminar is committed to bringing the fruits of his radical critical scholarship to the average Christian in the pew. According to Funk, Christians need to mature in their knowledge and realize that most of what Jesus is reported to have said in the Gospels was placed on His lips by later believers. As well, they need to realize that most authentic sayings of Jesus come from a hypothetical document, "Q," which some scholars believe is embedded in Matthew and Luke, and from the heretical Gnostic Gospel of Thomas. In 1993 Funk published a best-selling book, *The Five Gospels,* setting this heretical Gospel of Thomas alongside the four canonical Gospels as an equally valid source for access to Jesus.[35] This is like asking Christ and Belial to share the Sunday morning service. It can only confuse the average Christian and promote the coming of pagan religious syncretism.

Not every member of the Jesus Seminar comes from "Christian" roots. Indeed, for "objectivity" there are even non-Christian fellows. According to Seminar fellow Marcus Borg, in a taped public debate at the University of Oregon, Robert Funk is still attempting to live down his evangelical fundamentalist past. According to Borg, Funk as a youth, dressed in a white suit and white shoes, was pushed forward as a boy preacher. If anyone knows the hothouse atmosphere of certain milieux where children are used as cute "Christian" performers, one sympathizes with Funk. But escaping "out from fundamentalism" is anything but a cold objective affair.

Funk has come a long way. He dedicates his book to Galileo, "who altered our view of the heavens forever"; to Thomas Jefferson, "who took scissors and paste to the Gospels"; and to David Friedrich Strauss, who "pioneered the quest for the historical Jesus."[36]

Certainly the great scientist Galileo got an undeserving shaft from the church of his day. But should the work of Jefferson and Strauss on the Bible be seen as "science" in anywhere near the same sense? Would anyone today accept the subjective Bible-study methods of Jefferson? Concerning Strauss, as a so-called biblical scientist he is a most complex figure.

Strauss's biographer documents that though Strauss was held up as the great example of critical, dispassionate scholarship and the father of scientific research on the historical Jesus, he was in deep fellowship with the occult.[37] While his father Johann Friedrich Strauss was an orthodox Christian pietist,[38] early in his theological training David immersed himself in the mysticism of Jacob Böhme, and came to believe deeply in the supernatural, but "not . . . in any theistic sense, but rather as a belief in the pantheistic unity of the world."[39] Strauss himself later recounts a meeting with a medium:

> I cannot in my whole life remember such a comparable moment. I was absolutely convinced that as soon as I laid my hand in hers [the medium's] my whole thinking and being

would lie open before her . . . . it was as if someone pulled
the ground away from under my feet and I were sinking
into a bottomless abyss . . . . she [the medium] praised my
faith, and . . . [said] that I would never fall into unbelief.[40]

According to this seeress, the father of modern New Testament scholarship would always be a believer—*in occult pantheism,* something Strauss never repudiated. How can
someone with such deep religious convictions of a non-Christian nature, antipathetic to orthodoxy, make a believable
claim to objectivity when dealing with a theistic document
such as the New Testament?

Monists will *always* find theism unacceptable.* With
admirable consistency they will always eliminate any expressions of theism as a possible explanation of phenomena in the
life of Jesus. Miracles, a unique divine nature, Christ's atoning
death for sin, God distinct from the creation He made, and
inspired Scripture, to name just a few, are all elements
intrinsic to a theistic worldview that are "objectively" and "scientifically" screened out by monists as later additions to a
Jesus they want to make much more amenable to their theology. Such a theological agenda determines from the start
what Jesus can and cannot say. Monists can only produce a
monistic Jesus. This might be good (monistic) theology but it
is not science.

Marcus Borg: "Meeting Jesus Again for the First Time"

Marcus Borg, another fellow of the Jesus Seminar and
author of the recent book, *Meeting Jesus Again for the First
Time,*[41] is also a deeply religious man. Raised an evangelical
Lutheran, he now has discovered a new view of Jesus and of
the Spirit. The Jesus he met again for the first time is not the
Jesus of scriptural orthodoxy. Rather, he found that "like
Socrates, Jesus was a teacher of a subversive wisdom. Like the

---

* *Monism* sees all reality as "one." It is a parallel term for *pantheism,* which sees all
as God. *Theism* involves belief in a personal Creator-God who is distinct from the
creation.

Buddha, he had an Enlightenment experience. Like a shaman, he was a healer. Like Gandhi, he protested against a purity system."[42] Borg is not merely comparing Jesus with elements in the lives of other holy men. He is recognizing the validity of other religious traditions. As for his new view of the Spirit, it is actually rooted in the pantheism of Huston Smith.[43] So we need to ask not merely who is Jesus, but rather *who* is Huston Smith.

Huston Smith, born of missionary parents in China, is a well-known expert in comparative religions who is deeply committed to monistic spirituality. Significantly associated with New Age and occult Theosophical thinkers, Smith is a sponsor of the Temple of Understanding, an organism of the Theosophical Society devoted to global syncretism that now has the privileged status of a nongovernmental organization in the United Nations. Smith was a faculty member with well-known New Ager and Assistant Secretary-General of the U.N., Robert Mueller, the Dalai Lama, and Marilyn Ferguson (author of *The Aquarian Conspiracy*) at an interfaith gathering in Malta in 1985. In the same year, Smith gave a lecture at the Theosophical Society's "Blavatsky Lodge" in Sydney, Australia on the subject, "Is a New World Religion Coming?"[44] Smith believes *there is* a new world religion coming, by the work of the spirit—"an invisible geometry . . . working to shape [the great religious traditions of the world] into a single truth."[45]

Needless to say, this syncretistic view of the Spirit, when employed by Marcus Borg, will only consider believable a Jesus-guru who can blend into other religious systems. It will reject as unacceptable and thus inauthentic the exclusive claims of the Jesus of orthodox confession. In his personal testimony, Borg states quite honestly: "I do not believe that Christianity is the only way of salvation, or that the Bible is the revealed will of God, or that Jesus was the unique Son of God." Christianity is only one of many "mediators of the sacred."[46] One certainly has to respect Borg's belief system, but it is just that—*belief*.

So, at the end of the day, when all the science has been paraded, and all the claims of cold dispassionate scholarship have been touted, the Jesus Seminar is just one more ideologically-loaded attempt to serve the revival of pantheistic spirituality in our time. *Behind the science lies spiritual apostasy.*

The Unpardonable Sin–Calling a Spade a Spade

We live in a day of *open* apostasy—and a descent into paganism. Time does not permit a discussion of the advance of apostasy in the World Council of Churches, in the interfaith movement spreading like wildfire even in unsuspecting evangelical churches throughout the world, in the Parliament of the World's Religions, in the United Nations, and the many global agencies that espouse this new syncretistic form of spirituality.[47] What is both odd and strangely logical is that the leadership of this apostasy comes from Christian America. The coming of age of American New Testament scholarship as it introduces apostasy into the church's Scriptures is just one aspect of the coming of age of American spirituality as it becomes the world leader in an egalitarian, pan-sexual, and pantheistic religion that has nothing to do with America's Christian spiritual roots. The words of Jesus, inevitably considered inauthentic by the Jesus Seminar, certainly call for an answer: "What is a man [or a nation] profited, if he shall gain the whole world, and lose his own soul?" (Matthew 16:26).

In the history of the church, this has happened before. In the first three centuries, so-called "Christian Gnosticism" was a radically pagan re-interpretation of Christianity that was not simply an alternate and valid expression of the faith but, behind the subterfuge, was in fact its very antithesis. Inspired Scripture prophesied its coming (1 Timothy 4:1-10). Paul warned Timothy to (1) be on his guard against those who would apostasize from the faith; (2) denounce error; and (3) teach sound doctrine.

In the theistic world of the Bible where there is both truth and error, right and wrong, speaking the truth also involved

saying what the truth *is not.* In our day of diversity and tolerance, where God the Creator has been dethroned,
denouncing error has become the ultimate unpardonable sin.
Principal opposition to anything that others hold dear makes
you a bigot and a hate-monger. So why do it?

When Gnosticism became a massive challenge to orthodoxy, the church fathers of the succeeding centuries heeded
Paul's advice. They labored to acquaint themselves with these
"doctrines of demons," warn the faithful, and set alongside
error the great truths of the gospel. One of them, Hippolytus
(A.D. 170-236), stated his reasons. He sought to oppose error
not only to arm the church against false teaching but also to
"win those who are themselves teaching heresy." He believed
that "by proclaiming the folly of those who are persuaded by
[these heterodox tenets], we shall prevail on them to retrace
their course to the serene haven of the truth."[48] Hippolytus's
example is worthy of imitation in our day.

The Gnostics have resurfaced in various guises down through the centuries ever since their first appearance in the early church. Their goal was to co-opt the church in its formative days with a "higher revelation." Such Gnostics as the Docetists were identified and quickly repudiated by the early church leaders. Tertullian and others pointed out their errors while councils such as the Council of Nicea tried to prevent such heresies from ever entering the church by setting the boundaries of the Faith.

So what do Gnostics believe? The phrase "two completely separate beings" comes from the pen of a leading modern authority on ancient Gnosticism who shows that this esoteric school of thought consistently distinguished between the earthly, transitory Jesus of Nazareth and the eternal, heavenly Christ. For the Gnostics, "Christ" was the mysterious spiritual presence of the unknown God that inhabited the human Jesus and that inhabits every true Gnostic believer—a sort of ancient "cosmic Christ."

So, according to the *Apocalypse of Peter,* Jesus died on the cross, but the real Christ actually sat on the branch of a tree, watching and laughing. In the end, this distortion reaches a culmination when Christ is identified with the serpent of Genesis 3. We will now look at some of the latest Gnostics and their fellow spin doctors—a sobering lesson about a certain type of "leaven" that keeps reappearing.

4

THE NEW CHRIST
OF PAGANISM

Peter Jones

T hose raised on Disney, MTV, and Monday night football may find history a drag. Only nerds in libraries enjoy history, and only the nerd of nerds studies church history. But history can help Christians stand for truth, for the issues of the past have come back to haunt us. The wise solutions of our forebears can help us still.

In the early centuries, the church faced attacks on its central doctrine—the person of Christ. In the lovely town of Chalcedon on the Black Sea, in the balmy month of October, A.D. 451, the leading Christian teachers and pastors assembled to state with great clarity, against heretical and misinformed views, the church's doctrine of Christ. "One person in two natures" has ever since defined orthodox Christology. Jesus Christ is both truly God and truly man.

This is a great mystery. Who understands the mystery of the human person, let alone the person of God the Son in human form? This definition at Chalcedon did not claim infinite knowledge. It simply laid down some essential points of reference as indicated in Scripture.[1] Christ is one real person, like God the Father and God the Holy Spirit. He is not made up of multiple personalities. Of course, like every other person, Christ is unique. His uniqueness consists in being both divine and human—having two natures—and the mystery of

His person is that these two natures are both perfectly united and yet always remain distinct. The new paganized view of Christ, however, explodes this definition, disfiguring His person and work beyond recognition.

The New Christology: Two Persons, Two Natures

The Bible shows us what we do not like to see about ourselves and what we need to see about Jesus. But Aquarian (New Age) devotees twist the Scripture and use the Bible as a grotesque circus mirror—to flatter and bewitch. In this make-believe world, spiritual information comes from within. The magic mirror on the wall tells you that you are the fairest you can be—even godlike.

The new Christ is but a reflection of this divinized "New Human." A relativized Bible and a congenial (esoteric) Bible study method let the reader interrogate the text and discover new, personalized answers. Finding hidden meanings in Scripture, Christ is "seen" with new eyes. Not the "one person with two natures," Jesus is now viewed as a human imbued with "Christ consciousness," someone *you* can hope to be.

Shirley MacLaine reads the Bible and sees a Jesus "very much like metaphysical seekers in the New Age today."[2] Popular Christian novelist Madeleine L'Engle breaks from the unity of Chalcedon: "Jesus of Nazareth lived for a brief life span, but Christ always was, is and will be."[3] "New-look Christology" ditches the delicate unity of the divine with the human for a pagan notion of divinized humanity. Pagan witch Mary Daly affirms that "the idea of a unique divine incarnation in a male, the God man of the 'hypostatic union' [the Chalcedonian formula], is inherently sexist and oppressive. Christology is idolatry."[4]

This is not simply word-shuffling. The implications of these ideas are momentous for the future of the Christian faith. So we ask first, *who is Christ* according to the new pagan spirituality, and then, *who is Jesus?*

Who Is Christ?

The new spirituality answers the question, "Who is Christ?" in a number of ways, from the least innocuous to the most shocking. All, though, are on the same continuum, and in splitting Christ from Jesus, they depersonalize Christ and relativize the Incarnation.

The "Cosmic Christ"

The neopagan "Christian" theologian, Matthew Fox, promotes a brand of Christology that any religion (other than Christian orthodoxy) could buy.* Though he tries to maintain a link with Christianity by using certain Christian terms, Jesus Christ is no longer the unique mediator between God and man:

> Christ is not simply confined to the historical Jesus. Christ is the immanent Wisdom of God present in the whole cosmos. For Christians, Jesus is the paradigmatic manifestation of cosmic wisdom but he is only one such manifestation. This wisdom has been manifested in the Tao, the Buddha, the Great Spirit and the Goddess.[5]

Rosemary Radford Ruether, an influential Christian feminist, thinks that "Fox is basically on target in these affirmations."[6]

This perversion, of course, only happens in liberal churches, right? *Wrong!* Madeleine L'Engle,[7] in her book *The Irrational Season*, calls Jesus "the man who housed" the Christ.[8] Though she has denied any New Age connections, L'Engle was associated with institutions similar to Matthew Fox's Institute for Creation Spirituality,[9] so there is little doubt as to the intended meaning of this phrase.

Fox's "Cosmic Christ" also appears in L'Engle's writings. In her story, "Polly and the Episcopalian Priest," Polly, who is

---

* Ron Rhodes's chapter, "The Cosmic Christ of Matthew Fox," provides great detail on this.

posing as a goddess, is captured by an opposing tribe. The priest, a psychic healer, shows her the altar where he is going to kill her if the rains do not come. As she prepares to die at the hands of this pagan butcher, the following thoughts go through her mind:

> She thought . . . of her own experience of the healer holding his hands over hers, as warmth flowed through them. There had been incredible power and beauty in the old man's hands. Could he be a healer and yet with his healing hands take her blood to enhance his power? Could benign power and malign power work together? Mana power and taboo power were each an aspect of power itself . . . But there was [a key line] between Polly and the healer. Surely the loving power of Christ had been in those delicate hands . . .[10]

Samantha Scott and Brenda Smith researched L'Engle's writings and after reading the above paragraph concluded: "Utter blasphemy! Christ's power does not reside in the hands of a butcher."[11] Except, of course, if your notion of Christ is a "cosmic" pagan one, for then the yin and the yang belong together, nothing is ultimately good or bad, and the butcher can be Christ. Here the human and divine natures in the person of Jesus Christ are split. The divine is now called the Cosmic Christ, who is the Spirit in all religions. Jesus is a mere man who shares with others the divine Spirit. Christ and Christianity are no longer unique.

The "Christ Consciousness" or the Higher Self

According to this new spirituality, Christian orthodoxy's teachings about Jesus are not worth the paper they're written on. This goes especially for orthodoxy's "elitist belief that only one man has ever been of 'divine birth.'"[12] The new spirituality is much more democratic, and thus bound to please the "me generation" of "boomer" seekers. It views the union of the divine (which they call Christ) with the human (Jesus) as a particular example of what happens to *all* spiritual people.

Jesus is merely a paradigm or prototype of what should happen to every spiritual being.

In espousing this, Matthew Fox is just as "New Age" in his thinking as Chris Griscom, Shirley MacLaine's ex-guru. Says Griscom: "We don't have to wait for some booming voice from a male god to say, 'You are such and such.' "[13] "For inner peace, indeed, for ecstasy, all you need to do is to tune into your higher self. And the higher self will reply: 'Clothe yourself in love; awaken, stimulate your life force, then you will have the courage to be who you are.' "[14]

And who are you? "You are," says Griscom, "your higher self," a being of incredible power, able "on this planet to . . . conquer death, make choices, get rid of sickness . . . come into harmony with other planets and other realities and other dimensionalities." Griscom thus encourages her disciples: "You're worthy! And you have all the knowing. You'll never need anything but what's inside you." Armed with knowledge of the self, disciples will "walk this Earth as gods."[15]

From this perspective, everyone possesses the potential to attain "Christ consciousness." Jesus found the Christ in Himself. So should you.[16] "I found God in myself and I loved her fiercely," says Roman Catholic feminist theologian Carol Christ.[17] This new "god" or "Christ" consciousness is also flooding into liberal "Christian" writings. "Christian" systematic theologians Nimian Smart and Steven Konstantin speak of "a Divine Being who lies within and beyond the cosmos . . . but we also find the Divine within us, at the base of our consciousness. In searching inside ourselves through self-training[18] we can find her in the Light which lights our consciousness."[19] This is not "a fresh view of Christianity." It smells of ancient decadent paganism.

Though the names "Jesus" and "Christ" are used, such teaching is fundamentally anti-Christian, for it takes the focus off the unique person of Jesus Christ and elevates every seeking individual to Christhood status. The New Testament would call it pagan blasphemy, the worship of the creature rather than the Creator (Romans 1:25). Moreover, pagan blasphemy is the ultimate expression of diabolical seduction, exchanging the truth of God for "the lie."[20] Little wonder such misrepresentation of the truth leads finally to the promotion of the Antichrist.

Christ Is the Antichrist

Feminist witch Miriam Starhawk asserts that feminism is "the strongest mythogenic (myth-creating) force at work today."[21] Many in the West have failed to address this attack on Christianity; now, it is almost too late.[22] Anglican minister William Oddie, in his book *What Will Happen to God?* discusses the effects of feminism on the Christian faith. He believes that feminism may lead to "the substantial reconstruction of the Christian religion itself." Indeed, "Beliefs and values that have held sway for thousands of years will be questioned as never before."[23] While correct, this judgment expresses the understated reserve of an English gentleman with a stiff upper lip and a stiff collar to support it!

Radical Jewish feminist Naomi Goldenberg, now a witch, puts it much more forcefully: "The feminist movement in Western culture is engaged in the slow execution of Christ and Jahweh[24]. . . . the gods who have stolen our [women's] identity[25]. . . . We women are going to bring an end to God."[26]

She means, of course, the God of Scripture. For other gods are lurking in the shadows, particularly goddesses and the Antichrist, which have a strong likelihood of coming down to the same thing, if one is to judge by the goings-on at recent "Christian" feminist conferences. The goddess Sophia, worshiped by liberated women from mainline churches (most of whom were not self-confessed witches), was the new "re-imagined" Christ. Communicants received pagan sacred elements of milk and honey. Christa—the goddess of feminist deconstruction, lesbian love, and sinful play—now often replaces Christ the lamb of God bearing the sins of the world in His body on the tree. This is a palace revolution of unprecedented proportions. This is Antichrist in the temple of God, one more notable expression of the "abomination of desolation" (Matthew 24:15).

These "Christian" feminists seek to "re-imagine" Christianity by infusing "new" female-friendly notions of goddess worship and sexual liberation into biblical faith. Truly radical feminists know better and say so with candor and coherence:

> The radical Christian vision is, and always was [in early Gnosticism] a reemergence of paganism. To be truly revolutionary, Christianity would have to dissolve itself . . . [and] its male-dominated . . . hierarchies, . . . renounce most of the Old Testament, most of the New, . . . throw out Genesis to return us radically to an image of God based on the pre-biblical universal perception of a Great Mother—a bisexual being, both male and female. . . . But, as we said, if the Christian church ever changed itself this radically, it would become pagan.[27]

The Antichrist Is a Woman

Some readers blanched when I suggested in a previous book that perhaps the Antichrist would be a woman.[28] While no one knows for sure, I would hazard a further suggestion based on recent events—she/he could be an androgynous lesbian of diabolical spiritual power.

I am not out on a lonely limb. Already in the nineteenth century Mother Ann Lee, founder of the Shakers, and Mary Baker Eddy, founder of Christian Science, believed that at the second coming the Messiah would be female.[29] This is also what some very influential modern lesbian witch theologians think. One, Mary Daly, with two doctorates in theology and presently a professor of theology at the Jesuit Boston College, writes:

> I suggest that the mechanism of reversal has been at the root of the idea that the "Antichrist" must be something "evil." What if this is not the case at all? What if the idea has arisen out of the male's unconscious dread that women will rise up and assert the power robbed from us? . . . The

Antichrist dreaded by the Patriarchs may be the surge of consciousness, the spiritual awakening, that can bring us beyond Christolatry into a fuller stage of conscious participation in the living God.

Seen from this perspective the Antichrist and the Second Coming of Women are synonymous. This Second Coming is not a return of Christ but a new arrival of female presence, once strong and powerful, but enchained since the dawn of patriarchy . . .

The Second Coming, then, means that the prophetic dimension in the symbol of the great Goddess . . . is the key to salvation from servitude to structures that obstruct human becoming . . .[30]

Readers will forgive me for providing such a long quotation, but seeing and reading is believing.

This is a type of Christology few were expecting. In this line of thought, the earth, in crisis due to the fruits of patriarchy sown by the male Gods (the Father and Christ) will be saved by the return of the goddess. This fits perfectly with New Age speculation concerning the coming (some say *present*) Age of Aquarius, with its "yin, feminine energy."[31] We are witnessing the end of the Age of Pisces, the Age of the Fish (Christianity), and of masculine, yang energy. In astrology, Aquarius is pictured as "the water-carrier." Behold the goddess, the Great Mother/Creatrix who appears in ancient mythology as "the divine potter, the carrier of the heavenly water jar."[32] So the "dawning of the Age of Aquarius" is accompanied by the appearance of goddess morning star.

Such soft feminist rehabilitation of the serpent's lie is simply a new vaguely "Christianized" version of what New Agers and their precursors have been saying for some time— the welcoming of Satan as the bringer of wisdom, the bringer of poisoned water for the spiritually thirsty Aquarian believers. The line from this "Christian" devotion to Sophia to the diabolical and the occult is direct and rapid. David Spangler, a

THE NEW CHRIST OF PAGANISM

contemporary spokesman of the New Age, described the New Age as an age of Luciferic initiation.

> Lucifer works within each of us to bring us wholeness as we move into the New Age . . . Lucifer comes to give us the final . . . Luciferic initiations . . . that many people in the days ahead will be facing, for it is an initiation into the New Age[33]. . . . Christ is the same force as Lucifer. . . . Lucifer prepares man for Christ-consciousness."[34]

In one chilling example from the sixties, Charles Manson led his followers in the massacre of Sharon Tate and her friends, believing that everything he did was "good," an expression of karma. Thus his followers saw him both as Satan and Christ. The ultimate identification of Christ with Satan is a natural outcome of monism, where both good and evil are equally part of the whole, for everything belongs together in the monistic circle of existence.

If Christ is the mystic presence of the divine, what does the new spirituality have to say about the man, Jesus?

Who Is Jesus?

In the hallowed halls of New Testament learning it is often held as an unquestioned truth that Jesus did not proclaim Himself as the Messiah and Son of God, the divine Savior who came to die for the sins of the world.[35] This is considered a later addition imposed upon Jesus by the orthodox wing of the church. A logical question follows: Who, then, is Jesus?

Jesus Is Not Unique

The new answer, given by contemporary Bible scholars, in the context of the rehabilitation of ancient Gnostic heresy, is: Jesus is "Sophia's most trusted envoy,"[36] "Miriam's Child," "Sophia's Prophet,"[37] "Very Goddess and Very Man,"[38] "an epiphany of God, a 'disclosure'. . . of God."[39] Jesus is interesting—He was a prophet, "a charismatic healer, unconventional sage, and founder of an alternative community. . . . He is clearly one of the most remarkable figures who ever lived"[40]—but He is not unique. Certainly Jesus was a "spirit-possessed" revolutionary, but not in the classic, orthodox sense of the God-incarnate Messiah. "What he was like reminds us that there have been figures in every culture who experienced the 'other world.'"[41]

British New Testament scholar Francis Watson argues that in the Gospel of John the divine logos unites with the man Jesus at His baptism.[42] Watson admits that his interpretation is close to "the gnosticizing view that the heavenly Christ descended into Jesus at his baptism, and then abandoned Jesus again before his death."[43] Watson finds a parallel to what he is proposing as the original Christology of the Gospel of John in the Gnostic Second Treatise of the Great Seth. In this document the Gnostic Christ says:

> I visited a bodily dwelling. I cast out the one who was in it first, and I went in . . . And I am the one who was in it, not resembling him who was in it first. For he was an earthly man, but I, I am from above the heavens . . . I revealed that I am a stranger to the regions below.[44]

As we will see in the chapters on the Jesus Seminar later in the book, American New Testament scholarship now contends that the true Jesus is most likely the Jesus of the Gnostic Gospel of Thomas.[45] In this gospel, the Christological concerns of the canonical Gospels are considered "secondary, if not misguided."[46] For Jesus did not come talking about Himself, but really showed that He was no different than any of His disciples.[47] The new radical Q scholarship* agrees with Thomas in three significant areas: (1) *the person of Jesus*—Jesus did not proclaim Himself as the Messiah and the Son of God,

---

* **Radical Q scholarship**—Shorthand reference to the radical wing of New Testament studies, strongly represented in the Jesus Seminar, which sees in the common material between Matthew and Luke evidence of a document, Q. From this hypothetical document is extracted "evidence" of the earliest community around Jesus, who allegedly did not believe in the gospel of cross and resurrection theology.

the divine Savior who was to die for the sins of the world;[48] (2) *the work of Jesus*—the Jesus of Q is but a teacher of wisdom,[49] a sort of proto-Gnostic guru; (3) *the nature of the church*—the Q people did not focus "on the person of Jesus or his life and destiny. [Rather] they were engrossed with the social program that was called for by his teachings,"[50] including radical poverty, the lifestyle of the wandering beggar,[51] an attitude of political subversion,[52] and, needless to say, an egalitarian, antipatriarchal feminism.[53] Speaking of the "Q community," Burton Mack goes on to make the most radical of statements:

> The remarkable thing about the people of Q is that they were not Christians. They did not think of Jesus as a messiah or the Christ. . . . They did not regard his death as a . . . saving event. . . . They did not imagine that he had been raised from the dead. . . . They did not gather to worship in his name. . . . The people of Q were *Jesus people, not Christians* [emphasis mine].[54]

Publicity for Burton L. Mack's volume, *The Lost Gospel: The Book of Q and Christian Origins*, trumpets that the Book of Q "pre-dat[es] the New Testament by generations," that the New Testament "presents a fictionalized life of Jesus," and that Jesus' disciples "did not think of him as the Son of God . . . but . . . as a wise, anti-establishment . . . counterculture . . . teacher."[55]

If Jesus is not unique, He is interchangeable with other holy men, and with all Gnostic believers. This explains the disinterest of many today in Jesus as a person, and in the Gospels that describe the earthly Jesus.

Jesus is merely a human shell for the Cosmic Christ, just like the various bodies that our "Higher Self" occupies and then discards through multiple reincarnations. The uniqueness and dignity of His human person and His historical work are lost in the amorphous being, Christ, who inhabits all things, but has no personal identity.

Jesus Is Not the Lamb of God

For 2000 years the church has preached the gospel of Jesus, the Lamb of God. Paul considered this gospel "of first importance," the very basis of the truth in which the church stands.[56] The new spirituality begs to differ.

For Paul the "wisdom of God" was "Jesus Christ crucified," an event that was a stumbling block to unbelieving Jews and foolishness to unbelieving gentiles (1 Corinthians 1:18). This "wisdom" is roundly rejected by all sectors of the new spirituality, New Age gurus to radical feminists, many of them claiming to be Christians:

New Age Gurus. New Agers explain away the need for Jesus' atonement in a variety of ways—often by emphasizing that there's no need for an atonement since there's no real guilt. The "Voice" (supposedly Jesus) who in 1965 possessed Dr. Helen Schucman,* a Jewish atheist and psychologist, explained in *A Course in Miracles* that "evil is an illusion, and sin is the illusion that separates us from our own innate divinity, our own godhood."[57] This Jesus soothingly intones, "Forget your dreams of sin and guilt and come with me," and then goes on, quite naturally, to deny the reality of the cross.

Schucman's disciple, Marianne Williamson, also a Jewess involved in promoting this new-style Christianity, assures her many readers: "There is no place for hell in a world whose loveliness can yet be so intense and so inclusive it is but a step from there to heaven."[58]

Elizabeth Clare Prophet, leader of the Church Universal and Triumphant, considers the idea of blood-sacrifice an "erroneous doctrine" of dubious pagan origin.[59] Matthew Fox sees Jesus' death as a symbol of Mother Earth dying each day as a constantly sacrificed Pascal Lamb.

In a similar vein, the New Age spiritualizes and explains away the resurrection and the ascension of Christ. The mystical

---

* Tal Brooke's chapter, "The Cosmic Christ of Channeled Revelation," provides a thorough discussion of Helen Schucman and *A Course in Miracles.*

intellectual Joseph Campbell, guru of TV personality Bill Moyers, explains the ascension as the moment when Christ "has gone inward . . . to the kingdom of heaven within."[60] New Ager John White explains his view:

> The institutional Christian churches tell us that Jesus was the only Son of God, that he incarnated as a human in order to die on the Cross in a substitutionary act as a penalty for our sins, and thereby save the world. But that is a sad caricature, a pale reflection of the true story. . . . Jesus did not save people: he freed them—from the bondage of the ego. The significance of the incarnation and resurrection is not that Jesus was a human like us but rather that we are gods like him. . . .[61]

Radical Feminists. As noted in an earlier chapter, radical lesbian feminist Virginia Ramey Mollenkott "re-imagined" the future church's message: "We would avoid the androcentric language (Father, Son, etc.) and the dominant submission theology. . . . I can no longer worship in a theological context that depicts God as an abusive parent and Jesus as the obedient trusting child."[62]

Dolores Williams, professor at Union Theological Seminary, offers an equally radical opinion: "I don't think we need a theory of atonement at all. . . . I don't think we need folks hanging on crosses and blood dripping and weird stuff."[63] In *An Acceptable Time,* Madeleine L'Engle compares those who believe in the substitutionary atonement of Christ to murderous savages who slaughter human beings to satisfy Mother Earth.[64]

From these seemingly unrelated quarters come the same message. Individual and planetary redemption do not depend on the objective work of God in the historical death of Jesus that removes the objective stain and guilt of sin. Redemption is a *human* work, the inner capacity to realize one's divine nature and limitless potential. Such realization includes the rejection of any "externally imposed" creational structures and scriptural laws. Liberation consists in knowing that these things are without meaning. Knowing oneself to be god is *power* knowledge—the power of the human god unto human salvation! This is the saving gnosis (secret knowledge) of which the ancient Gnostics constantly spoke. For them, too, Christ was not a Savior, bearing in His body the curse of our sin. Christ was rather the revealer of knowledge, whispering to people to look inside.

These ideas are not fruitful insights into the original gospel. They are *another* gospel, mutually exclusive of the New Testament's gospel. Two gospels, according to Paul, are an oxymoron. One eliminates the other. Which one should the church choose? The gospel of Q, of the Jesus Seminar and the Gnostic texts, or the gospel of the apostles and the historic creeds?

Jesus Is a Guru

It is no coincidence that we hear so much about the rediscovery of the goddess Sophia (Wisdom) while New Testament studies emphasize Jesus as a wisdom (*sophia*) teacher.* Female mainline feminists meet (mostly) male mainline New Testament scholars at this new confessional intersection: Jesus is "Sophia's Most Trusted Envoy."[65]

The modern approach is to see "Jesus as Sage," not a teacher of dogma or morals, but "of a way or path, specifically a way of transformation . . . similar to the other great sages . . . include[ing] Lao Tzu . . . and the Buddha."[66] The work of Jesus according to the Jesus Seminar is to be a teacher of wisdom.[67]

In this new perspective, Jesus is "a renewal movement founder . . . [who] points us to human community and history, to an alternative culture which seeks to make the world more compassionate."[68] This compassion emanates not from the wisdom of the gospel of the crucified Christ but from

---

* The Greek word of "wisdom" is *sophia.*

wisdom found within the self. The newly discovered Jesus is not the preacher of the Cross and the final revelation of the God of Old Testament Scripture but Sophia's most trusted envoy—which ultimately makes Jesus (the true founder of Christianity) a pagan worshiper of the goddess.

New Testament scholars thus open the door of the church to the spirituality now prevalent in radical feminism and New Age religion. In current New Age thinking the female principle holds the key to salvation. James Lovelock, a New Age spokesman, calls for a return to goddess spirituality to save the earth from ecological disaster and avoid the destruction to which the Semitic/Christian God will inevitably lead. Shirley MacLaine dedicates her book *Going Within* to "women and men who seek the spiritual feminine in themselves."[69]

The Jewish feminist theologian, Rita Gross, advocates borrowing from Hindu goddess traditions to affect the "second coming of the goddess."[70] Since the goddess increasingly symbolizes an amalgam of all peoples and faiths, Jesus will doubtless be heralded as the great Christian prophet of interfaith communion. Jesus—the envoy of Sophia—has prophetically shown us the way of the "Cosmic Christ," the unifying spirit of a new religious world order.

The pieces fit. Philosophical deconstruction eliminates rational (left-brain masculine) thought, leaving intuition and personal taste. Radical New Testament scholarship reconstructs Jesus, envoy of Sophia, as a blueprint for a compassionate, tolerant, politically correct, multicultural, multisexual, feminist egalitarian society, liberated from notions of sin, guilt, and the New Testament theology of the Cross. Radical religious feminism worships the goddess Sophia, rejecting all hints of orthodox Christianity. Both scholarship and feminism restore Gnostic teaching on the same theme.

At the same time, New Age thinking awaits a global transformation based upon the rediscovery of the feminine, right-brain "yin" intuition of the Age of Aquarius. It decries rational, male-inspired "yang" "theories of the atonement" of the Age of Pisces. These disparate movements come together in the confession of a brand new "Christology" (really quite old), which replaces the historic confession of the crucified Jesus as the true wisdom of God.

A new "Christ" consciousness appears, calling for new birth. Receiving Jesus as Savior, however, no longer means regeneration by the work of Christ on the Cross, an act of God that reconciles the world to Himself. Believers experience rebirth when they come to see that all wisdom is contained within the self. According to modern guru Carolyn Anderson:

> Right now a transformation is occurring in the hearts and minds of countless people on earth. The process begins with the individual, with the willingness of those of us who are consciously awakening to know ourselves by exploring the depths of our essence . . . the integrating our humanity with our divinity. . . . The healing of the planet resides in the "wholing" of humanity.[71]

This rebirth produces no Christians, ready to die for their Savior, Jesus of Nazareth. This New Age "Great Awakening" bears children in the image of its gods—pagan idols set on the thrones of hearts: *the gods within.*

Have New Age leaders penetrated the church to teach a new Christ, or is this idea merely the hysteria of backwards minds? There is probably no better example of such genuine penetration than Matthew Fox, a priest who has stood in the center of San Francisco's grand historical Grace Cathedral to conduct a Planetary Mass. What is this mass? It celebrates the divinity of the earth, the coming "cosmic Christ," and a consequent paradigm shift.

Matthew Fox, an excommunicated Roman Catholic priest now fully embraced by the Episcopalian hierarchy, has constructed a cosmic theology (and Christology) that has wide appeal. His stand against patriarchal religion makes him popular with the feminists. His pantheism and mysticism make him popular with New Agers. His focus on "rescuing mother earth: makes him popular among the ecologically minded. His version of the cosmic Christ—nonjudgmental about sin and especially "inclusive" of homosexuality—makes him popular with the "lesbian-bi-gay" community. His emphasis on deep ecumenism makes him popular with all those who hold to the politically correct idea that all religions lead to God. And couching his theology in Christian terminology makes him popular with a wide range of cultural Christians in the major denominations. Matthew Fox's million-selling books epitomize the phenomenon of the cosmic Christ, and that makes his inclusion in this book a necessity.

5

THE COSMIC CHRIST
OF MATTHEW FOX

Ron Rhodes

His name is Matthew Fox, and he is one of the most influential New Agers today. This chapter will focus on his version of the "Cosmic Christ" against the broader backdrop of his theological system known as creation spirituality.

- His Institute for Culture and Creation Spirituality has included on its staff a witch, a shaman, a voodoo priestess, a Zen Buddhist, a T'ai Chi master, and a Jungian analyst.

- Hundreds of thousands of people around the world—including New Age seekers, disgruntled Catholics, free-spirited Protestants, and people turned off by institutional religion—have attended his creation spirituality workshops.

- His creation spirituality has even been taught to children, with each class beginning with a "Pledge of Allegiance to the Earth."

Fox became a Dominican in 1960 after graduating from college, and was ordained in 1967. That same year, as a result of mystic Thomas Merton's (1915-1968) influence, Fox entered the doctoral program at the Institut Catholique de Paris. His degree was in the history and theology of spirituality. He focused heavily on medieval mystics.

Two of the more important mystics Fox studied are Hildegard of Bingen and Meister Eckhart. These mystics, more than any others, played a role in molding Fox's thinking on key theological issues—especially the doctrine of Christ. Fox went on to write books on these individuals—*Breakthrough: Meister Eckhart's Creation Spirituality in New Translation* (1980) and *Illumination of Hildegard of Bingen* (1985).

Fox has wielded tremendous influence in the world through his 16 books. There is no question that the three most important of these are *Original Blessing: A Primer in Creation Spirituality* (1983), *The Coming of the Cosmic Christ* (1988), and *Creation Spirituality* (1991). Because the present chapter focuses on Fox's cosmic Christology, primary attention will be focused on his million-selling *The Coming of the Cosmic Christ.*

The controversial teachings contained in these books— along with Fox's lack of accountability and submission to the Catholic hierarchy—caused such intense conflict with the Vatican that he was finally dismissed from the Dominican order in 1993. He then became an Episcopalian priest in good standing in December 1994. The publicity caused by his conflict with the Vatican has proved to be a blessing in disguise— Fox's creation spirituality is more well known and more popular than ever. The saga continues . . . .

Today's Spiritual Crisis

Before one can properly appreciate Fox's views on creation spirituality, it is necessary to grasp what he says about today's "spiritual crisis." The components of this crisis, Fox says, include the survival of Mother Earth, the despair of our youth, the inadequacy of Western worship, the loss of the mystical tradition in all religions, and justice toward women, the poor, and all the native peoples of the world.

Ecologically, Fox says we are devastating Mother Earth. He claims we are destroying topsoil at a rate of six billion tons per year; the world's forests are disappearing at an alarming rate (one-third of the planet's total will be destroyed in the next 15 years); numerous species are disappearing (one every 25 minutes); birds are constantly dying; and the human race is self-destructing.

Fox also points to the gross expenditure of wealth on militarism and its effect on Mother Earth. He claims that man is spending $1.8 million per minute on weapons of mass destruction. In nuclear bomb tests alone, Fox says the United States has ruptured Mother Earth's womb 845 times. "Mother Earth is in great pain—a pain inflicted by her own children as they commit matricide."[1] In this statement alone one can detect hints of Fox's disdain for patriarchy and great sympathy for a feminist model of religion.

Creation spirituality sets out to deal directly with the above "spiritual crisis."

A Symbol for Our Day

Fox acknowledges that Jesus died on the cross. However, ignoring all biblical evidence to the contrary (Matthew 20:28; 2 Corinthians 5:18,19; 1 Timothy 2:6; 1 John 2:2), he explains Jesus' death *not* in terms of the substitutionary atonement but in terms of His so-called stand against patriarchal religion. Jesus' "invitation to divine motherhood seriously challenged the religious system of his day. The crucifixion of Jesus was the logical result of His frontal assault on patriarchy." Jesus "died at the hands of men . . . just as Mother Earth is dying at the hands of a patriarchal civilization gone mad with its attraction to matricide. Both Jesus and Mother Earth appear to be victims of the same pathology."[2]

The crucifixion of Jesus is viewed by Fox as an appropriate symbol for the suffering of Mother Earth. After all, like Jesus of Nazareth, Mother Earth is not guilty of any crime. Both are innocent. Moreover, Mother Earth has "loved" us for billions of years—providing us with flowers, plants, water, food, and much more. Yet, despite the fact that she has loved us, *she is being crucified daily.*

If *crucifixion* is an appropriate symbol for the suffering of Mother Earth, then *resurrection* is an appropriate symbol for relieving Mother Earth's pain. Fox says that a revival of mysticism is a resurrection story for our times. "If we can awaken to an authentic mysticism, then a resurrection of Mother Earth is possible."[3] This reawakening to mysticism, Fox says, will lead to a deep spiritual conversion of everyone on earth. As mysticism is "resurrected" in the world, so Mother Earth herself is "resurrected."

The mysticism Fox speaks of centers on a personal experience of the divine and a sense of interconnectivity. "Ours is a time of emerging awareness of the interconnectivity of all things. Mysticism is all about interconnectivity. Thus ours is a mystical time."[4]

This revival of mysticism must of necessity involve the right hemisphere of the brain, for "mystical ability is physiologically located in the right lobe of the brain." Fox argues that "a crucial dimension of the imbalance in the West is the stunted growth of our mystical awareness and the underdevelopment of our mystical brain." This must be remedied in order for a global spiritual renaissance to occur. We must follow the example of Jesus, who Himself employed His right brain: "He was not a lawyer or a theologian but a storyteller who announced the Good News. Storytellers work out of the right brain and speak to the right brain of others."[5]

Fox sometimes refers to this awakening to mysticism in humanity as the "second coming." Ignoring biblical verses that speak of a *literal, physical* second coming of Jesus Christ (for example, Acts 1:11), Fox believes the "second coming" of the Cosmic Christ (an awakening to mysticism) will usher in a global renaissance that can heal Mother Earth and save her by changing human hearts and ways.[6]

More specifically, Fox believes that if we humans can simply come to see ourselves as pieces of divinity in the universe, then we will begin to see the interconnectivity of all things— *including* our interconnectivity with the Earth and all the lifeforms on the earth. This realization will generate compassion,

THE COSMIC CHRIST OF MATTHEW FOX

and this, in turn, will compel us to protect the Earth from further degradation.

The Ancient Tradition: Creation Spirituality

Creation spirituality is nothing new, according to Matthew Fox. It may *seem* new to twentieth-century Westerners, but it is actually an ancient tradition long propagated in the nature religions of the native peoples of the world. These peoples have *always* recognized the presence of the divine in the world. Fox claims this ancient tradition has been represented in church history in the writings of such luminaries as Basil of Caesarea, Gregory Nazianzus, Hildegard of Bingen, Mechtild of Magdeburg, Meister Eckhart, Julian of Norwich, and Nicholas of Cusa.

Creation spirituality is both a theological system *and* a movement that focuses on the "original blessing" instead of on "original sin" (a deviant doctrine Fox blames on Augustine). When Fox speaks of "original blessing," he is referring to "those blessings of healthy soil, living forests, singing birds, clean waters, and healthy DNA in our reproductive systems."[7] Fox says that because the original blessing *is greater* than the effects of man's sin, man should focus his attention on the creation and on discovering God *in* the creation. After all, God's creation is sacred. *It is divine.*

The Pantheistic Backdrop

In creation spirituality the emphasis and focal point is the creation. Fox views the divine as being *present in* the creation. Creation spirituality thus rests on the foundation of Fox's basic worldview—*pantheism.*

Fox asserts that "divinity is not outside us. We are in God and God is in us. That is the unitive experience of the mystics East or West. Its technical name is panentheism, which means that 'God is in all things and all things are in God.' "[8]

Fox utterly rejects the idea that God is "out there." He abhors the "dualistic manner" that separates creation from divinity. "Pantheism melts the dualism of inside and outside—like fish in water and the water in the fish, creation is in God and God is in creation."[9]

Jesus Himself was a pantheist, Fox argues. Jesus was allegedly teaching pantheism when He spoke of God's kingdom in our midst (Luke 17:20,21). "Jesus has seen something that so many others have missed: that all is in God and God is in all. Or, that all is in the kingdom/queendom of God and the kingdom/queendom of God is in all. For Jesus the kingdom/queendom of God is a pantheistic realm."[10]

Moreover, says Fox, the very fact that believers can do greater things than Christ (John 14:12) proves that pantheism is true. "This is possible because of our mystical and pantheistic relationship to the Creator. . . . Jesus teaches us about the vast dream of the Cosmic Christ yearning to be born in us—a dream about glory and fruitfulness."[11]

The Emerging Paradigm Shift

Borrowing the term "paradigm shift" from science historian Thomas Kuhn, author of *The Structure of Scientific Revolutions*, Fox says there is a paradigm shift before us in which the old is passing away and the new is being issued in. What is passing away? Fox says the religious model that focuses on man's sin, his need for redemption, and Jesus' death on the cross is a model that is passing away. Patriarchal religion—which calls God "Father" and involves a male priesthood—is passing away. The mode of thinking that there is a separation of the sacred and the profane (the Newtonian mechanistic way of thinking) is passing away. Man's abuse of nature is passing away. Man's sole reliance on the left sphere of the brain, where logical and analytic abilities reside, is passing away. In place of the old, the new model embraces the creation, God's presence *in* the creation, wholeness, ecology, feminism, and right-brain mysticism.[12]

Fox also calls for a shift from a quest for the historical Jesus to a quest for the Cosmic Christ. He says it is time to "reclaim" the Cosmic Christ. We need to move from a "personal Savior" Christianity to a "Cosmic Christ" Christianity.

The emphasis on the Cosmic Christ was allegedly lost during the eighteenth-century Enlightenment. The Enlightenment, Fox says, challenged Christian theologians to engage in a quest for the historical Jesus. For two centuries now, the quest for the historical Jesus has dominated theological discussions. "We need to let go of the Enlightenment and its worldview that denies mysticism."[13]

Who Is the Cosmic Christ?

In Fox's theology, the Cosmic Christ is a divine presence that permeates all of creation (note the close connection with pantheism). The term "cosmic" refers to that which is related to the whole universe. Fox believes the Cosmic Christ is present *in all* of creation.

The Cosmic Christ is "the divine mirror glistening and glittering in every creature." It is a "pattern that connects." Indeed, the Cosmic Christ "connects heaven and earth, past and future, divinity and humanity, all of creation: 'everything in heaven and everything on earth.' " The Cosmic Christ connects "all the atoms and galaxies of the universe." It is the "image of God present in all things." The Cosmic Christ "ushers in an era of coherence, of ending the separations, divisions, dualism, piecemealness that characterize a world without mysticism."[14]

The Cosmic Christ Common to All Religions and All People

Fox stresses that the Cosmic Christ is not the sole possession of Christianity. The Cosmic Christ has been and continues to be manifested in all the religions of the world. "Does the fact that the Christ became incarnate in Jesus exclude the Christ's becoming incarnate in others—Lao-tzu or Buddha or Moses or Sarah or Sojourner Truth or Gandhi or me or you? Just the opposite is the case."[15]

The concept of the Cosmic Christ is pre-Christian. The image of God in every atom and galaxy is not exactly a property of Christians. The divine "I am" in every person and every creature is no particular tradition's private legacy. Indeed, many non-Christians and post-Christians have written at length and quite happily about the "Cosmic Christ" including Paramahansa Yogananda, Rudolf Steiner, and Carl Jung.[16]

The presence of the divine in human beings is a thread that runs throughout Fox's *The Coming of the Cosmic Christ.* He boasts, "One of the most common themes in Cosmic Christ theology is a celebration of how common and omnipresent divinity is. Divinity is found in all creatures." The Cosmic Christ says to every individual, "Be still and know that I am God . . . *and you are too.*" A theology of the Cosmic Christ "is not embarrassed by the deification of humans."[17]

Fox quotes often from Meister Eckhart (thirteenth-century German mystic) and St. Hildegard of Bingen (twelfth-century Benedictine abbess) in arguing that the Cosmic Christ manifests itself in human beings. Citing these mystics, Fox is sure that all of us are called to "give birth" to the Cosmic Christ within ourselves and in society.

As noted above, Fox refers to this divine presence as the "I am" presence, noting that just as Jesus embodied the "I am" presence, so all human beings can embody the "I am" presence. This sounds quite similar to the view of Elizabeth Clare Prophet, who heads the (New Age) Church Universal and Triumphant.[18] Ultimately Jesus is no different from other humans. We've all got the "I am" presence. And because Jesus is not unique in Fox's theology, He receives very little attention in *The Coming of the Cosmic Christ.* The Cosmic Christ, *not Jesus,* is on center stage.

It is this manifestation of the Cosmic Christ in humans everywhere, Fox says, that ultimately leads to the saving or healing of Mother Earth. "What is needed if there is to be a twenty-first century for Mother Earth and her children is a spiritual vision that prays, celebrates, and lives out the reality of the Cosmic Christ who lives and breathes in Jesus and in all God's children, in all the prophets of religions everywhere, in all creatures of the universe."[19]

The Call for a Deep Ecumenism

Matthew Fox calls for a "deep ecumenism." By this he refers to the coming together of the world religions at a mystical level. "Without mysticism there will be no 'deep ecumenism'.... The promise of ecumenism, the coming together of religions, has been thwarted because world religions have not been relating at the level of mysticism."[20]

This coming together of world religions is made possible by the Cosmic Christ, the "pattern that connects" and "the divine mirror glistening and glittering in every creature" *of every religion.* Ecumenism becomes a genuine possibility because the kingdom/queendom of God is *among us all.*

Deep ecumenism will enable us as a race to draw from the wisdom of *all* the world religions.

> Deep ecumenism is the movement that will unleash the wisdom of all world religions—Hinduism and Buddhism, Islam and Judaism, Taoism and Shintoism, Christianity in all its forms, and native religions and goddess religions throughout the world. This unleashing of wisdom holds the last hope for the survival of the planet we call home.[21]

A key component of this "wisdom" is the realization of the interconnectivity of all things. Taking care of the earth is a natural outgrowth of this mystical recognition of interconnectivity.

Redefining Sin and Salvation

Earlier we noted Fox's view that Jesus died on the cross because of His "frontal assault" against patriarchal religion. This raises the important issue of how sin and salvation fit into Fox's theology.

While Fox on occasion uses the words "sin" and "salvation," his version of these doctrines bears no resemblance to the biblical view. For Fox, sin does not involve acts that the church has condemned as morally evil. Nor does it relate to so-called "original sin." Rather, sin ultimately amounts to thinking wrongly about God, the creation, the ecosystem, women, and native peoples.[22]

Fox's weak view of sin is more than apparent in his openness to homosexuality:

> All too many Christians have been led to believe that Christ is not present in lovemaking. That makes no sense. In fact, the Cosmic Christ is radically present to all sexuality in all its dimensions and possibilities. The Cosmic Christ celebrates sexual diversity—"in Christ there is neither male nor female," says Paul (Galatians 3:28). The Cosmic Christ is not obsessed with sexual identity. The Cosmic Christ can be both female and male, heterosexual and homosexual.[23]

Theologians have long recognized that a weak view of sin always produces a weak view of salvation. Such is the case in Fox's theology. In his thinking, salvation is not individual but is rather *creation-wide.*

> Only a Newtonian worldview of piecemealness could have spawned the popular heresy that salvation is an individualistic or private matter. In a world of interdependence there is simply no such thing as private salvation. . . . Salvation is about God becoming "all in all," as Paul tells us (1 Corinthians 15:28).[24]

In place of the biblical view of salvation, then, Fox offers us a cosmic redemption based on a revival of mysticism rather than on the work of the historic Jesus. Again, Fox says we must move from a "personal Savior" Christianity to a "Cosmic Christ" Christianity.

A Critique

It is hard to know where to begin in critiquing Matthew Fox's theology. There is *so much* that is wrong here. I am very sympathetic with one scholar who, after examining Fox's work, found himself reduced to "helpless, gibbering fury."[25]

On the positive side, Fox is to be commended for being concerned about such things as ecology and the environment, justice in the world, and help for the poor. These positive aspects aside, Fox's version of Christianity is a total departure from the faith. His Christianity is not just a distortion of biblical faith, *it bears no resemblance to it.*

Perhaps the place to begin in evaluating Fox's theology is to challenge his scholarship—*or lack thereof.* Bible scholar Mitchell Pacwa, in his cogent critique of Fox's creation spirituality, has provided substantial evidence that Fox frequently abuses Hebrew etymology and mistranslates Greek words.[26] Words are often translated in a way that supports creation spirituality. For example, Fox claims the Hebrew word for blessing, *berakah,* is closely related to the word for create, *bara,* which is utter nonsense.[27] There is virtually no relationship between these two words.

Pacwa cites two other well-respected scholars who have examined Fox's interpretation of St. Hildegard of Bingen and Meister Eckhart (the two mystics Fox appeals to most in support of creation spirituality). Contrary to the feminist Hildegard portrayed by Fox, Dr. Barbara Newman notes that the *real* Hildegard "firmly defended social hierarchies, and believed in divinely ordained gender roles." Hildegard also called God "Father" and used masculine pronouns for God. Hildegard's theology was *Incarnation-*centered, not *creation-*centered. Dr. Newman, after examining Fox's book on Hildegard, said the book "raises serious questions about the editor's integrity." Fox's book is "rife with errors about Hildegard's work."[28]

Dr. Simon Tugwell, who examined Fox's book on Meister Eckhart, says Fox inaccurately translates the text with "an extraordinary number of mistakes." Tugwell says, "It is difficult to avoid the feeling that the mistranslation is deliberate, intended to minimize anything that would interfere with the alleged 'creation-centeredness' of Eckhart's spirituality."[29]

Fox is unreliable as a scholar. If he makes so many mistakes in the original Hebrew and Greek of the Bible, as well as with major historical sources, then how can anything else he says be trusted? Whether these errors are the result of poor scholarship or outright deceit, the result is the same: *faulty information.*

Beyond problems in scholarship, one must also call into question Fox's dependence on mysticism. Mysticism is utterly insufficient as a ground upon which to build our knowledge of God. It is too uncertain in every way. The Christian points instead *to history*—in particular to the historical Jesus Christ— as the arena of God's personal, objective self-revelation to humankind.

It is noteworthy that the historical Jesus did not seek to find mystical interpretations in Scripture (as does Fox), but rather interpreted Scripture literally—including the creation account of Adam and Eve (Matthew 13:35; 25:34; Mark 10:6), Noah's ark and the Flood (Matthew 24:37-39; Luke 17:26,27), Jonah and the whale (Matthew 12:39-41), Sodom and Gomorrah (Matthew 10:15), and the account of Lot (Luke 17:28,29). Jesus was always *objective* in His approach to Scripture.

Contrary to the mystical subjectivism of Matthew Fox, Scripture indicates that God *is a God of reason* (Isaiah 1:18), and He created humans as rational creatures in His image (Genesis 1:27; Colossians 3:10). Moreover, the Bible is filled with exhortations to *use* our reason. Jesus commanded, "Love the Lord . . . with all your *mind*" (Matthew 22:37, emphasis added in all quotes here). Paul also "*reasoned*" with the Jews (Acts 17:17) and with the philosophers on Mars Hill (verses 22–34), winning many to Christ (verse 34). Bishops were instructed to be able "to *refute* those who *contradict*" (Titus 1:9 NASB). Paul declared that he was "appointed for the *defense* of the gospel" (Philippians 1:16 NASB). Jude urged us to "*contend* earnestly for the faith which was once for all delivered to the saints" (Jude 3 NASB). And Peter commanded us to be "ready to make a *defense* to everyone who asks you to give an account for the hope that is in you" (1 Peter 3:15 NASB). No right-brain stuff here! (It is ironic to note in passing that Fox uses plenty of left-brain reasoning to argue his case for right-brain mysticism in *The Coming of the Cosmic Christ*.)

As we utilize reason to consider the biblical concept of God, it quickly becomes clear that God is *eternally distinct* from what He created. God, who is infinite and eternal, created all things *out of absolute nothingness* (Hebrews 11:3; see also Genesis 1:1; Nehemiah 9:6; Psalm 33:8,9; 148:5). And while God is omnipresent (Psalm 139:7-9), He most certainly is not pantheistically "in" the universe, and He remains distinct from humankind (see Numbers 23:19; Ecclesiastes 5:2; Hebrews 11:3).

Fox's mysticism has led him to believe in a Cosmic Christ that has manifest himself (itself) not just in Jesus but in Buddha and all the other leaders of the world religions. One would think that if this were really the case, however, these leaders would teach very similar concepts about God. *They do not.*

- Jesus taught that there is only one personal God who is triune in nature (Matthew 28:19).
- Muhammad taught that there is only one God, but that God cannot have a son.
- Confucius believed in many gods.
- Zoroaster taught that there is both a good god and a bad god.
- Buddha taught that the concept of God was essentially irrelevant.

Are we to conclude, then, that the Cosmic Christ inspires people to come up with radically different concepts of God? What does this say about the Cosmic Christ? (Cosmic Multiple Personality Disorder?!)

Furthermore, if there really is a genuine divine presence in all human beings, one wonders why it is necessary to buy books from Matthew Fox to find out about it. If we are all divine, wouldn't we already know it?

Certainly Jesus did not consider Himself one of many vehicles for the Cosmic Christ. In fact, He claimed that what He said took precedence over all others. He said He is humanity's only means of coming into a relationship with God, affirming, "I am the way and the truth and the life. No one comes to the Father except through me" (John 14:6). In Acts 4:12 Peter similarly affirmed, "Salvation is found in no one else, for there is no other name under heaven given to men by which we must be saved."

Moreover, contrary to Fox, "Jesus" and "the Christ" are not two distinct persons or entities. Jesus and the Christ refer to one and the same person. Jesus did not merely embody the Cosmic Christ as an adult, but rather was (is) *the one and only* Christ from the very beginning (see Luke 2:11,26).

Jesus made His identity as the Christ the primary issue of faith on several occasions in the New Testament (Matthew 16:13-20; John 11:25-27). When Jesus was acknowledged as the Christ, He did not say to people, "You, too, have the Christ within." Instead, He warned them that others would come falsely claiming to be the Christ (Matthew 24:4-5,23-25).[30]

We should also note that while Jesus sought to elevate the status of women in a society where they were looked down upon, He certainly did not engage in a "frontal assault" against patriarchy, as Fox claims. Throughout His three-year ministry He always referred to God as His "Father" (for example, John 14:2,6,7,9,10,11,14), and He summoned *exclusively* male disciples to follow Him and spread the gospel on His behalf (for example, Matthew 4:18-22; 9:9-13).

Finally, if Fox thinks Augustine was hard on humans regarding sin, he should consider the words of the historical Jesus. Augustine's words pale next to the indictment of Christ. Jesus taught that man since the Fall is evil (Matthew 12:34) and is capable of great wickedness (Mark 7:20-23). He said that man is utterly lost (Luke 19:10), that he is in need of repentance before a holy God (Mark 1:15), and that he needs to be born again (John 3:3,5,7). Jesus described sin as blindness (Matthew 23:16-26), sickness (Matthew 9:12), being enslaved in bondage (John 8:34), and living in darkness (John 8:12; 12:35-46). Moreover, Jesus taught that sin is a universal condition and that all people are guilty before God (Luke 7:37-48).

Jesus also taught that both inner thoughts and external acts render a person guilty (Matthew 5:28). He said that from within the human heart come evil thoughts, sexual immorality, theft, murder, adultery, greed, malice, deceit, envy, slander, arrogance, and folly (Mark 7:21-23). And He affirmed that God is fully aware of every person's sins; nothing escapes His notice (Matthew 22:18; Luke 6:8; John 4:17-19). Fox's call for a dismissal of "personal Savior" Christianity in favor of a "Cosmic Christ" Christianity becomes *sheer madness* in view of the words of the historic Jesus.

A closing thought. It is human sin—with its unrestrained greed, envy, passion for money and wealth, power, and prestige—that drives so many entrepreneurs on this planet to generate money with little concern for the environment (polluting streams with chemical waste, cutting down forests for paper production, and so forth). To *not* deal with human sin, then, is ultimately to ignore the biggest environmental hazard there is: *fallen man's heart.*

Among the most prolific sources of the various counterfeit Christs in our time are the psychics and channelers whose revelations appear to come out of thin air like radio waves broadcast through a receiver. In the eighties and nineties such revelations have come at such a high "baud rate" that they are like some kind of high-powered fax machine from another dimension that has been spitting out thousands of pages. The result has been a wide range and variety of teachings from various cosmic masters. Consider the best-selling books and media phenomena of such revelations—from TV miniseries to a dedicated "psychic channel." It is all hugely influential.

In the present spiritual marketplace, it is every seeker for himself. Some will opt for the Christ in *A Course in Miracles;* some will go to Edgar Cayce, J.Z. Knight, or Kevin Ryerson; others will go further back to *The Aquarian Gospel of Jesus the Christ.* We need to probe behind this psychic veil and discover what is really going on. What happens when channelers twist their faces and talk in foreign or alien voices? Are some in it for the fame and the money? Yes. But from time immemorial other channelers have been under the influence of what the Bible refers to as familiar spirits. At some point in their lives they surrendered to an invisible presence. The goal of these beings is to steer peoples' lives, by deception, away from the truth and into ultimate destruction, fostering allegiance to alien Christs.

6

THE COSMIC CHRIST OF CHANNELED REVELATION

Tal Brooke

I t is mid-January of 1987, and the big TV miniseries that everyone has been waiting for is finally on the air. Famed actress Shirley MacLaine has found the "truth" in the New Age movement—and it all started when she inadvertently attended a channeling session. She is telling the world about it in this autobiographical miniseries, *Out On a Limb,* which is based on her best-selling book. ABC television network has sunk a fortune into this one, while media previews and feature articles have netted everyone's attention months ahead.

Weeks later, in early February, I am driving past the Pasadena Convention Center. It is typically mid-70s in greater Los Angeles and downtown Pasadena has thousands of people with badges flowing through the streets. They are attending a New Age convention, among the largest in the nation. I am there to check it out. A line stretches for blocks leading into the main auditorium.

New Age channeler Jach Pursel is there to channel "Lazaris." Kevin Ryerson, who may be channeling "the apostle John," shares the bill with Pursel. It is common knowledge that in MacLaine's TV miniseries, Ryerson plays himself, performing "live" channeling in a full trance during the actual filming. Mediumship invades millions of homes, knowingly or unknowingly. At the Pasadena Convention Center, channeling is the key attraction. "We are taking over," someone announces in line, smiling while hoping to hear some cosmic spirit unveil new mysteries to excite perhaps an otherwise dull and jaded life.

Channeled Revelations in the Ancient World

Revelations from voices that proclaimed themselves to be deities and spirits passed through the mouths of channelers and mediums and then flowed across the ancient world like a vast rumbling spiritual Euphrates. These voices flooded through India, Persia, Babylon, ancient Greece, and Egypt. At the summit of such revelations, priestly oracles in mediumistic trances spoke the will of the gods, at times divulging cosmic mysteries.

The more common mediums claimed to communicate with the dead. It was to such a medium—the witch of Endor—that Israel's first king (Saul) secretly went in an attempt to communicate with the recently deceased prophet Samuel. He was instantly judged for practicing this forbidden occult abomination, and his kingship ended by God's decree as the mantle passed on to King David (1 Samuel 28).

Channeled communications were a central part of the ancient mystery religions, especially in Babylon. The Old Testament repeatedly and clearly warned that these mediumistic utterances were not coming from gods, but—when they were not mediums pretending to be oracles so as to gain power themselves—were in fact demonic powers masquerading as deities, polluting beliefs and darkening cultures.

The priests, mediums, and sorcerers who uttered such supernatural revelations were not holy conduits of divine revelation but instead defiled vessels who had come under the influence of evil powers and principalities by knowingly opening their minds and souls to "familiar spirits." The outcome of channeled revelation was invariably to twist the truth, deceive the hearer, and obscure the true God through an enticing counterfeit, thus preventing genuine revelation.

By contrast, God's true human messengers—prophets and priests—were set apart by Him and led lives of integrity, obedience, and moral purity. They were true lights in a darkened world and their words were cautionary and sobering, never flattering.

Isaiah the prophet communicated an insightful warning about the ancient mediums of his day: "And when they say to you, 'Consult the mediums and the wizards who whisper and mutter,' should not a people consult their God? Should they consult the dead on behalf of the living?" (Isaiah 8:19 NASB). God had repeatedly warned ancient Israel from the time of Moses to avoid the defiling occult practices of the Canaanites—"Do not turn to mediums or spiritists; do not seek them out to be defiled by them. I am the LORD your God" (Leviticus 19:31 NASB). "A man or a woman who is a medium or spiritist shall surely be put to death. They shall be stoned with stones, their bloodguiltiness is upon them" (Leviticus 20:27 NASB). This was serious business, not something to play around with. Again God warned:

> There shall not be found among you any one that maketh his son or his daughter to pass through the fire, or that useth divination, or an observer of times, or an enchanter, or a witch, Or a charmer, or a consulter with familiar spirits, or a wizard, or a necromancer. For all that do these things are an abomination unto the LORD: and because of these abominations the LORD thy God doth drive them out from before thee. (Deuteronomy 18:10-12 KJV)

The channeled sources usually promised great things while glorifying and seducing the hearers—that is, when these supernatural powers were not commanding their terrorized subjects to drag someone into the fires of Baal or some similar brutal and deadly ceremony. The false god Moloch required the sacrifice of infants. The appeasement of these "gods" was often a terrible thing, revealing their demonic nature.

We now stand at the end of the twentieth century and watch a growing onslaught of mediums. It started with the Romantics at the end of the last century and has been progressing to the present New Age movement—all while the Christian presence in the West has been slowly retreating, millions having left it behind. At the same time, almost all of these contemporary channeled revelations have altered and redefined the nature and person of Jesus Christ, a significant signal in itself.

A Course in Miracles

In recent years a major new revelation has hit the stands creating a New Age furor. It is called *A Course in Miracles,* composed of the alleged teachings of "Jesus," channeled through a Jewish atheist—now deceased—who worked in the department of psychiatry at Columbia University. *A Course in Miracles* is a much sought-after source of teaching among New Agers and even some churches. Here, too, is an event—a phenomenon—that should not entirely escape our scrutiny. It is a classic case of spiritual deception by means of mediumship, or "channeling," as New Agers prefer to call it. This route to higher revelation is repeatedly and expressly forbidden in the true canon of revelation. What emerges is pure deception.

The channeler, Helen Schucman, Ph.D., in the mid-1960s was an associate professor of medical psychology at Columbia University's College of Physicians and Surgeons. Her department was riddled with strain, tension, and academic competition. This job stress ate into her personal life, creating anxiety and pessimism, as it did also with her boss, Dr. Bill Thetford. Department and faculty meetings were like war zones as medical egos displayed themselves. The two—constantly at odds—made a joint commitment to straighten things out at almost any cost. One technique involved acknowledging and selectively seeing only the positive in the other person.[1]

Schucman had always possessed a strange psychic faculty, yet she only peripherally acknowledged it, remaining an atheist. The "mental pictures" she had been seeing in her mind for as long as she could remember soon changed from black and white to color. Then they started moving, motion picture style, and indeed began invading her dreams. In the summer of 1965 the psychic process heightened. Schucman got a flash of herself as an Egyptian priestess. In a "vision" she discovered a large black book in a treasure chest. A silent voice then began to accompany the moving psychic pictures. It told her that it was "her" book.

Schucman told Dr. Thetford that she might need to undergo a psychiatric examination herself. It might be pathological. Thetford was soon drawn to psychic Edgar Cayce in looking for explanations. Cayce was a vital link, he felt.[2] By September of 1965 Schucman had a premonition that something major was about to happen. The inner voice was appearing more and more.

Schucman finally phoned her boss reporting that the inner voice would not leave her alone. He asked her what it was saying.

"You're not going to believe me," she responded.

Bill countered with "Try me."

Schucman announced, "It keeps saying, 'This is *A Course in Miracles*. Please take notes.' What am I going to do?"[3]

Thetford encouraged her to take notes.

That night the voice came through loud and clear with the first words: "This is *A Course in Miracles*. It is a required course." The atheistic scribe resisted, but then followed her colleague's recommendation, skeptically doubting every word that came through. At first the inner dictation frightened her, but she went through with it anyway. This was in the fall of 1965.

In seven years, by 1973, the entire course was transcribed, resulting in a 622-page text and a 478-page workbook as well as a short manual. Since then, the three-volume set has sold well over 900,000 copies. Years later her colleague, Dr. Thetford, described *A Course in Miracles* as "a spiritual document very closely related to the teachings of the non-dualistic Vedanta of the Hindu religion."[4]

What is interesting about this is that the voice never divulged its identity. It stayed anonymous. Adherents of the course, however, have adopted Schucman's hunch that the voice was that of Jesus. It implies as much in the first pages of the course.

The emerging document produced by "the Voice" was coherent and authoritative, but Schucman did not intellectually believe in its source. What was eerie was that if the dictation was broken off at any point, when it was taken up again (hours or days later) it began exactly where it had broken off—like a computer modem, beginning again after a pause in protocol. *A powerful intelligence was behind this event.*

Schucman's biographer, Robert Skutch, observes with irony:

> On the one hand, she resented the Voice, objected to taking down the material, was extremely fearful of the content and had to overcome great personal resistance, especially in the beginning stages, in order to continue. On the other hand, it never seriously occurred to her not to do it, even though she frequently was tremendously resentful of the often infuriating interference."[5]

Skutch also observes that "throughout the writing . . . the acute terror Helen felt at the beginning did gradually recede, but part of her mind simply never allowed her to get completely used to the idea of being a channel for the Voice."[6] Even though the intellectual and skeptical part of Schucman's mind still resisted absolute belief in these channeled revelations, nevertheless, as time went on, another side of her became increasingly willing to open up to them.

When Schucman asked the Voice why it was communicating through her, it responded with this statement:

The world situation is worsening to an alarming degree. People all over the world are being called on to help, and are making their individual contributions as part of an overall prearranged plan. . . . Because of the acute emergency, however, the usual slow, evolutionary process is being bypassed in what might best be described as a "celestial speed-up."[7]

A Course in Miracles is not concerned with filling in the missing "bio" of Jesus. It is a spiritual teaching couched in Christian terms but giving them new cosmic meanings. As Dr. Thetford observed, it is essentially Vedanta. When Thetford gave the manuscript to Edgar Cayce's son, Hugh Lynn Cayce of the Association for Research and Enlightenment, Hugh Lynn became very encouraging. This was the same mystery-Christos that his father, the famous psychic, had channeled.

Soon the guiding powers brought some key figures connected with the New Age movement into the lives of the two New York psychologists, and proposals for publication were well underway. The inner voice of Robert Skutch's wife, Judith, directed her to Schucman. In fact, Judith's inner voice ordered her to commit to publishing the work before finances were even available. Their foundation was already stretched to the limit in helping to fund ex-astronaut Edgar Mitchell's Institute of Noetic Sciences as well as Stanford Research Institute's breakthrough in "remote viewing."[8] When Judith first saw the manuscript, she said to herself, "Finally . . . here's my map home."[9] In little time the Skutchs published A Course in Miracles.

What new facets did the course provide about the Cosmic Christ? None, beyond a coherent supernaturally based document that itself was seen as a miracle and proof of higher guidance. Ironically, not far away in New Jersey, the spirit-entity Seth had been dictating similar revelations through Jane Roberts.

The course is totally positive and reassuring. It is the kind of thing an anxiety-ridden New York professional woman such as Helen Schucman needed for reassurance. It is a revelation that uses the Hindu concept of *maya* to dispel the threat of evil. Evil is an illusion, a projection of the mind. With enough positive thinking, it will disappear. We can reshape reality because we have the godlike power to govern reality through expanded consciousness because all that is is Spirit, and spirit alone. We get into trouble when we vacillate between the two modes of consciousness: the old and the new.

If evil is not real, neither is any misguided sense of sin. As *A Course in Miracles* states, sin is the illusion that separates us from our own innate divinity, our own godhood. We are extensions of the "Thought of God." So our natural inheritance is a state of "Pure Love." The Hindu word for such cosmic bliss is *ananda*. One of the course's exercises in consciousness is to replace all fear, and other negative emotions, with love.

Christ is our exemplar, model, and elder brother. But we are His equal, being already perfect like Him. The course even claims that we are more powerful than Christ. Our manufactured illusions of sinfulness have made the world a prison for Christ. Thus we are the ones with the power to free Christ by perceiving the world in the higher mode—that is, free of all evil. The course encourages one to say, "God himself is incomplete without me,"[10] and, "there is no difference between your will and God's."[11]

Clearly, if *A Course in Miracles* is right, Jesus is the most misunderstood figure in history. History for 2000 years has had it wrong. The church never even got off on the right foot. And the long-promised Paraclete—the Holy Spirit, who was to guide the church throughout history—has not even managed to get through to Christians about their misguided understandings. They have uniformly, all of them, believed a counterfeit gospel for this extended time. And Christ's messianic act of sacrifice on the cross, that central historical fact of Christianity, was wasted blood and pain. He never even needed to come to earth if all He needed was a good channel.

For there was no real sin to atone for, and our separation from God was just an illusion all along—that is, *if* you believe Helen Schucman.

Edgar Cayce—the Channeler of the Century

Though Edgar Cayce died in 1945, the books concerning this famous psychic and channeler still flood bookstores. They are top sellers among Bantam's New Age paperback series. Cayce spent years going into trances in which he claimed to gain access to the hall of records of the cosmic mind—better known as the Akashic records. He had the look and bearing of a simple Bible Belt Christian. His demeanor of kindly innocence made him believable. For years all he did was diagnose physical illnesses in this trance state. Even if the subject were halfway across America, the impersonal "we" voice would almost always accurately diagnose the problem of a subject whom he had never met, giving the method of cure.

Then one day a wealthy Jewish theosophist in the Midwest paid for his trance time, but then started asking the Akashic mind questions concerning the nature of ultimate reality. The startling revelations that came from the other side confused and even frightened Cayce. When he woke out of trances he had never remembered anything, nor had he ever "met" the "voice" that worked through his body using it as a medium. When this groundbreaking channeler was told what he had said in his first nonmedical reading, he was almost undone. For he was revealing a cosmos identical to that of the theosophists, mystics, and Hindus.

The loving, personal God whom Cayce had read about in the Bible as a child turned out to be a "myth of the dualistic mind." What Cayce's channeling revealed was the impersonal Godhead, like an infinite ocean of consciousness, without attributes, yet composed of and beyond all qualities and forms of being. The cosmos was made not ex nihilo (out of nothing) but *out of God.* The pantheistic system was therefore true after all.

Along with reincarnation came the inevitable law of karma, the Akashic records simply being a cosmic recording of all prior events and past lives. Cayce began to give "life readings" of past lives. Presto! What came out were accounts of Atlantis, the occult civilization that blew itself up. Now we learn that these "evolved" souls who had perished in Atlantis would soon be streaming into rebirth on "the earth plane." Though Cayce died in the 1940s, this would have been the sixties generation he was talking about. These advanced souls had a mission: to restore to the earth the Atlantian spiritual secrets while taking civilization beyond Atlantis. Thus, there would soon be a New Age with new powers unleashed. There would also be the return of the occult priesthood and adepts, oracles, psychics, astrologers, channelers, high mystics, and godmen who were here to change the "earth plane." (This revelation helped spur me to meet my spiritual destiny in India at any price.)

Not just God, but the character of Christ changed as well. Christ was the perfect yogi, avatar, incarnation of the God-head, and God-man. He had already reincarnated on the earth a number of times to set up His messianic mission, perfecting Himself even more each time. Melchizedek was but one embodiment in Christ's genealogy of past lives. In that sense He is a model for all men to follow in order to attain what is now called "Christ-consciousness." Strategically, the Akashic "voice" channeling through Cayce targeted the hidden years in Christ's life about which the Bible is nearly silent. Now there was room to fill in the blanks.

With an elaborate explanation of astrological forces, the Akashic voice depicted the young "Perfect Master" traveling to Egypt to study at the temples of wisdom and beauty, where He learned certain psychic arts. Then the young Jesus went on to India and Tibet to learn levitation and transmutation from certain Tibetan masters: While in India, He learned healing, weather control, telepathy, and ultimately reached "at-one-ment" (the "real" meaning of atonement) with the cosmic overmind. From there, at age 29, He returned to the Holy Land as the promised Messiah.

Perhaps what initially bothered Cayce most about this channeled revelation was the fact that the apostles left all these critical bits of history out of the New Testament. Cayce knew that the Bible did not mention so much as a hint about any of these mystical sojourns. None of the historians of antiquity ever saw the dimmest traces of this. Nor, from all the hundreds of letters from out of the era of the early church, soon after the life of Christ, was a word ever uttered about these trips to India. You would think *someone* would have written about it then. No, Cayce had to trust the invisible voice coming through him, and this took a certain leap of faith.

Thomas Sugrue, the major biographer of Edgar Cayce, in *There Is a River*, makes an observation about Cayce and all other channels of the Cosmic Christ:

> The system of metaphysical thought which emerges from the readings of Edgar Cayce is a Christianized version of the mystery religions of ancient Egypt, Chaldea, Persia, India and Greece. It fits the figure of Christ into the tradition of one God for all people, and places Him in His proper place . . . He is the capstone of the pyramid.[12]

Levi Dowling and *The Aquarian Gospel of Jesus the Christ*

Edgar Cayce was hardly the first channeler to come up with revelations about the Cosmic Christ. Another major source was Levi Dowling, a late nineteenth-century medical practitioner who traveled from town to town in the Midwest in a covered wagon. In the early hours of the morning he channeled and recorded, through automatic writing, the famed occult classic, *The Aquarian Gospel of Jesus the Christ.* Dowling gave his body to a "higher force." Its purpose was to complete what the apostles had left out, updated for our coming "Aquarian Age."

Dowling had already rejected the New Testament. He considered his channelings to be higher scriptures, and numbered them chapter and verse like the Bible. One could almost lament at this point—Oh, if only the scholars would bring their weighty redactive and critical methodology to bear on these channeled teachings from around the world. Surely they would bounce all over the map. What is a believer to do? And which channeled revelation do we trust!

Dowling portrays the "young Master" as a sort of Siddhartha, passing tortuous tests, transcending the limited ego, and going on sojourns through India, Tibet, Persia, Assyria, Greece, and Egypt. During this time Jesus learned magic and gained psychic powers.

According to Dowling's revelations, Christ learned herbal arts in Benares, India. *The Aquarian Gospel* reveals:

> Benares of the Ganges was a city rich in culture and learning; here the two rabbonis tarried many days. And Jesus sought to learn the Hindu art of healing, and became a pupil of Udraka, the greatest of Hindu healers. Udraka taught the uses of the waters, plants, and earths; of heat and cold; sunshine and shade; of light and dark (23:2-4).

We also learn that "Jesus was accepted as a pupil in the temple of Jagannath: and here learned the Vedas and Manic Laws"(21:19). Yet the reality is this: the only scriptures Christ quotes from in the New Testament are from the Jewish Old Testament. Not a breath about the Vedas, but plenty from the prophets, psalms, David, and Moses. Not a single reference to Udraka or the Jagannath Temple with its thousands of Hindu gods.

Perhaps in a pantheistic mood, the Aquarian Christ reveals: "With much delight I speak to you concerning life— the brotherhood of life. The universal God is one, yet he is more than one; all things are God; all things are one" (28:3-4).

At the feast of Persepolis honoring the Magician God, the Aquarian Christ has some good things to say at the invitation of the ruling magician: "Your purity in worship and in life is pleasing unto God; and to your master Zarathustra, praise is due" (39:5). When he goes on to Delphi, he has some great things to say about the oracle: "The Delphic age has been an age of glory and renown; the gods have spoken to the sons of men through oracles of wood, and gold, and precious stone. . . . The gods will speak to man by man. The living oracle now stands within these sacred groves; the Logos from on High has come" (45:8-10).

By the time Dowling's young master arrived in Egypt he was ready to go through the seven tests of mystical brotherhood to become a full master. In the chamber of the dead he became a pupil of the Hierophant. Here he learned the mysteries of life and death and "the worlds beyond the circle of the sun." Faced with the body of a young boy whom He was to embalm, the Cosmic Christ told the boy's grief-stricken mother that "death is a cruel word; your son can never die" (54:6-7). Indeed, these words can be found in the Bible, but spoken by one other than Christ, to be sure. "Ye shall not surely die" (Genesis 3:4 KJV).

Today we are 10,000 channels down the road from the days of Levi Dowling and Edgar Cayce, and there has been a lot of history and words added to the Cosmic Christ. It has been a most extensive and elaborate dress rehearsal. Currently, contemporary channels such as J. Z. Knight, who channels Ramtha, Jach Pursel, who channels Lazaris, and Elizabeth Claire Prophet, figurehead of the Summit Lighthouse, who channels multiple ascended masters, echo similar teachings as Cayce and Dowling. They have added sophisticated makeup to this Cosmic Christ along with Helen Schucman. *It is a powerful potion.*

Who are the doubters? Among them are the orthodox Christians who do not recognize the new gospel coming from the Cosmic Christ. They are still "hung up" over their carefully transmitted 2000-year-old canon that has survived the centuries intact. They claim it has already worked the miracle of grace upon their lives and does not need changing. For they have encountered Christ *personally*, and when they read the New Testament, that is indeed the one being described whom they have fallen in love with. Through the New Testament they have encountered the true historical person of Jesus Christ, and He in no way resembles this new Cosmic Christ. This should be a warning to all, for Christ Himself warned that impostors would arise (Matthew 24:24-25).

Westerners in the main are completely unaware of the harsh reality of religious persecution of Christians in Israel and Islamic lands—that Christians can face *enormous* social consequences for their faith. The fact is, both Judaism and Islam have altered the message and identity of Christ over the centuries, distorting Jesus (and His gospel) in different ways. The result has been that both have created a pervasive anti-Christian prejudice among their followers, in a sense immunizing them against the gospel of Christ.

Christians in the Middle East today are in particularly difficult circumstances. Pressed hard from both sides, they have essentially two options: (1) leave their ancestral homeland; (2) suffer in silence and anonymity. This situation also explains the difficulty and rarity of Christian conversions in the Middle East. It helps explain the bill before the Israeli parliament to essentially ban all Christian activity in Israel. Similarly, Christian converts from Islam face harsh physical reprisals from their former co-religionists.

Christians in the West may occasionally experience mild public opposition for an "offensive" view that is at odds with secularism, political correctness, and so on. Indeed, adhering to Christ and the gospel has social consequences for anyone who takes his faith seriously. But in Jewish and Islamic lands, Christians are in a far more precarious situation—one in which the opposition can be lethal.

7

BETWEEN ISAAC AND ISHMAEL

JEWISH AND ISLAMIC
ANIMOSITY TOWARD CHRIST

Brooks Alexander

W hat would happen if Jesus returned to the land of His birth today? What would His reception be? That question has been asked (and answered) in drama and speculative fiction. Authors who handle the theme usually assume Jesus would be rejected a second time as well, and use the ironic twist as a literary device.

But we don't have to resort to literary speculation to know how Christ would be received today. Christ's brothers and sisters—believers in the "Good News," His family of faith—are being received *as He* would be in the Holy Land right now. To know how Christ would be treated, we have only to look at the way Christians are being treated in the land where their faith began.

Triangle of Anathema

The picture we see is disturbing. The plight of Christians in the Middle East today is always difficult, often dangerous, and sometimes desperate—caught as they are in the crossfire between Arab/Moslem/Palestinian interests and Zionist/Jewish/Israeli interests.

Both the Moslem nations and the Jewish State pursue policies that bring pressure to bear on Christians in the territories under their control. And both the Moslem and Jewish cultures foster a popular hostility toward Christianity that routinely produces social discrimination and sporadically erupts into violence against believers.

The worst news is that this kind of dual pressure is having its intended effect. The overt and covert purpose of all such discrimination is to either ghettoize other religions or drive them out completely. This serves to "religiously cleanse" the society so it can become a purer expression of either the "Jewish State" or the "Islamic State," depending on who is doing the cleansing.

It is working. The double pincer of Moslem and Jewish pressure against Christianity is driving Christians out of the Holy Land at a rate that can only be described as "mass flight."

> According to a survey conducted by Dr. Bernard Sabella of Bethlehem University, the great majority of Christian Palestinians have already left. Sabella's work shows that . . . there are now more Jerusalem-born Christians living in Sydney than in Jerusalem. . . . Most observers agree that if emigration continues as at present it is only a matter of time before Christianity becomes extinct in the land of its birth.[1]

The prospect seems almost unthinkable—Christians and Christianity driven from the land of Christ! But the prospect is quite thinkable to the extremists of both Judaism and Islam, for whom the gospel is equally an affront to their religious claims and an impediment to their political aims.

Moslem extremists would like to see Jews and Christians simply gone from the Middle East, and are ready to help it happen. Jewish extremists, for their part, would like to see Moslems and Christians gone, and are also ready to push the process along. Unfortunately, both Moslem and Jewish extremists not only inflame existing cultural attitudes, they influence—and sometimes determine—official policies as well.

The reality of power politics in the Middle East pits Jewish Israel against the Islamic nations. Those who bear the name of Christ are therefore caught in the middle of a struggle between those who lay claim to Isaac's legacy and those who point to Ishmael as their ancestor. Unfortunately, Christians in the Holy Land today stand where those overlapping bigotries converge.

Not only are Christians subject to double discrimination, they have no place of refuge to which they can escape. The Muslims have their countries and the Jews have their State, but Christians have no local nation of their own. It is therefore the Christians who are leaving the Holy Land in droves, as their presence in the land of their heritage dwindles to the vanishing point.

The persecution of Christians in Moslem countries is becoming relatively well-known because of the media's attention to the threat of Islamic fundamentalism. Many people already know, for example, that Egypt's Coptic Christians live in daily danger of terrorist attack from Moslem extremists in that country. And many already know of the harsh anti-conversion laws and the virtual ban on any form of Christianity in Saudi Arabia. Operation Desert Storm brought that reality into our living rooms by way of satellite on CNN. Some people even know of Muslims who have converted to Christ and faced legal penalties as a result—up to and including the death penalty.

Not many people know that Christians also live under threat and pressure in Israel itself. For various reasons, the plight of Christians in Israel is less publicized, though it is no less difficult for believers who have to endure it. Anti-Christian attitudes in the Jewish State (as in the Moslem nations) are both official and unofficial. They include everything from limits on where Christians may live, to laws against evangelism, to religiously incited and socially tolerated vigilante attacks on the person and property of Christians themselves.

The legal, social, and cultural bias against Christianity in both the Jewish State and the Moslem nations clearly reflects a deep religious conflict. The plain and simple fact is that

Judaism, Christianity, and Islam all make absolute claims for themselves, each of which invalidates the claims of the other two. Mingled together in the same geography, they create a unique "triangle of anathema." When you stir in the fact that all three profess to speak truly in the name of the same God, and to be true heirs of the same religious tradition, you have the recipe for a conflict more intense than most people can imagine.

The Koranic View of Jesus

Christianity and Islam have been refining their antagonistic relationship for 1,400 years. The interesting thing about the conflict, however, is that it has been largely political and military in its historical expression. It is not *scripturally* based in the same way the Jewish/Christian conflict is. There is no deep-seated aversion to Christ and Christians woven into the (Moslem) Koran the way it is woven into the (Jewish) Talmud, for example.

The Koran speaks approvingly of Christians in most of the 15 passages in which they are mentioned directly.[2] Mohammed was greatly influenced in his views by the Hebrew Scriptures (the Old Testament), which he knew directly, and by Christian teaching, which he knew indirectly. In general, the Koran treats Christians as sincere believers in the one God who will be rewarded for their faith at the last judgment, though they lack the full knowledge of Allah through his prophet, Mohammed.

The Koran does criticize Christians in some ways, but even its complaints are mild. Mohammed finds fault with Christian believers for their tendency to disagree among themselves and to form warring sects around their points of contention— an ironic judgment in view of Islam's later sectarian bloodbaths. The Koran also criticizes the emerging Christian institution of monasticism. The idea struck Mohammed as strange. He viewed the practice with distaste and its practitioners with suspicion.

Still, by the standards of religious rhetoric (especially those of the day), the Koran's attitude toward both Christians and Jews is remarkably generous. Mohammed's fiercest religious fight was with the grossly idolatrous Arab culture that surrounded him, and especially with the militant paganism of its leaders. In that context, he looked at the other two biblical religions as allies (or at least cobelligerents) in his struggle against idol-worshiping superstition. Thus, the Koran exhibits a high regard for the Jewish and Christian Scriptures.

On a personal level, Mohammed engaged in cordial dialogue at times with Jews and, apparently, with Christians. Toward the end of his life, however, he was more favorably disposed toward Christians than Jews, whom he increasingly regarded as hard-hearted and reprobate.[3]

There was hence a basis for mutual respect between Muslims and Christians, not only in the Koran, but even in the life of Mohammed himself. Nevertheless, the actual encounter between Christianity and Islam has been marked by struggle and conflict. It was one thing for Mohammed to deal with Christians as people who could believe in God without benefit of the Prophet's (Mohammed's) message. It was another thing for Muslims to deal with Christians who rejected the Prophet's message altogether—a common response when they were pressed on the issue.

The problem is that while the Koran took a generous view of Christians, it also took a view of Jesus that no Christian could accept. Mohammed lauded Jesus as a prophet of God, and respected His words accordingly. He treated Jesus as one of history's greatest prophets. His bottom-line view, however, was that Jesus failed in His prophetic mission. After the Jews finally rejected Him, Jesus simply disappeared from view and someone else was crucified in His place. In the wake of that spiritual debacle, Mohammed was sent from God to fulfill the mission Jesus couldn't accomplish.

The Koran never states how Jesus ended His days. A common assumption of Islamic scholars is that God supernaturally took

Him out of the world. God "recalled" Him, as it were, once it was obvious that His mission had failed and His message had been rejected. The Koran makes it clear that Jesus did not die as the Gospels describe, and was never resurrected.

Since the sacrificial death and resurrection of Christ are the heart of Christianity, the Koran's denial of them rendered the rest of its "respect" for Christianity irrelevant. Christians rightly saw Mohammed's message as a direct contradiction of their own beliefs and a radical attack on the foundation of their faith. Islam's claim that Jesus Himself had prophesied Mohammed's coming didn't help much either. Christianity is not prepared to accept such a derogation of Christ's role and identity—and Islam is certainly not prepared to accept the Christian rejoinder that the Prophet was simply wrong. To whatever extent either viewpoint is insisted upon, the other is equally stirred to resist— by definition.

To put it simply, the message of the Prophet collided with the good news of the Savior. Very soon thereafter, those two religious worlds clashed politically as well. After the death of Mohammed (A.D. 631), the religion he founded swept westward through North Africa, reaching Morocco and the Atlantic Ocean within 60 years. Islam's collective military might grew along with its territorial conquests, and it soon gathered enough strength to invade Christian Europe. A Berber army crossed the Straits of Gibraltar in A.D. 711; they easily routed the forces of King Roderick—the last of the Visigothic rulers. The Islamic invaders conquered Spain with amazing speed and ease, and even pushed their way into France.

The wave of Moslem power finally crested, however, and the growth of its empire was arrested by the French under Charles Martel ("the Hammer") at the Battle of Poitiers in 732. There followed over 700 years of slow Islamic retreat in Spain. Meanwhile, Christian militants tried to retake the land of Christ's birth from its new Moslem overlords. The see-saw battles of the Crusades (1096-1270) ended with the situation essentially unchanged—that is, with Muslims still in control of the Holy Land.

Facing a stalemate against Catholic Christianity in the West, militant Islam struck north against the Byzantine empire. The Ottoman Turks finally overthrew Constantinople in 1453. From there they threatened Eastern Europe for another 230 years until the Ottoman army was driven off its siege of Vienna in 1683 by Christian troops under John III of Poland.

For almost a millennium and a half, Muslims have faced religious hostility and military belligerence from the Christian West. European colonialism and the conduct of the Western powers in the Moslem conflict with Israel have added deceit and betrayal to the list as well. History has given the Prophet's followers ample reason to nurse their grievances and plenty of time to simmer their resentments.

The legacy of that conflict still burdens both of its heirs today. In the "apostate" Christian West, guilt about Christianity's part in the religious wars of the past creates vacillation and compromise in the face of Islam's modern missionary offensive—a bewilderment reinforced by the trendy politically correct ideologies of "pluralism" and "diversity."

Islam's inheritance from that conflict is less diluted with confusion. Whatever its other deficiencies may be, Islam understands its own identity well enough to know that Christianity is not only a competitor, but a standing denial of the Prophet's claims. Therefore, a strong rejection of Christianity and a deep hostility toward Christians remains an integral part of popular culture throughout the Moslem world.

Christianity in Moslem Lands Today

Official policies toward Christianity vary to some degree among Moslem nations, depending on their official commitment to Islam. But popular attitudes toward Christianity vary very little. Several illustrations can be given. Among the North African nations, Tunisia is the most secular in its approach to religion. This is in contrast to Libya, which under Khaddafi has tried to wrestle itself into conformity with eighth-century Koranic law. Despite those official differences, on the popular level

> all hold to the unalterable attitude that to be a North African is to be a Muslim. To become "Christian" is understood to mean a traitorous abandonment of one's heritage, family and nation. Almost nothing could bring greater disapproval.[4]

Official attitudes toward Islam also vary among the Arab nations and elsewhere in the Middle East—from Syria's secular socialism to Iran's reactionary fundamentalism. Regardless, the traditional Islamic bias against Christianity remains entrenched among the general population. Visible Christians in Islamic cultures face social and economic isolation. Muslims who convert to Christianity face ostracism at best and murderous revenge (martyrdom) at worst.

Moslem prejudice against Christians is not confined to the countries of Islam's birth and early expansion. Islam is a universal religion, and it has carried its allergy to Christianity with it wherever it has traveled and taken root, including Asia. Anti-Christian discrimination tends to exist wherever Muslims predominate socially, and especially where they rule politically. Islam's spite against Christianity readily turns to irrational fury and even mob action, including (sometimes lethal) physical abuse.

> In Malaysia's Pahang State legislators have legalized mandatory whippings and imprisonment for Muslims who apostatsize or preach other religions. In China's Sinkiang Province, eyewitnesses report that apostates—in this case Christian converts from Islam—are tied to the ground while soapy water is poured down their throats over a period of three days to wash out evil spirits. They are then forced to

endure a week-long crash-course in the Qur'an after which they must recant their faith in Christ or face possible exile or death.[5]

Statistics confirm a worldwide pattern of anti-Christian discrimination in Islamic countries. In 1996, Open Doors (a Christian ministry) examined and compared over 100 nations, assessing the level of religious freedom they afforded Christianity. They published their findings as *The World Watch List,* an authoritative index of religious persecution. Of the ten countries most active in persecuting Christians, all but two are Moslem-dominated. The top ten list (from the most oppressive to the less so) reads as follows: Somalia, Saudi Arabia, Southern Sudan, Comoro Islands, Iran, Northern Sudan, China, Morocco, North Korea, and Egypt.[6]

Jesus and Judaism

Islamic persecution isn't the only thing driving Christians out of the Holy Land. There is also pressure against Christianity within Israel itself—a pressure that is severe enough to make local Christians abandon their ancestral homes in alarming numbers.

Christianity and Judaism have had a vexed relationship from the beginning. The tortured history of that relationship has been well publicized in recent years, and it doesn't need to be repeated here. What does need to be emphasized is that the vexation has been bipolar from the outset. The Judeo-Christian conflict, throughout its history, has been mutual, conscious, and deliberate—on both sides.

In Europe Christians have held the upper hand socially and politically, and they have acted out their vexation with the Jews accordingly. In the early days of the church, however, the situation was reversed. Jews held the upper hand of power, and they expressed their vexation with Christianity in direct and often brutal ways. One of the most shocking instances of anti-Christian persecution by religious Jews was the stoning of deacon Stephen (Acts 6:8-15).

Almost two millennia later (1948), the State of Israel was born in blood and controversy. Now an explicitly Jewish power dominates the Holy Land again. What does that mean for Christians living there today? The earliest believers found themselves a despised and beleaguered community, living under the hostile attention of Jewish authorities. What has changed in the intervening 2000 years? More to the point, what has remained the same?

Most commentators on the Middle East avoid dealing with that question directly. Interestingly, it has taken Jewish activists to break the surface of public discussion on the issue. Some Israeli Jews are attuned to the difficult plight of non-Jews in Israel today. The so-called "secular left" has often complained about Israel's treatment of its Moslem and Christian citizens—as have some religious Jews. But few of those voices have added the weight of scholarly knowledge to their complaints.

Dr. Israel Shahak is an exception. Shahak is a Holocaust survivor (Belsen camp), an emeritus professor of organic chemistry at Hebrew University, a resident of Israel since 1945, and a longtime human rights activist. A seasoned student of Jewish scripture and tradition, Shahak candidly discusses the roots of the Judeo-Christian conflict—from the Judaic side.

Shahak believes that the State of Israel's prevailing ethnic and religious discrimination is a threat to its own moral legitimacy, and ultimately to its very existence. He believes that Israel will inevitably entangle itself in problems that are literally impossible to solve unless it can confront the *religious* sources of its own problem-making behavior.

Specifically, Shahak puts his challenge of conscience to Israel in terms of two historical questions: (1) "How do Jewish scripture and Jewish tradition shape current Jewish extremism?" and (2) "How does Jewish extremism shape current Israeli policy?"

His answers are likely to unsettle the views many conservative Christians hold about Judaism in general and the State of Israel in particular. He concludes from his studies that

> Judaism is imbued with a very deep hatred toward Christianity, combined with an ignorance about it. This attitude was clearly aggravated by the Christian persecutions of Jews, but is largely independent of them. In fact, it dates from the time when Christianity was still weak and was persecuted (not least by Jews), and it was shared by Jews who had never been persecuted by Christians, or who were even helped by them.[7]

Today, says Shahak, those same attitudes continue in force. Their expressions have changed to reflect the ways of the modern world, but the religious distaste and cultural resentment Judaism harbors toward Christianity has not abated. Jewish extremists merely extend and apply Jewish tradition in a particular way. We cannot understand Jewish extremism, much less the influence it exerts in modern Israel, unless we understand the pervasive anti-Christian attitude that runs throughout Jewish religion and Jewish cultural lore. A visceral loathing for Christianity is woven into Jewish scripture and is plainly displayed in Jewish history.

Jesus the Magician

The long-standing Jewish sense of revulsion toward Christianity described by Shahak has its origins in a conflict that has existed between them from the beginning. The main dispute between the first Jewish Christians and the Jewish leadership of the day was about the role of Jesus Himself. Was He God's promised Messiah, as He had plainly claimed, or was He an impious impostor?

The choices were clear—and so were the consequences. If you thought Jesus was an impostor, you aligned yourself with the ruling powers of the day, including the Jewish religious establishment. If you thought Jesus was God's Messiah, you aligned yourself against them, and you could expect to be harassed, jailed, chased out of town—or maybe just killed on the spot.

The clash between Jew and Christian was as inevitable as the clash between Jew and Muslim, but it happened faster and was more fundamental. The Judeo-Christian conflict was more immediate and more intense on both sides because Christianity emerged, not *outside* of Jewish religion, but *within* it. Thus the tension between them was instantaneous. Christianity's claim that Jesus is God's promised Messiah challenged the legitimacy of rabbinic Judaism far more directly than anything Mohammed said or did.

Islam was an external threat; Christianity was an internal danger. For that reason, Christ and Christianity have been singled out for special rejection in Jewish scripture and special revulsion in Jewish tradition.

Rabbinic nullification of the gospel was quickly institutionalized. Jewish religious authorities reacted swiftly to "the Jesus affair," and began to teach about Christ in ways designed to harden the Jewish people against Christianity. The rabbis circulated demeaning tales about Jesus Himself, and described Christians as creatures so low on the scale of existence that no Jew would ever think of becoming one. Their anti-Christian teachings were eventually written down in the Jewish scripture known as the Talmud—the sprawling compendium of rules, interpretations of rules, and general commentary on life that has guided the belief and behavior of religious Jews for thousands of years.

Shahak has studied the Talmud critically, and regards it as a defining document of the Judeo-Christian conflict. He finds within the Talmud two major strands of bigotry against Christians and Christianity. The first strand consists of "hatred and malicious slanders against Jesus" Himself; the second indicts Christianity as a form of idolatry and accuses Christians of being idolators.[8]

To say that the Talmud reviles and despises Jesus would be an understatement. It depicts Jesus as a bastard, a black magician, and a blasphemer. The Talmudic judgment on Jesus can be summed up in a litany of scandalous accusations: He was the illegitimate son of a Jewish whore (Mary) by a Roman soldier named Pandira.[9] Jesus learned sorcery and black magic,[10] and by their means deceived many.[11] He falsely claimed to be the Messiah promised by God, and thereby led His followers to spiritual destruction. "According to the Talmud, Jesus was executed by a proper rabbinical court for idolatry, inciting other Jews to idolatry and contempt of rabbinical authority."[12] In punishment for His blasphemy, His eternal fate is to be immersed in boiling excrement forever.[13]

> The very name "Jesus" was for Jews a symbol of all that is abominable, and this popular tradition still persists. The Gospels are equally detested, and they are not allowed to be quoted (let alone taught) even in modern Israeli schools.[14]

The Talmud reinforces its negative view of Christ with an equally negative view of Christians. The charge of idolatry the rabbis brought against the early Christians is more serious than it sounds to us today. Idolatry is the ultimate spiritual crime in Talmudic terms, and the accusation meant that Christians were relegated to a special class of spiritual outlaws—renegades who had forfeited their basic rights as human beings before both God and man. The Talmud's attitude toward Christians effectively assigned them the judgment God meted out to Cain (who was made an outcast and alien because of his high crime of murder), while denying them the protective "mark of Cain" (that whoever took vengeance on Cain would suffer God's punishment sevenfold—see Genesis 4:11-15).

Just as Christians were viewed with disgust and treated with derision, their Scriptures were viewed with a burning hatred. Pious Jews were forbidden to handle, read from, or listen to the Christian Scriptures, and the New Testament was to be publicly burned whenever it was possible to do so.

The Talmud's appraisal of other religions in general isn't exactly "friendly," but its assessment of Jesus and His followers is uniquely hostile. When we look at Judaism's history of treating Muslims and Christians respectively, it becomes obvious that a special category of malice has been reserved for Christianity. Comparatively speaking, Judaism's

> attitude towards Islam is relatively mild. Although the stock epithet given to Mohammed is "madman" (*meshugga*), this was not nearly as offensive as it may sound now, and in any case it pales before the abusive terms applied to Jesus. Similarly, the Koran—unlike the New Testament—is not condemned to burning. It is not honored in the same way as Islamic law honors the Jewish sacred scrolls, but it is treated as an ordinary book . . . Therefore the Halakha (the legal system of classical Judaism) decrees that Muslims should not be treated by Jews any worse than "ordinary" Gentiles.[15]

Christians, on the other hand, definitely *were* to be "treated worse by Jews than 'ordinary' Gentiles." As officially designated idolators, the followers of Christ were put beyond even the minimal regard that the Talmud extends to non-Jews who accept the "Noahide precepts"—the seven biblical laws considered by the Talmud to be addressed to Gentiles. Since the Noahide laws feature a ban on idolatry, Christians were deemed to be in violation of its standards by definition. In the Talmudic scheme of things, then, Christians were ranked even lower than Gentiles in general, and Jews were taught to revile them accordingly.

The Talmud's command to burn copies of the Christian Scriptures that come to hand is still observed in Israel, both in principle and in practice. Public burnings of the New Testament are carried out today with the direct blessing of Jewish religious authorities and the indirect blessing of the Jewish State.

Thus on 23 March 1980 hundreds of copies of the New Testament were publicly and ceremonially burnt in Jerusalem under the auspices of Yad Le'akhim, a Jewish religious organization subsidized by the Israeli Ministry of Religions.[16]

The Talmud and the Jewish State

The Talmud's view of Christ as a spiritual criminal and Christians as spiritual outlaws has shaped the view of classical Judaism toward Christianity for the last 2000 years. And, as we can see in the case of Scripture-burning, it continues to do so today.

In Israel, Jewish religious attitudes have secular implications. The outside world needs to know in what other ways Talmudic teachings affect the policies of the Jewish State. In particular, as Christians, we need to know how Talmudic attitudes affect the treatment of Christians and other non-Jews who live under Israel's rule today.

Those are straightforward questions, but their answers won't be found by polling Jews on what they think about the Talmud. Most modern Jews don't think about the Talmud at all. Today, only Orthodox (and "Ultra-Orthodox") Jews study the Talmud directly and attempt to follow it. Conservative Jews know it mostly by reputation, and Reform Jews ignore it almost completely. Secular Jews, for the most part, are ignorant of the Talmud; those who do know something about it are often critical of it.

Modern Judaism is anything but monolithic, and modern Jewry as a whole is even less so. There are religious Jews who strictly follow the Old Testament rules of living; there are secular Jews who ignore their religion altogether; and there are atheistic Jews who attack their religion outright. Yet all are considered to be Jews by the State of Israel.

Ironically, the very breadth and diversity of modern Jewry illustrates how basic the Talmud is to the identity of Israel as a Jewish State. Israel's *inclusive* view of Jewishness embodies a Talmudic view that is rigidly *exclusive* of one particular *kind* of

Jew. The Talmud absolutely excludes Christian Jews from its definition of who is Jewish—and so does the State of Israel.

Israel's 1950 "Law of Return" guarantees to all Jews worldwide automatic entry into the country as immigrants, plus "national" (that is, first-class) citizenship on arrival. Also guaranteed are all manner of material support—from free school kits and Hebrew language lessons all the way up to housing and financial subsidies—as a matter of right, *because they are Jews*. All stripes of Jewish belief and unbelief are accepted for entry and enrolled for benefits based on those guarantees.

Jews who profess Jesus as their Messiah, however, have no such rights. They are automatically classified as non-Jews by Israeli Law and Israeli courts.

> Messianic Jews ask, "Why is it that a Jew may embrace atheism, agnosticism, or even practice an eastern religion and still be regarded as Jewish, while only those who believe in Jesus are seen as having abandoned their heritage?"[17]

The simple answer to their query is that Christian Jews alone are singled out as Jewish traitors because of the indirect effect of Talmudic thinking—conveyed through Zionism—on the official conduct of the State of Israel. It is probably safe to say that the majority of Jews in Israel, including those involved in politics, know little or nothing of the Talmud *per se*. But the weight of Jewish cultural history means that the Talmud's view of gentiles—and especially its view of Christians—still guides Israel's uneven-handed treatment of the people under its rule today.

> The persistent attitudes of classical Judaism toward non-Jews strongly influence its followers, Orthodox Jews and those who can be regarded as its continuators, Zionists. Through the latter it also influences the policies of the state of Israel. Since 1967, as Israel becomes more and more "Jewish," so its policies are influenced more by Jewish ideological considerations. . . . This ideological influence is not usually perceived by foreign experts, who tend to ignore or downplay the influence of the Jewish religion on Israeli policies.[18]

Talmudism shapes Zionism, and Zionism in turn sets the agenda for Israel as a "Jewish State." By official self-definition, the State of Israel "belongs" to the Jewish people (that is, to all Jews, whether they have ever set foot in Israel or not) and to them alone. By direct implication, then, Israel does not and cannot in any sense "belong" to a non-Jew, though his family may have lived there for a thousand years.

Defining Israel as a Jewish State defines the non-Jew as a literal "foreign body"—an alien who may be accepted temporarily for reasons of necessity, but who is inherently under pressure to remove his non-Jewish presence and go away. Thus the normal concept of who is a "native" and who is an "alien" gets turned upside down. By decree, all Jews are made natives of a land to which many of them are strangers, while non-Jewish natives are declared to be strangers in their own land.

That same Talmudic-Zionist attitude shapes many Israeli policies, domestic as well as foreign. Non-Jews within Israel face a labyrinth of official discrimination and bureaucratic harassment that works to oppress them and ultimately to vex them into leaving—or if they can't leave, simply to vex and oppress them. Gentiles (and especially Christians) who live in Israel awaken every day to the fact that they are unwelcome among their Jewish neighbors. They arise every morning with the certain knowledge that their unwelcomeness will be made clear to them in numerous personal and official acts committed during the course of the day.

> Almost every morning, Palestinian merchants find fresh Hebrew graffiti spray-painted on their doors with messages like "Arabs Out!" and "Jerusalem is for Us!"
> "What can we do?" shrugged one shop owner after he translated the bright red Hebrew characters on his door for me early one morning. "If we cover it, it's always back; and besides, they all have guns. They do what they want here."[19]

Dr. Shahak identifies the Talmud as the source of that persecution. Whatever its roots, however, you don't have to be a
Talmudic scholar to recognize its results. In 1992 a U.S. State
Department report on human rights drew a clear picture of
Israel's rule over non-Jews in the "occupied territories." In
effect, said the report, there is a dual system of law. Jewish set-
tlers in the territories are subject to Israeli law, while the resident non-Jews live under the much harsher standards of
military occupation law. As the *Christian Science Monitor* noted,
the system creates a two-tiered society with

> a favored minority and a majority that is essentially an
> underclass and suffers legally instituted and sanctioned dis-
> crimination of various sorts. The State Department's report
> described the actual conditions in the occupied territories:
> "Sentences given to Israelis for killing Palestinians are
> generally much lighter than sentences handed down to
> Palestinians convicted of killing either Israelis or Pales-
> tinians."
> Israeli settlers are immune from many other forms of
> punishments and restrictions to which the Palestinians are
> subject, including restriction on movement and travel, deten-
> tion without charge or trial, closure of schools and universi-
> ties, and many others. In brief, as the State Department's
> report puts it, there is a "dual system of governance applied
> to Palestinians and Israelis" in the occupied territories.[20]

The Dual System in Israel

America's dual system between blacks and whites was
called "Jim Crow"—and America underwent a social revolution to get rid of it. The South African system of dual ethnic
classification was known as "apartheid"—and the world condemned South Africa because of it. South Africa accepted the
world's chastisement, and now struggles with a social revolution of its own.

For whatever reason, Israel's dual system has escaped
widespread condemnation. Israel openly enforces a two-tiered

system of justice that is openly based upon ethnic standards—
but only its victims stand up to complain.

> Israel's enemies have always found it easy to make
> unjust comparisons with the old South Africa. But it gets
> easier when you read that the government is preparing
> plans to corral Israeli Arabs in Galilee into blocks of flats to
> prevent them from having a majority of the land . . . and
> when you witness the casual contempt with which Orthodox
> Jews in Jerusalem deal with Palestinians.[21]

The "enemies of Israel," however, are not the only ones to
make such comparisons. Some of the strongest criticisms
come from within Israel itself, and are uttered by Israelis who
are plainly committed to Israel's validity and existence.
Shahak speaks eloquently for many of them. He describes
Israel's regime in terms that few Western journalists would
dare to use. He calls the Israeli treatment of Palestinians in
the occupied territories "in some respects worse than that of
South Africa's apartheid regime at its worst."[22]

Worse comes to worse when it is realized that Israel's dual
system of government is not confined to the occupied territories, with their special "security problems." Even within Israel
itself, there is a two-tiered system of administering the law that
makes it easy for Jews to move through the bureaucratic maze,
and difficult for everyone else.

The double bureaucratic standard in Israel extends from
matters of land ownership and use, through the selective allo-
cation of public resources, up to selective restrictions on personal mobility. Non-Jews in Israel (essentially meaning
Christian and Moslem Arabs) are issued color-coded ID cards
that determine where they are authorized to travel within the
country. Non-Jews find it next to impossible to acquire land or
transfer it to their descendants. Arabs in Jerusalem who wish
to make repairs or improvements to their existing property
face a daunting gauntlet of forms, fees, and permits that can

drag the process out virtually at the whim of Israeli bureau-crats.

It should be obvious at this point that the "whim" of Israeli bureaucrats is not really "whimsical" at all, but systematically prejudicial.

> It is clear that Israeli Interior Ministry actions are aimed at reducing the number of Palestinians entitled to live in Jerusalem and to have access to such services as public schooling and national health insurance.
>
> By entangling Palestinians in a bureaucratic web, and by denying their right to live in their place of origin or with their families, the Israeli occupation authority is conducting a campaign of "ethnic cleansing" to erase East Jerusalem's Palestinian character and create an Israeli rather than an Arab majority.[23]

Israel's discriminatory policies also take the form of "malign neglect." Sheldon Richman, senior editor for the Cato Institute in Washington, DC, points out that the very concept of a Jewish State

> affects the way that people are treated day to day in Israel. Since the government dominates the economic life of Israel, the distribution of many goods and services is directly affected by the basic discrimination against non-Jews.[24]

Perhaps the clearest example of malign neglect is the way that basic life-sustaining civic services like water, power, and sanitation are withheld from Christian and Moslem towns and villages, while the taxes that are supposed to support those nonexistent services continue to be rigorously collected—sometimes at bayonet-point.

Worse Than the IRS

In 1989 the Christian town of Beit Sahour felt the sharp point of the Israeli bayonet. Beit Sahour claims to be built on the site where the angels first appeared to shepherds "once upon a midnight clear" to announce the birth of Christ. For nearly 2000 years the village has survived and prospered—under both Moslem and Christian rule. Under Israeli rule, however, Beit Sahour has not thrived but withered, becoming a poor, unpleasant, and unsanitary place to live.

> The roads are pitted with potholes, there are no phone boxes or street lamps, the rubbish lies uncollected at the bottom of every driveway. It was this neglect on the part of the Israeli military occupation authorities, combined with crippling taxation rates, two or three times the Israeli norms, that led the town into a non-violent tax revolt in April 1989.
>
> Raising the Bostonian cry of "No Taxation Without Representation," the people of Beit Sahour held a sit-in at the Greek Orthodox church, and announced that they were refusing to pay any more taxes until the authorities showed some sign of providing services in return. The response was brutal.[25]

The Israeli army surrounded Beit Sahour and declared a security curfew. The next day, soldiers went house-to-house demanding that residents pay their taxes on the spot or face dispossession. The case of Nicola Ghattas is typical. Ghattas is a small-scale craftsman; he owns a workshop and tools with which he makes items from mother-of-pearl—a local specialty since the fourth century. A member of the Orthodox Church whose basilica dominates the town's skyline, he caters mostly to the tourist trade with religious souvenir items. On the second day of the curfew, Israeli soldiers

> came to Ghattas's house and asked him to pay a minimum of 1,000 shekels from his tax bill. When he refused, they removed everything he owned: his machinery from the workshop, the television, fridge, vacuum cleaner, stove, washing machine, beds, tables, chairs and gold-plated icons. They left him with an empty house, with no source of income and no food.

The curfew continued for week after week, as the army went around each house in the village, performing the same operation. There were no breaks to allow people to stock up on food and water. If the people had fruit trees in their back garden, then they could eat. Otherwise, when their food stocks ran out they went hungry.[26]

The curfew was extended into a second month, becoming the equivalent of a siege. A coalition of churches in Jerusalem sent a delegation to lift the siege and relieve the suffering of Beit Sahour's residents by bringing them food and humanitarian aid. They were turned back with teargas. The Israeli authorities were determined to starve Beit Sahour into submission, and they showed little restraint and less hesitation in brushing aside any effort to interfere with that purpose.

Eventually, after 56 days, the town capitulated, but no one received their confiscated possessions back. "Our family business supported 23 mouths," said Ghattas. "Now with our machinery gone, we couldn't find the price of a loaf of bread, we couldn't even afford an aspirin. . . . Muslim neighbors from other villages would occasionally bring us bread."[27]

Beit Sahour is an extreme example, to be sure. But the travail of the church in Israel today lies precisely in the fact that Beit Sahour is *only* an extreme example of an otherwise pervasive and routine discrimination. Indeed, "it is not difficult to point to Arab villages in Israel whose residents have been left for decades without electricity or sewage, often to the present day."[28]

Popular Persecution

Another example of the dual system within Israel is the selective way the state enforces its own laws against racism and racist incitement. Israeli laws

> proscribe public expressions of racism and utterances hurtful to human dignity . . . [but] they are almost always applied against the Arabs and hardly ever against the Jews. . . . Racist and inciteful pronouncements of Jews against non-Jews,

especially against Arabs, abound in the State of Israel. Yet I
do not recall a single instance of a Jew being convicted for
such an offense, although many Arabs have been convicted
for incitement against the Jews.[29]

The public burning of New Testaments also plainly vio-
lates those laws. Yet such acts are subsidized by the Israeli government. In Israel, Jewish extremists know they can light the
fires of religious spite with impunity—and so does everyone
else. In Israel, everyone understands that fact of life because
everyone sees it happen on a daily basis. Christians, as always,
are special objects of that spite. They are the targets of a comprehensive cultural hostility against which the Jewish State of
Israel provides no real protection and no effective recourse.

That double standard is the most dangerous one of all,
because it endorses the second-class status of non-Jews and
validates the traditional Jewish (Talmudic) prejudice against
them. Extremist Jews are thus encouraged to ventilate their
exaggerated scorn against gentiles (especially Christians) in
public ways—while the objects of their scorn are constrained
from responding in word or deed. It doesn't take a social scientist to figure out what the results of that imbalance will be.

Inflammatory words kindle inflamed behavior. When the
popular bias against gentiles and Christians is affirmed by the
structure of law and reinforced by a pattern of bureaucratic
discrimination, Jewish extremists feel free to act out fantasies
of anathema drawn from the most regressive elements of Talmudic tradition.

The standard expression of anathema is profaning and
desecrating the holy things of your religious opposition. The
Talmud clearly identifies its religious enemies, and declares it
the *religious duty* of pious Jews to profane the enemy's holy
things. In Israel today,

> one can read quite freely—and Jewish children are actually
> taught—passages such as that which commands every Jew,
> whenever passing near a cemetery, to utter a blessing if the

cemetery is Jewish, but to curse the mothers of the dead if it is non-Jewish.

Without facing this real social fact, we all become parties to . . . the consequences . . .[30]

One consequence of this "real social fact" is that Christians in Palestine have had their cemeteries, churches, holy sites, places of pilgrimage, and places of worship routinely vandalized and desecrated over the years since Israel's founding. The desecrations are normally performed by individual Jews and groups of Jews, acting on their own or under the direct inspiration of their extremist rabbis. In a number of cases, however, they have been carried out by units of the Israeli army, acting under the indirect influence of the same extremist ideology.

The pattern of profaning Christian sites began early in the history of Israel, and has continued to the present day. Outrageous incidents of anti-Christian desecration have led to official protests—in some cases by the UN, in some cases by other countries, and sometimes by interdenominational Christian bodies. The Christian Union of Palestine (CUP) led the way in 1948 by issuing a statement denouncing the destruction and desecration of Christian holy places that took place as a part of the war to establish the State of Israel. In the preamble to their statement, the CUP said:

> Because of this dreadful situation, We, the representatives of the Christian Communities, deem it our solemn duty to raise our voice of protest against the violation of the sanctity of our Churches, convents and institutions.[31]

The report that followed detailed 26 of the worst cases that had occurred during the course of the war. As it turned out, that was only the beginning. Since then, incidents of anti-Christian vandalism have increased rather than diminished. Many reports and objections have been filed by various churches and church groups over the years, but they don't appear to have had any lasting effect. The UN has passed a number of resolutions deploring Israel's treatment of its minorities, but has never effectively enforced them.

The problem of aggressive religious spite in Israel (or anywhere else) is intractable through bureaucratic fiat and moralistic resolutions because its momentum comes from the weight of fallen human nature. Until the connection between the Talmud's anti-gentile prejudice, Israel's anti-gentile discrimination, and the extremists' anti-gentile violence is addressed—on some level—within Israel itself, the situation will not change. Jewish extremism that compulsively desecrates another faith perpetuates the most regressive elements of Talmudic tradition. Shahak puts the matter with characteristic brutal candor:

> Dishonoring Christian religious symbols is an old religious duty in Judaism. Spitting on the cross, and especially on the Crucifix, and spitting when a Jew passes a church, have been obligatory from around AD 200 for pious Jews. . . . This barbarous attitude of contempt and hate for Christian symbols has increased in Israel.[32]

It is not a surprise that interreligious hatred continues to exist in the modern world. No one who understands fallen human nature will be baffled by the persistence of pogroms and persecutions. The fallen human tendency to divide ourselves from and despise one another is an ancient problem that will never be overcome entirely until the Lord returns. Meanwhile, however, it *can* be constrained and corrected to some degree—*provided it is acknowledged and identified as a problem.*

That is exactly why Christians in Palestine regard their future with such a sense of grim despair. Their difficult status is not acknowledged or identified. It is little noted in Israel itself, even less so in the Western press, and hardly at all in America. One example of this is that after the Christian cemetery on Mount Zion had been desecrated for the eighth time in a row during the span of a few years, one Western reporter finally visited the scene. He was shocked at what he found. In his description,

> the tombstones had almost all been shattered, metal crosses lay twisted in their sockets, and the sepulchers had been broken open; the one standing mausoleum was riddled with bullet-holes. "Had we been Jews and our churches been synagogues, desecration like this would have caused an international outcry," said the monk at the Martyrion. "But because we are Christians, no one seems to care."[33]

Persecution and Indifference

It is difficult for most of us to imagine what it is like to live under such conditions—in which pervasive discrimination, continual hostility, and an ever-looming sense of danger dominate one's moment-by-moment attention. Among Christians in Palestine, however, the real temptation to despair (and exodus) is the fact that almost everyone agrees that the problem will get worse instead of better.

There are things that could be done to help—but they won't be. Experience has shown that political and economic pressure from other nations would help relieve the kind of persecution that Christians are undergoing in the Middle East, whether in Israel or in Moslem countries. But no such pressure is forthcoming.

The clash of Arab and Israeli agendas sends tremors throughout the international community. But the persecution of Christians doesn't register to anyone as a matter affecting their national interests.

Christians are caught in the collision between two massive power blocs. Since they are overshadowed by the contending forces that swirl around them, the condition of Christians in Palestine has been and continues to be a nonissue for most of the world. Therefore no serious action will soon be taken on their behalf. Israel and the Moslem countries are occasionally "reminded" by the U.S. State Department or the UN that their policies are not entirely approved of. But rarely is anything actually done. The Christians of Palestine already know that the most they can hope for from the "world community" (including the United States) is empty rhetoric and occasional empty gestures.

In the absence of any significant protest from the rest of the world, the double pincer of Moslem and Jewish hostility continues to tighten, and the Christians who actually live under it know what that means for their future. The Jewish side of the pincer pinches the most at the moment because it is the less recognized of the two. Ironically, though discrimination against Christians is (almost) publicly unknown outside of Israel, it is publicly flaunted within Israel itself.

The prejudice against Christians in the Holy Land suggests an unpleasant answer to the question of how Christ would be received if He returned for a visit today. The short answer is that He would get the same treatment He got on His first visitation. My confidence in saying that comes from the fact that Christians are already getting the treatment He got, and Christ Himself made it clear that rejecting His followers is the same as rejecting Him.

In the week before His crucifixion, Jesus delivered the last major sermon of His ministry—the so-called "Olivet Discourse." Knowing that His death was near, He spoke of cosmic themes and final things. He described the last judgment, at which time the Son of Man will separate people from one another "as a shepherd separates the sheep from the goats" (Matthew 25:32). To the "sheep," He promised His Father's blessing, saying, "For I was hungry and you gave me food, I was thirsty and you gave me drink, I was a stranger and you welcomed me, I was naked and you clothed me, I was sick and you visited me. I was in prison and you came to me" (Matthew 25:35-36 RSV).

To the "goats," however, He promised judgment, exile, and "the eternal fire prepared for the devil and his angels," saying that they had turned away from Him when He was hungry, thirsty, naked, and so forth.

Both groups protested that all of this was news to them. Both asked when they had ever behaved in such a way. The "goats" were almost indignant in their query—but to no avail:

> "Lord, when did we see You hungry, or thirsty, or a stranger, or naked, or sick, or in prison, and did not take care of you?"
> Then He will answer them, saying, "Truly I say to you, to the extent that you did not do it to one of the least of these, you did not do it to Me." (Matthew 25:44-46 NASB)

In His time on earth, Christ was beset and plotted against by His enemies and abandoned in His hour of need by His friends and disciples. Today on earth, the Body of Christ is replaying that same role in the same part of the world. Not only are the Christians in Palestine beset by religious extremists from both sides, their suffering is largely ignored by their brothers and sisters around the world.

"Because we are Christians, no one seems to care." It is an all too familiar cry. Those Christians who are able to leave are doing so, because they can only see worsening conditions ahead. Experts estimate that at the present rate of emigration, Christianity will have essentially vanished from its birthplace by sometime in the early twenty-first century—if the world lasts that long.

Things *have* changed since Jesus first came among us. For Christ there was no room at the inn (Luke 2:7). For His followers today, it seems, there is not even room in the manger.

Why is there a chapter on the Jehovah's Witnesses in this book when this group has been written about exhaustively in hundreds of countercult books and exposes? Because the Jehovah's Witnesses are perhaps the clearest textbook example of how Christ has been reinvented to create a cult. Yet this heresy did not begin in the modern era. It is a cultic distortion with ancient roots—one that has taken a considerable toll since the time of the early church. Like some of the other distortions of Christ we're looking at in this book, the Watchtower distortion is based on an ancient error—in this case, that of Arianism (based on the heretical ideas of Arius). The new is reflected in the old. This heresy became refined in the last century to create a movement, the Jehovah's Witnesses, that has spread around the world to become one of the most popular and aggressive cults of all time.

Ron Rhodes, who has written a 440-page book on the Jehovah's Witnesses among his many books, is one of the world's experts on this particular cult. He does a masterful job of unraveling the teachings of the Jehovah's Witnesses and shows how they are very much a part of the "den of thieves" who are detracting from the person of Christ.

8

THE JESUS OF
THE WATCHTOWER SOCIETY

Ron Rhodes

Arius, the fourth-century heretic, maintained that Jesus was a pretemporal superhuman creature—the *first* of God's creatures. Jesus was not God, Arius said, but He was much more than a man. He was created out of nothing before the world began. He is thus not eternal, nor does He possess the divine essence. He was brought into being so the world might be created through Him. If Jesus were without beginning, Arius argued, then He would be the Father's brother, not His son.

Arius has long passed from the scene, but his theology lives on. Indeed, the Watchtower Society has developed Arius's deviant ideas into a full-fledged theology that strips Jesus of His divinity and exalts Jehovah as the only personage with whom we have to do.

Jehovah's Witnesses are told through Watchtower publications that God's true name is Jehovah. They are taught that superstitious Jewish scribes long ago removed this sacred name from the Bible. There is no need to worry, however, for the Society's New World Translation has "faithfully" restored the divine name in the Old Testament where the Hebrew consonants "YHWH" appear.[1]

Moreover, the name "Jehovah" has been inserted in the New Testament in verses where the text is believed to refer to

the Father.[2] They have taken the liberty to do this despite the
fact that it blatantly goes against all the thousands of New Testament Greek manuscripts in our possession—some of which
date from the second century.

Anatomy of a Lesser God

A central feature of Watchtower theology is that Jesus is
not Jehovah. The Jehovah's Witnesses concede that Jesus is a
"mighty god," but they deny that He is God Almighty like
Jehovah is.[3] *The Watchtower* magazine asks: "If Jesus of the
'New Testament' is Jehovah of the 'Old Testament,' as many
claim, should there not at least be one biblical reference
saying that Jesus is Jehovah? Yet there is not one."[4]

The *Watchtower* teaches that Jesus is a mere angel—the
first being God created in the universe. As *The Watchtower*
magazine puts it, "there is Scriptural evidence for concluding
that Michael was the name of Jesus Christ before he left
heaven [to become a man] and after his return [to heaven following his 'resurrection']."[5]

Jehovah's Witnesses argue that it was through this created
angel that God brought "all other" things into being (they
mistranslate Colossians 1:16 toward this end). The Watchtower book, *Aid to Bible Understanding,* explains:

> Jehovah's first creation was his "only-begotten Son"
> (John 3:16), "the beginning of the creation by God" (Revelation 3:14). This one, "the first-born of all creation," was
> used by Jehovah in creating all other things, those in the
> heavens and those upon the earth, "the things visible and
> the things invisible" (Colossians 1:15-17).[6]

The Witnesses say that Michael (Jesus) conceivably
existed in his prehuman state for billions of years. At the
appointed time, he was born on earth as a human being—
ceasing his existence as an angel. To "ransom" humankind
from sin, Michael willingly gave up his existence as a spirit

creature (angel) when his life-force was transferred into Mary's womb by Jehovah.

This was *not* an incarnation (God in the flesh). Rather, Jesus became a perfect human being—nothing more and nothing less. He was equal in every way to Adam prior to the Fall. He lived His life as a human being, fulfilled the ministry appointed to Him by Jehovah, and died faithfully for the ransom of humankind.

Like Arius, the Jehovah's Witnesses often appeal to a set of proof-texts to demonstrate that Jesus is lesser than the Father (Jehovah). For example, Jesus Himself said, "the Father is greater than I" (John 14:28). First Corinthians 11:3 tells us that "the head of Christ is God." Jesus is called "the firstborn over all creation" in Colossians 1:15. He is also referred to as "a God" in John 1:1 and a "mighty God" (as opposed to God Almighty) in Isaiah 9:6. Clearly, the Jehovah's Witnesses say, Jesus is not God in the same sense Jehovah is.

In keeping with this, the Watchtower Society teaches that Jesus was not worshiped in the same sense that the Father was. "It is unscriptural for worshipers of the living and true God to render worship to the Son of God, Jesus Christ."[7] Even though the same Greek word used for worshiping Jehovah (*proskuneo*) is used of Jesus, the Watchtower Society says the word should be translated "obeisance" and not "worship" when used of Christ. Hence, the New World Translation renders Hebrews 1:6b: "Let all God's angels do obeisance to him."

The Watchtower Society teaches that Jesus died as a sacrifice for sin, but they do not interpret Christ's sacrificial death the same way evangelical Christians do. They teach that the human life Jesus laid down in sacrifice was *exactly equal* to the human life Adam fell with. "Since one man's sin (that of Adam) had been responsible for causing the entire human family to be sinners, the shed blood of another perfect human (in effect, a second Adam), being of corresponding value, could balance the scales of justice."[8] Christ's "ransom" at the cross served only to remove the effects of Adam's sin. This having been accomplished by Christ, it is now up to each Jehovah's Witness to engage in works that will lead to salvation (contrary to Ephesians 2:8,9 and many other verses).

When Jesus died on the stake (not a cross), He allegedly became nonexistent and was raised (or, more accurately, *recreated*) three days later as a spirit creature (that is, as Michael the Archangel). A physical resurrection did not occur. "We deny that He was raised in the flesh, and challenge any statement to that effect as being unscriptural."[9]

One reason Jesus did not raise from the dead in a body of human flesh is related to His work of atonement. The Watchtower publication *You Can Live Forever in Paradise on Earth* says that "having given up his flesh for the life of the world, Christ could never take it again and become a man once more."[10] Christ *forever* sacrificed His human flesh at the cross. Hence, at the "resurrection" He became not a glorified human being but rather was recreated as the Archangel Michael.

In keeping with this, the Watchtower Society teaches that Jesus did not appear to His disciples in the same body in which He died. In *"The Kingdom Is at Hand"* we read: "Therefore the bodies in which Jesus manifested himself to his disciples after his return to life were not the body in which he was nailed to the tree."[11] To convince Thomas of who He was, "He used a body with wound holes."[12]

What, then, happened to the human body of Jesus that was laid in the tomb? *The Watchtower* magazine reports that it "was disposed of by Jehovah God, dissolved into its constituent elements or atoms."[13] Indeed, "the human body of flesh, which Jesus Christ laid down forever as a ransom sacrifice, was disposed of by God's power."[14]

Consistent with Jesus' alleged spiritual resurrection is the teaching that a spiritual second coming of Christ occurred in 1914. Words normally translated "coming" in contexts dealing with the second coming are translated by the Jehovah's Witnesses as "presence." Hence, the second coming refers to Christ's spiritual presence with man since 1914. Beginning that year, Christ has allegedly been ruling as King on earth through the Watchtower Society.

Now, it is quite clear from the above that the Jehovah's Witnesses offer us a Jesus completely unlike the one espoused by historic Christianity. In what follows I will briefly respond to some of the more blatant Christological distortions of the Watchtower Society.

A Created Creator?

In Isaiah 44:24 God Almighty said, "I, the LORD [Yahweh], am the *maker of all things*, stretching out the heavens *by Myself*, and spreading out the earth *all alone*" (NASB, emphasis added). This verse makes it impossible to argue that Christ was created first by Jehovah and then Jehovah created all other things "through" Christ. The fact that Jehovah is the "maker of all things" who stretched out the heavens "by myself" and spread out the earth "all alone" (Isaiah 44:24)— *and* the accompanying fact that Christ Himself is the Creator of "all things" (John 1:3; Colossians 1:16; Hebrews 1:2-10)— proves that Christ is God Almighty, just as the Father is. As Norman Geisler put it,

> There is no doubt that the Old Testament presents God alone as Creator of the universe (Genesis 1, Isaiah 40, Psalm 8). And when the disciples of Christ declare Jesus to be the one through whom all things were created, the conclusion that they were thereby attributing deity to him is unavoidable.[15]

Mistaken Identity

Jesus was most certainly not the Archangel Michael in the Old Testament. For one thing, Michael in Daniel 10:13 is specifically called "*one of* the chief princes." That Michael is "one of" the chief princes indicates that he is *one among a group* of chief princes. How large that group is, we are not told. The fact that Michael is one among equals, however, proves that he is not unique. By contrast, the Greek word used to describe Jesus in John 3:16 is *monogenes*—meaning "unique" or "one of a kind." He is not a "chief prince" but is rather the "King of kings and Lord of lords" (Revelation 19:16).

Moreover, in Hebrews 1:5 we are told that no angel can ever be called God's son: "To which of the angels did God ever say, 'You are my Son. . . .' " Since Jesus *is* the Son of God, and since no angel can ever be called God's son, then Jesus cannot possibly be the Archangel Michael.

Further, we are explicitly told in Hebrews 2:5 that the world *is not* (and *will not be*) in subjection to an angel. The backdrop to this is that the Dead Sea Scrolls (discovered at Qumran in 1947) reflect an expectation that the Archangel Michael would be a supreme figure in the coming messianic kingdom. It may be that some of the recipients of the book of Hebrews were tempted to assign angels a place above Christ. Whether or not this is true, Hebrews 2:5 makes it clear that *no* angel will rule in God's kingdom. This being so, Christ cannot be Michael since He is repeatedly said to be the ruler of God's kingdom in Scripture (Genesis 49:10; 2 Samuel 7:16; Psalm 2:6; Daniel 7:13-14; Matthew 2:1,2; 9:35; Luke 1:32,33; Revelation 19:16).

In addition, Scripture portrays Christ as immutable. Immutability refers to the fact that Christ as God is unchangeable in His being. Hebrews 13:8 tells us that "Jesus Christ is the same yesterday and today and forever." If Christ is the same *yesterday, today,* and *forever,* then He couldn't have been an *angel,* become a *man,* and then been recreated as an *angel.*

Finally, the Archangel Michael does not have the authority in himself to rebuke Satan. In Jude 9 we read, "But Michael the archangel, when he disputed with the devil and argued about the body of Moses, did not dare pronounce against him a railing judgment, but said, 'The Lord rebuke you' " (NASB). By contrast, Jesus rebuked the Devil on many occasions (for example, Matthew 4:1-11; 17:18; Mark 9:25). Since Michael *could not* rebuke the Devil in his own authority and Jesus *could* (and *did*) rebuke the Devil in His own authority, Michael and Jesus cannot be the same person.

It is highly revealing that Jesus is often called "Lord" (Greek: *kurios*) in the New Testament (for example, Philippians 2:9-11). So, when Michael said "the Lord [*kurios*] rebuke you," he was directly appealing to the authority of Jesus Christ, the King of kings and Lord of lords (Revelation 19:16).

Much More Than "a God"

John's Gospel is the richest book in the New Testament concerning various evidences for Christ's deity. In this Gospel Jesus claims to be God (John 8:58), is recognized by others as God (20:28), is portrayed as preexistent and eternal (1:15,30; 3:31), self-existent (1:4; 5:26), omnipresent (1:47-49), omniscient (2:25; 16:30; 21:17), omnipotent (1:3; 2:19; 11:1-44), and sovereign (5:21,22,27-29; 10:18). He is recognized as the Creator of the universe (1:3), and He claims to be the theme of the entire Old Testament (5:39-40).

Obviously, the Watchtower Society must do something to take the wind out of the sails of John's Gospel. They do this by mistranslating key verses in this Gospel. The most blatant example of this is their mistranslation of John 1:1 in the New World Translation: "The Word [Christ] was a god" (insert added).

The Watchtower magazine states that "because there is no definite article 'the' (*ho*) in John 1:1, it means Christ is only a god, not the God."[16] The Greek of John 1:1 "is not saying that the Word (Jesus) was the same as the God with whom he was but, rather, that the Word was godlike, divine, a god."[17]

In response, we must note that if John had intended an adjectival sense in John 1:1 ("godlike" or "divine"), he had an adjective (Greek: *theios*) ready at hand that he could have used. Instead, John emphatically says the Word *is God* (*theos*)!

Moreover, it is not necessary to translate Greek nouns that have no definite article as having an *in*definite article. In other words, *theos* ("God") without the definite article *ho* ("the") does not need to be translated as "a God" as the Jehovah's Witnesses have done in reference to Christ in John 1:1. It is significant that *theos* without the definite article *ho* is used of

Jehovah-God in the New Testament (Luke 20:38). Because the lack of the definite article in Luke 20:38 in reference to Jehovah does not mean He is a lesser God, neither does the lack of the definite article in John 1:1 in reference to Jesus mean He is a lesser God. The fact is, the presence or absence of the definite article does not alter the fundamental meaning of *theos*.

To drive one further nail into the Watchtower coffin, let us note that some New Testament texts *do* use the definite article and speak of Christ as "the God" (*ho theos*). One example of this is John 20:28 where Thomas says to Jesus, "My Lord and my God." The verse reads literally from the Greek: "The Lord of me and the God [*ho theos*] of me" (see also Matthew 1:23 and Hebrews 1:8). So it does not matter whether John did or did not use the definite article in John 1:1—the Bible clearly teaches that Jesus is God, not just *a* god.

The Myth of the Lesser God

What about all the supporting verses—Colossians 1:15, John 14:28, 1 Corinthians 11:1, and Isaiah 9:6, for example— that the Watchtower cites to "prove" Jesus is a lesser deity? Do they not make a convincing case? It may appear so to the biblically uninformed, but not to those familiar with these verses in context.

Christ the "Firstborn." It is true that Jesus is called the "firstborn" in Colossians 1:15. But "firstborn" (Greek: *prototokos*) does not mean "first-created" (*protoktisis*). (The latter term is never used of Christ in the New Testament.) Rather, "firstborn" means "first in rank, preeminent one, heir."[18] The word carries the idea of positional preeminence and supremacy (see Genesis 41:50,51 [compare with Jeremiah 31:9] and Psalm 89:27 for proof of this). Christ is the "firstborn" in the sense that He is positionally preeminent over creation and is supreme over all things.

The Father Greater than Jesus? In John 14:28 Jesus acknowledged that the Father was "greater" (Greek: *meizon*) than He was. It is critical to recognize, however, that Jesus was not speaking about His nature (Christ had earlier said "I and the Father are *one*" in this regard—John 10:30), but was rather speaking of His lowly *position* in the Incarnation.[19] The Athanasian Creed affirms that Christ is "equal to the Father as touching his Godhood and inferior to the Father as touching his manhood."[20]

The Father was seated upon the throne of highest majesty in heaven; the brightness of His glory was uneclipsed as He was surrounded by hosts of holy beings perpetually worshiping Him with uninterrupted praise. Far different was it with His incarnate Son—despised and rejected of men, surrounded by implacable enemies, and soon to be nailed to a criminal's cross.

The Father the "Head" of Christ? While the Father is indeed called the "head" of Christ in 1 Corinthians 11:3, this does not mean Jesus is an inferior deity. A close examination of this verse shows that it has nothing to do with inferiority or superiority of one person over another; rather, it has to do with patterns of authority. Notice that Paul says the man is the head of the woman, even though men and women are utterly equal in their essential being. Men and women are both human, both created in God's image (Genesis 1:26-28), and are *one* in Christ (Galatians 3:28). These verses, taken with 1 Corinthians 11:3, demonstrate that *equality of being* and *social hierarchy* are not mutually exclusive. Though men and women are completely equal in terms of their nature, there is nevertheless a functional hierarchy that exists between them.

In the same way, Christ and the Father are utterly equal in their divine nature (John 10:30), though Jesus is functionally under the Father's headship (1 Corinthians 11:3). There is no contradiction in affirming both an *equality of being* and a *functional subordination* among the persons in the Godhead.

Jesus a "Mighty God"? The Watchtower Society is correct in affirming that Jesus is called a mighty God in Isaiah 9:6, and they do this thinking they've dealt a fatal blow to the view of orthodox Christians. What they fail to recognize is that in the very next chapter in Isaiah (Isaiah 10:21) Jehovah Himself is called "mighty God." The fact that Jehovah is called "mighty God" obliterates the Watchtower argument that the expression must refer to a lesser deity. Because Jehovah is called "mighty God," the fact that Jesus too is called "mighty God" points to His equality with God the Father.

From the brief treatment above I think you can begin to see my point. The Watchtower cites a number of verses together in machine-gun fashion to make it appear that Jesus is lesser than the Father. But these verses, considered individually and in context, fully support the undiminished deity of the Lord Jesus Christ. (A fuller treatment of these and other verses may be found in my book, *Reasoning from the Scriptures with the Jehovah's Witnesses*.)

Worthy of Worship

It is highly revealing that the Watchtower Society once endorsed the worship of Jesus. An early issue of *The Watchtower* magazine said that "to worship Christ in any form cannot be wrong."[21] Indeed, "We believe our Lord Jesus while on earth was really worshiped, and properly so."[22]

Many years later, however, *The Watchtower* magazine dogmatically asserted that "it is unscriptural for worshipers of the living and true God to render worship to the Son of God, Jesus Christ."[23] The magazine warned, "Do not erroneously conclude that Christians are to worship Christ; that is not what he taught."[24]

The fact is, Christ *was often* worshiped as God according to the Gospel accounts—and He always accepted such worship as appropriate. Jesus accepted worship from Thomas (John 20:28); the angels (Hebrews 1:6); the wise men (Matthew 2:11); a blind man (John 9:38); Mary Magdalene (Matthew 28:9); and the disciples (Matthew 28:17). In the book of Revelation, God the Father (4:10) and Jesus Christ (5:11-14) are portrayed as receiving *the exact same worship*. Why? Because both are equally divine.

A Bodily Resurrection

Contrary to the Watchtower claim, the New Testament is brimming with evidence that Jesus was physically raised from the dead. For example, the resurrected Christ told the disciples, "See My hands and My feet, that it is I Myself; touch Me and see, for a spirit does not have flesh and bones as you see that I have" (Luke 24:39 NASB). Notice three things here: (1) The resurrected Christ said He is *not a spirit*; (2) The resurrected Christ said His resurrection body is made up of *flesh and bones*; (3) Christ's physical hands and feet represent physical proof of the materiality of His resurrection from the dead.

Along these same lines, we are told in Acts 2:31 that Christ's "flesh did not see corruption." Why didn't His flesh see corruption? Because Jesus was raised from the dead in a material, fleshly body. The body "sown" in death was the *very same body* raised to life (1 Corinthians 15:35-44).

Note also that Jesus' resurrection body retained the physical wounds from the cross. Indeed, the resurrected Christ revealed His crucifixion scars to the disciples (Luke 24:39), and even challenged doubting Thomas to touch His wounds (John 20:27). Moreover, the resurrected Christ ate physical food on four different occasions to prove He had a genuine physical body (Luke 24:30; 24:42-43; John 21:12-13; Acts 1:4). It would have been deceptive on Jesus' part to have offered His ability to eat physical food as a proof of His bodily resurrection if He had not been resurrected in a physical body.

Further, the Greek word for body (*soma*), when used of a person, always means *physical body* in the New Testament. There are no exceptions to this. Greek scholar Robert Gundry, in his authoritative book *Soma in Biblical Theology*, points to "Paul's exceptionless use of *soma* for a physical body."[25] Hence, *all* references to Jesus' resurrection "body" (*soma*) in the New Testament must be taken to mean a resurrected *physical* body. It is in this body that Jesus will *physically* and *bodily* return to earth one day in the future (Matthew 24:29-30; Acts 1:9-11; Titus 2:13; Revelation 1:7).

Jesus Is Yahweh

A comparison of the Old and New Testaments provides powerful testimony to Jesus' identity as Yahweh. Support for this is found, for example, in Christ's crucifixion. In Zechariah 12:10, Yahweh is speaking prophetically: "They will look on me, the one they have pierced." Though Yahweh is speaking, this is obviously a reference to Christ's future crucifixion.[26] We know that "the one they have pierced" is Jesus, for He is described this same way by the apostle John in Revelation 1:7.

The Septuagint—a Greek translation of the Hebrew Old Testament that predates Christ—provides additional insights on Christ's identity as Yahweh. It renders the Hebrew phrase for "I AM" (God's name) in Exodus 3:14 as *ego eimi*.[27] On a number of occasions in the Greek New Testament, Jesus used this same term as a way of identifying Himself as God.[28] In John 8:24, for example, Jesus declared: "Unless you believe that I AM [*ego eimi*] He, you shall die in your sins" (NASB). The original Greek for this verse does not have the word *he*. The verse literally reads, "If you do not believe that I AM, you shall die in your sins."

Then, according to John 8:28, Jesus told the Jews: "When you lift up the Son of Man, then you will know that I AM [*ego eimi*] He" (NASB). Again, the original Greek reads, "When you lift up the Son of Man, then you will know that I AM" (there is no *he*). Jesus purposefully used the phrase as a means of pointing to His identity as Yahweh.[29]

In keeping with this, it is highly revealing that Old Testament passages about Yahweh were directly applied to Jesus in the New Testament. For instance, Isaiah 40:3 says: "In the desert prepare the way for the Lord [*Yahweh*]; make straight in the wilderness a highway for our God [*Elohim*]" (inserts added). Mark's gospel tells us that Isaiah's words were fulfilled in the ministry of John the Baptist preparing the way for Jesus Christ (Mark 1:2-4).

In Isaiah 6:1-5 the prophet recounts his vision of Yahweh "seated on a throne, high and exalted" (verse 1). He said, "Holy, holy, holy is the Lord [*Yahweh*] Almighty; the whole earth is full of his glory" (verse 3, insert added). Isaiah also quotes Yahweh as saying, "I am the LORD; that is my name! I will not give my glory to another" (42:8). Later, the apostle John—under the inspiration of the Holy Spirit—wrote that Isaiah "saw Jesus' glory" (John 12:41). Yahweh's glory and Jesus' glory are equated.

Christ's deity is further confirmed for us in that many of the actions of Yahweh in the Old Testament are performed by Christ in the New Testament. For example, in Psalm 119 we are told that it is Yahweh who gives and preserves life. In the New Testament, however, Jesus claims this power for Himself: "For just as the Father raises the dead and gives them life, even so the Son gives life to whom he is pleased to give it" (John 5:21).

In the Old Testament the voice of Yahweh was said to be "like the roar of rushing waters" (Ezekiel 43:2). Similarly, we read of the glorified Jesus in heaven: "His voice was like the sound of rushing waters" (Revelation 1:15). What is true of Yahweh is just as true of Jesus.

Further, in the Old Testament Yahweh is described as an "everlasting light," one that would make the sun, moon, and stars obsolete (Isaiah 60:19,20). The same is said of Jesus regarding the future eternal city: "The city does not need the sun or the moon to shine on it, for the glory of God gives it light, and the Lamb is its lamp" (Revelation 21:23).

When all the facts are known, it becomes undeniably clear that Jesus is not the lesser God of the Watchtower Society but is rather God Almighty—He who is the First and the Last, the Alpha and the Omega, the God of glory who is infinite in perfections (Revelation 1:8,17; 22:13). With the Father and the Holy Spirit, Jesus is everlastingly the Living God.

Long before the "Jesus Seminar" made headlines with its bold pronouncements about the "true" Jesus, the groundwork for the organization had already been laid. The story of the "quest for the historical Jesus" is a sobering tale of academic arrogance and folly that begins in the early nineteenth century. Theologians seeking to be relevant adopted the latest assumptions about reality that came from prestigious faculties of philosophy—often down the hall from their own departments. As philosophical trends changed—say, from neo-Kantianism to logical positivism—so did theological views.

Theologians desperate for peer respectability quickly adopted the latest views. They abandoned the very gospel they had been entrusted to preserve, altering it to fit current philosophical vogue. Early in the game they declared there were no such things as miracles. After this, they proceeded to "unearth" the true Jesus beneath the strata of "myth."

As we reach the end of the twentieth century we now witness where this journey has taken us—to final bankruptcy, as today's academic elite declare that the "true" Jesus is merely the Jesus of our own imaginations. The Jesus Seminar has merely borrowed from this academic quest that has gone on for the better part of two centuries as great sectors of Christendom have continued to fall behind these blind guides. The wreckage has been staggering.

9

THE QUEST FOR THE HISTORICAL JESUS

John Moore

O ver the past several hundred years there has been a unique assault on the "faith which was once for all delivered to the saints" (Jude 3 NASB). It has come from the most prestigious and influential universities in the West where theologians, biblical "critics," and other scholars have been relentlessly destroying the pillars of the faith—first chipping away, then tearing them down.

The byproduct of this organized campaign of intellectual skepticism can be seen in the West—across Europe and America—in the empty churches that were once bastions of robust faith and orthodoxy. These often beautiful, at times grand edifices had much happier days before their riches were plundered. Once full of steadfast believers who knew their Lord and God, they have been robbed by a unique den of thieves. Today they stand largely empty, little more than a quaint reminder of bygone days.

When the grand universities and academies ceased to believe, they passed their sepsis of unbelief down the hierarchy of learning, from theologians to clerics. Reverends in long, flowing robes could show off their newfound bankruptcy of faith. From the pulpits, this high sounding doubt was passed down to parishioners. At first these new ideas became fashionable among the educated, a sign of being ahead socially and intellectually. Gradually, other sheep wandered into this wasteland of emptied meaning in a general "falling away," which is now the state of much of Christianity's former bastion, Europe. The church in the United States, all evidence would indicate, is not far behind.

One of the most potent forms this intellectual and academic plundering took was through what is known as "the quest for the historical Jesus." The development of this quest provides us a unique glimpse into the process of apostasy. It is a glimpse into history that has had an impact on all Christians. The Jesus Seminar that we see today is just the latest, and perhaps the final, chapter in a tale of academic arrogance and pride that spans the centuries since the eighteenth-century Enlightenment. What follows is a brief tour of the various stages of this quest.

The First Quest

The first leg of the story begins in the late eighteenth century and runs through the whole of the nineteenth, and is mainly a story of German New Testament scholarship, beginning with Herman Reimarus. Reimarus's work, published posthumously in 1778, was a skeptical account, the first that tried to separate Jesus' words from those supposedly given to Him by His disciples. Reimarus believed that Jesus had originally preached a this-worldly message in line with Jewish nationalistic hopes. The disappointed disciples later reworked His message into that of a universal Savior.[1] In believing that Jesus' words as recorded in the New Testament were not His own, or at least not *entirely* His own, but that they had been conscripted into the service of a later socioreligious movement, Reimarus gave birth to the idea that there was a true "historical" Jesus hidden somewhere behind the layers of tradition and theology in the New Testament documents. The quest to find that true Jesus of history was begun.

The roots for Reimarus's work had been laid earlier, however, by the Englishman John Locke (1632–1704) and his contemporaries. Locke, whose thought and writings were to play a significant role in shaping the thinking of the founding fathers of the United States, was a champion of the resurgence of the Stoic (ancient Greek) idea of natural law, according to which miracles were a violation of sound thinking. Locke and his contemporaries, notably Matthew Tindal, wrestled with two philosophical problems in particular: the problem of miracles as reported in the Scriptures, and the particularity of the gospel.

Miracles were an affront to natural law, which sought to explain all activity in terms of the orderly, predictable operation of scientific principles (naturalism). And the particularity of the gospel was an affront to the seventeenth-century sense of justice: how could a gracious, just God reveal Himself to just *one group* of people at just *one time* and this be considered the saving event of the universe?[2]

These questions flowed naturally out of the upheavals in religious and political thought of the preceding century, the Reformation, and the Enlightenment. The Reformation, with Martin Luther's translation of the Bible into German, had opened the Scriptures to the common man, paving the way for critical evaluations of its contents. The Enlightenment, with its emphasis on man's reasoning ability as the supreme good and the measure of all things, gave birth to the intellectual streams of *rationalism* (the reliance on reason as the basis for establishment of religious truth) and its sister *naturalism* (the doctrine that scientific laws are adequate to account for all phenomena).

In response to these problems, Locke published (anonymously) a little book called *The Reasonableness of Christianity As Delivered in the Scriptures* (1695). In it, he called on Christians to approach the Scriptures from the common ground of reason, and work toward interpretations of Scripture that would not conflict with reason, as understood by natural law.

This book and other similar works laid the groundwork for a naturalistic approach to the interpretation of Scripture that was adopted, with great gusto, by a generation of German scholars almost a century later, starting with Reimarus.

In fact, this approach to biblical interpretation has endured, and has become almost the defining mark of modern critical scholarship. The view that true miracles do not happen, and therefore the miracles reported of Jesus were in fact something else—pious fictions, misunderstood natural phenomena, or myth "pure and simple"—is the stated or unstated presumption of all of the nineteenth century quest, the later twentieth century "New Quest" (a second quest), and now much of the so-called "Third Quest" for the historical Jesus (more on the "New Quest" and "Third Quest" shortly). The tenet of modern thought that evangelical scholar Phillip Johnson calls "atheistic naturalism," and that is elsewhere referred to as "philosophic naturalism," enters biblical scholarship here, with Locke.

In response to the skeptical naturalistic reconstructions being produced by the First Quest, several German orthodox scholars attempted orthodox, naturalist reconciliations by proposing rational explanations for the miracles: when Jesus walked on water He was actually in the shallows—fog helped create the illusion of a miracle; the transfiguration was actually the result of a strange interplay of clouds and sunlight; and so forth. Unfortunately, as might be imagined, the result of this "scholarship" was simply to cast the Gospels as naive misinterpretations of the historical events, or, at worst, as crude deceptions. As Howard Clark Kee put it, these interpretations seemed to transform the Gospel accounts from "Good News" into "gross misunderstanding."

Into this milieu, David Friedreich Strauss interjected another possibility. In his 1835 book *The Life of Jesus*, Strauss was the first to propose with "thoroughness and consistency" that the miracles recorded by the evangelists were not lies or deception, nor were they misunderstandings of natural events.

They were, in fact, augmented perceptions of reality—*deeper truths*—not confined to the strictly historical record.[3] In other words, they were *myths*. Strauss's work offered, for some, a more satisfying answer to the question of the origins of the "Christ of creed and dogma." The early disciples could, from this view, be seen not as deceivers or simpletons, but as simply operating from a different conception of reality.

Of course, it required a jump from understanding the Gospels as concrete history to understanding them as "historico-spiritual" history—an understanding that is incompatible with the orthodox view. To the world of liberal criticism, however, Strauss's mytho-poetic solution was a seemingly brilliant compromise—it allowed the exclusion of miracles as historical fact, as required by naturalism, but it offered the possibility of retaining the "spiritual reality" of the miracles. Strauss's reconstruction was to prove corrosive as its implications spread from the realm of biblical criticism into that of theological instruction, and from there into the church.

Meanwhile, the First Quest for the historical Jesus continued throughout the rest of the century. Space forbids a detailed discussion of the various remaining aspects of this initial quest. I will, however, mention two more scholars from this period: Adolph von Harnack, because of many interesting parallels between his work and that of the Jesus Seminar, and Albert Schweitzer, whose work is credited with bringing the First Quest to its stumbling end.

Adolph von Harnack (1851-1930) is widely regarded as one of the most accomplished scholars of his day. His work represents both the high point *and* the ultimate futility of the scholarship of the First Quest. By the end of the century, problems with the First Quest had become apparent: the many studies that had been conducted using "purely objective" techniques of historical analysis had produced many divergent and contradictory pictures of the "historical Jesus."

Von Harnack determined to ignore the problems of trying to recreate the events of Jesus' life and simply concentrate on

His *teachings*. Howard Kee outlines the problems with this approach in a way that sounds like it could have been written with the Jesus Seminar in mind:

> This decision [to dismiss the question of the life of Jesus and concentrate on his teachings] is a value judgment: that the enduring significance of Jesus does not lie in his historical existence, in the activities and events of his life, but in the content of his teachings. But even in this more limited field of investigation, certain choices must be made as to which among the array of sayings attributed to Jesus are to be regarded as authentic and which are later accretions. . . . Once certain criteria for authenticity have been adopted, an impressive case can be made for reconstructing what Jesus "really" taught—but only if the reader is willing to accept the presuppositions of the reconstructor.[4]

In 1900 von Harnack produced a popular work called *What Is Christianity* that set out, essentially, to strip Jesus' message of any apocalyptic elements. He acknowledged the presence of apocalypse—the revelation of the truth about God's activities at the end of time—in Jesus' teachings, but found the concepts distasteful—"wretched miserablisms." His reconstruction of the "true" message of Jesus became, in effect, the message that he wished Jesus had delivered. Von Harnack, in an incredible act of presumption, set out to correct the theology of Jesus to make it conform to his own nineteenth-century liberalism and universalism.

To make the point again, it was not that von Harnack did not believe that Jesus had delivered an eschatological message—he did. It was simply that von Harnack felt that Jesus' message would be "better" if it were stripped of this offensive material.

As Albert Schweitzer was soon to show, however, there were only two options with regard to Jesus' message as presented in the Gospels. Either Jesus' message was one of "thoroughgoing eschatology" or the entire record was a fiction (more on Schweitzer shortly). Von Harnack took an untenable third route, one which he must have known as a scholar was historically impossible: the apocalypticism of Jesus' message had been *added later* to the otherwise trustworthy records of His teachings.

The idea that God would judge the peoples of the earth at the end of time, sending some to eternal glory and some to eternal damnation, was a major stumbling block not only for von Harnack, but for much of the rest of liberal nineteenth-century scholasticism. As B.A. Pearson notes:

> Eschatology as such, involving ideas of the last judgment, resurrection, and the supernatural deliverance of the elect from temporal earthly existence, is quite foreign to the modern (or "postmodern") ways of thinking, and it was inevitable that a scholarly struggle would be mounted against it as holding the key to Jesus' teaching.[5]

That Jesus would teach such things was inconceivable to these scholars. And many, such as von Harnack, attempted to set the record straight. This attempt was quelled for a time by the black eye that the First Quest received from the work of Albert Schweitzer.

Albert Schweitzer—The End of the First Quest

The result of the entire enterprise of the nineteenth-century First Quest was the conformance of the "historical Jesus" to the personal views of those seeking Him. This is the message driven home by the thesis of the young Albert Schweitzer (1875-1965), which is credited with more or less putting an end to the German First Quest.

Schweitzer's work, *The Quest of the Historical Jesus* (1906), is almost universally regarded as demonstrating two things: First, in conjunction with the work of Johannes Weiss (1827-1918), Schweitzer showed that the message of Jesus was one of "thoroughgoing eschatology" (in direct contradiction to von Harnack, among others). In Schweitzer's view, Jesus was an apocalyptical fanatic who tried to force the hand of God and paid with His life at the hands of the Jewish and Roman authorities. Schweitzer was operating from the naturalistic, rationalistic assumptions common to the rest of the First Quest. Nevertheless, though he found Jesus' eschatological message personally offensive, he persevered in presenting it faithfully as the core of Jesus' message.

Second, Schweitzer showed, in a scathing analysis, that the conflicting historical "Jesuses" of the previous century's quest were uniform in one respect—they *all* mirrored the philosophical preconceptions of the scholars doing the questing. Evangelical scholar Scot McKnight sums it up nicely: "Everybody simply claimed Jesus for his own cause."[6]

Schweitzer's thesis was so acidic to the scholarship that had gone before him that it was not accepted by the department to which he submitted it at his university. This is no doubt part of the reason Schweitzer subsequently abandoned a career in theology and turned to music, and then medicine. In fact, the "scholarly struggle" over Schweitzer's work continues to this day. The Jesus Seminar has optimistically made the overturn of Schweitzer's thesis the fifth of their "seven pillars of scholarly wisdom."

Rudolph Bultmann and the Period of "No Quest"

Schweitzer's work seems to have produced in liberal criticism a kind of crisis in confidence. From the publication of *The Quest of the Historical Jesus* through the end of World War II, there was a period that is now termed the "No Quest." Rudolph Bultmann summed up the prevailing mood during this period when he pronounced in his 1934 book *Jesus and the Word,* "We can now know almost nothing concerning the life and personality of Jesus, since the early Christian sources show no interest in either, are moreover fragmentary and often legendary."[7]

In this now famous quote, Bultmann dismisses the scholarship of the nineteenth-century quest, and at the same time reveals the prejudices that have become the hallmarks of later twentieth-century liberal criticism. Bultmann's defeatist complaint about the lack of objective evidence is the tip of a deeper iceberg: a more general defeatism about the possibility of truly objective historical research.

Schweitzer's *Quest* drove home the defeat of nineteenth-century rationalism, naturalistic reason had been shown to be an inadequate basis for the interpretation of history. Since rationalism had already replaced revelation with reason as the ultimate basis for understanding, *and reason had failed,* those who had placed their faith in rationalism were at a loss. Maybe the whole understanding of reality implied by rationalism was fundamentally flawed. One possibility would have been to return to revelation as the basis of epistemology.* As we know, this was not the option chosen. Instead, modern criticism began to search for something beyond rationalism as its foundation.

At this juncture in history—the beginning of the twentieth century—in a move that has had profound consequences, Rudolph Bultmann had an epiphany about the true meaning of Jesus. He declared that the true meaning of Jesus was not in His activities as a person on earth, but in His *message as proclaimed by the church.* Bultmann was acting on the suggestion of another, earlier theologian, Martin Kähler (1835-1912). Kähler had stated in an address in 1892 that

> the real, that is the actual Christ, who strides through the history of his people, with whom millions have had communion in childlike faith, with whom the great witnesses of faith have communed as they struggled, accepted, conquered and surrendered—*the real Christ is the preached Christ.*[8]

Kähler, who was a mentor of Paul Tillich, and who also heavily influenced Bultmann, conceived the "real Christ" as a way to make an end-run around the vagaries of the First

---

* Epistemology is the study of the nature and grounds of knowledge, especially with respect to its limitations and validity.

Quest. Instead of depending on the results of the critics to tell theologians who Jesus was, Kähler envisioned a "real" Jesus—the "preached Christ"—who was distinct from the historical Jesus. In a sense, this was just the reverse of the "quest"—*the real Jesus was now the Christ of creed and dogma.*

All of this sounds vaguely comforting to Protestant ears with its emphasis on the proclamation of the Word of God in preaching. The underlying assumption of this position, however, is that Jesus of Nazareth, whoever He might have been, is not as important as whatever the church has chosen to say about Him, or (and here is where the Devil's bargain really becomes plain) what it may choose to say about Him in the future. In fact, in Bultmann's view, Jesus of Nazareth was an important impetus behind the start of the church, but His message is actually pre-Christian, *because it pre-dates the creation of the Christian gospel.* This is the same conclusion arrived at by those who assumed the "historical Jesus," but come at it from the other side.

The "quest" originally assumed that the true Jesus was a person whose real life and message were obscured by the later theological encroachments of the church. Bultmann, and those who follow him, assume that the true "Jesus" is the dynamic creation of the church, which bears, perhaps, only an incidental likeness to the Jesus of Nazareth, a first century Jew about whom not much can be known.

This proposal of Kähler and Bultmann, if accepted, has important implications for the modernist conception of objective reality. For if the *message* about Jesus assumes primacy over the *actual* Jesus, and the message is controlled by the messengers (the Gospel writers), then the messengers have control over the "reality" of Jesus. Bultmann's view means that classic modernism—the view of reality that came out of the Enlightenment—is no longer tenable. Truth, like beauty, is in the eye of the beholder. In fact, this is the belief at the root of all Eastern philosophies. What has taken place in this switch is the triumph of Strauss's mytho-poetic paradigm.

It is no longer of final importance what Jesus *did* or *said.* What is of final importance is *what is believed* about Him.

Bultmann was also tremendously influential as a critic who pioneered the use of form criticism on New Testament texts. Form criticism originated among Old Testament scholars who were trying to determine the way texts were used in the "cultic" (that is, liturgical) practices of ancient Judaism. For example, it is widely agreed by the form critics that the book of Esther was originally an oral tradition commonly recited as part of the ancient Jewish festival of Purim, only later codified as the written book of Esther.

From such beginnings, however, form criticism soon mutated into complex and esoteric systems for identifying the "layers" of tradition found in Old Testament documents, producing such things as the infamous JEDP "Documentary hypothesis" about the authorship of the Pentateuch.* When imported into the world of New Testament criticism, form criticism exacerbated the tendency of liberal critics to view the Gospels as composite documents, assembled over decades and centuries by multiple authors from multiple competing traditions.

Out of form criticism came another of the "higher" criticisms, redaction criticism, which attempts to determine the theological biases of the authors of the ancient texts. Combined with the Bultmannian view of reality, form criticism and redaction criticism inevitably provide pictures of Bible texts as complex assemblages of individual traditions—layers of sometimes competing tradition—combined by later "redactors" (or editors) who assembled them to suit their own theological agendas. These ancient scissor-and-paste specialists were not concerned with reality as "we" understand it, assert the higher

---

* The JEDP theory is a form of higher criticism which holds that the five books of Moses were not the works of a single author. Rather, the contributions of several anonymous authors could allegedly be identified by the names they used for God and other factors. These hypothetical authors came to be known as the Yahwist (J), the Elohimist (E), the Deuteronomist (D), and the Priestly Source (P).

critics, because they did not share our rationalist preconceptions about history.

All of this may have some elements of truth, of course. If one assumed a *completely* literal interpretation of the Gospels, for example, the higher critics would no doubt have something to tell us about the kinds of ancient history writing practices that would go into creating a passage such as the "Sermon on the Mount" (Matthew 5–8). The higher critics would tell us that Matthew assembled various sayings of Jesus and couched them in the narrative framework of Jesus going up a mountain with His disciples and teaching them. That is to say, the Sermon on the Mount is not a court-reporter's transcription of one actual sermon that Jesus delivered on one particular mountain on one particular date. This is interesting, perhaps, but hardly earthshaking; unless one assumes a kind of "straw-man" literalism (such as the kind the Jesus Seminar identifies with all of its "fundamentalist" opposition). As Craig Blomberg, an evangelical New Testament scholar at Denver Seminary, points out:

> Take the Sermon on the Mount. We know it's not a straight, stenographic account. When you look up those passages in *Matthew*, they can be read in a matter of minutes. Whereas a teacher who spoke to a large crowd like that might have held forth much of a day.[9]

Whether the Sermon on the Mount is a condensed version of a single, historical address, or a collection of Jesus' sayings that have been "framed" in a traditional first-century narrative device, is a matter of reasonable debate, well within the confines of orthodoxy. But asserting that Matthew collected various connected sayings of Jesus and presented them as a single discourse is a long way from asserting that Matthew actually *made up* most of the words and has Jesus speak them in order to advance his (Matthew's) own theological position. That, however, is exactly the jump that the criticism of the "quest" takes as its starting point. It is an even bigger jump to assert that these supposed "made up" words of Matthew's are actually the message of the "real" Jesus; that is, that they represent the reality of the "proclaimed Christ." But that is the underlying, usually unstated assumption of the leg of the quest that comes after Bultmann—the New Quest.

The New ("Second") Quest

The New Quest (the *second* quest) was started by former students of Bultmann after World War II, when they eventually grew dissatisfied with his pronouncement that nothing could be learned about the Jesus of history. The New Quest left behind some of the radical agnosticism of Bultmann's position, but took with it the new tools of "higher" criticism, and a modernist framework substantially altered from that of the original quest.

The certainties of the nineteenth-century First Quest were based on the assumption that the reality of the first century and that of the nineteenth century were congruent. Human events in any century were of a piece, and the application of rational analysis to the records of a prior epoch, no matter how encrusted with irrational beliefs, would yield the true picture that was desired.

The New Questers, after Bultmann, could entertain no such confidence. The reality of the first century was a creature of the first-century mind, and to fully analyze it, one would have to map the contours of that mind. This would involve moving into the world of unreason, a world in which irrational beliefs were often as not the basis of reality, as now understood. This was a project that had no assurances of success under rationalist principles.

The fractured modernism of the New Quest is an odd creature. It maintains the essentially naturalistic view of the world of the nineteenth-century, but it has been forced to make room for the irrational in the makeup of reality; *it believes in the reality of myth.* The New Quest is a "transitional form," straddling the boundaries between modern and postmodern.

Evangelical scholar Michael J. Wilkins and J. P. Moreland comment on the effects of this strange mix:

> This [fractured modernism] has produced intriguing contradictions in methods and presuppositions among scholars who combine "modernism's" optimistic scientific quest with "postmodernism's" skepticism. On the one hand, these scholars attempt to be objective in their quest for the historical Jesus, establishing criteria that sift nonhistorical elements in historical records from truthful ones. On the other hand, these scholars are influenced by postmodernism's declaration that objectivity is impossible: we all look through our own eyes, bringing our own perspectives and biases, so we can only make the best of what we see.[10]

It is not surprising, given its lineage, that the New Quest has been able to identify little in the New Testament documents that it considers reliable. What is perhaps surprising is that it finds *anything* that can be relied on—but it does, or at least did. For example, Norman Perrin, one of the best known scholars of the New Quest, in 1974 summarized a list of things that could be confidently asserted about the life of Jesus:

> His baptism by John, the proclamation especially in parables of the present and future kingdom of God, a ministry of exorcism, his gathering of disciples across socioeconomic boundaries, his sharing a common meal that celebrated their new relationship to God, his challenge to the Jewish teachers of his day, the arousal of opposition that led to his arrest, his trials by the Jewish authorities on charges of blasphemy and by the Romans for sedition, and his crucifixion.[11]

This list is substantially longer than anything that would be admitted to by the Jesus Seminar. Even so, it leaves out plenty. When it is understood that the term "exorcism," to the modern mind, is synonymous with psychological healing, it is clear that this list leaves nothing of Jesus' miracles, none of His prophetic statements, none of His claims of a unique relationship with the Father, no claims of being the Messiah, and no resurrection.

The Third Quest

The aging New *(second)* Quest was never really anything very "new." It amounted to the First Quest with a postmodern facelift and a post-Bultmann historical agnosticism. Within the past 15 to 20 years, however, another branch of scholarship has arisen that may in fact deserve the designation "New." This is the so-called "Third Quest," which is made up of scholars who have concentrated on placing Jesus' life and message in the context of first-century Judaism. This includes such scholars as Ben Meyer at McMaster University in Canada, E. P. Sanders of Duke University, James Charlesworth of Princeton, Gerd Theissen from Heidelberg, and A. E. Harvey and Geza Vermes (a leading Jewish scholar) from Oxford. Although rooted in the same naturalistic framework as the rest of the "quest," the Third Quest has "spawned a substantial optimism concerning how much of the first three Gospels reflect historically trustworthy material."[12]

Many scholars of the Third Quest have imported tools from the fields of sociology and anthropology to understand better the social world of first-century Palestine. These scholars use these tools to create models of the first-century Jewish-Palestinian culture using evidence from all the available resources, including biblical texts, extrabiblical texts, and archeological evidence. They then analyze the picture of the first century presented in the New Testament texts in light of the picture generated by the sociological-anthropological models. The degree to which the biblical evidence "agrees" with the larger picture is used to gauge its historical accuracy.

The results of this type of analysis have been quite positive for the view that the New Testament documents, or at least the Synoptic Gospels,* are authentic, historically reliable texts arising from within the framework of first-century Judaism.

---

* The Synoptic Gospels are Matthew, Mark, and Luke. These Gospels can be "seen together"—that is, they present the details of Jesus' life and ministry using a consistent timeline.

Craig Blomberg summarizes the findings of this scholarship with respect to the Synoptic Gospels:

> Indeed, major studies of almost every theme or segment of the Synoptic tradition have advanced plausible arguments for accepting *the historical reliability* of substantial portions of Matthew, Mark, and Luke, once they are interpreted in light of the early first-century Palestinian Jewish setting.[13]

As has been noted, the Third Quest is rooted in the same naturalistic tradition as the rest of the "quest," and therefore generally rejects the more spectacular of Jesus' "nature" miracles—such as walking on water and raising the dead—as mythical. It tends to regard as questionable instances where the Synoptics differ considerably in relating the same event, and it puts less weight on traditions that are recorded in only one source (that is, only one of the Synoptic Gospels). It also shares the rest of modern criticism's suspicion about the historical reliability of the Gospel of John. Still, in looking outside the inbred world of biblical criticism for sources of academic insight, the Third Quest has escaped the existentialist malaise of the New Quest. From a believer's point of view, the Third Quest's ability to make rational findings based on objective historical evidence is positively refreshing, especially after spending any amount of time in the brackish backwater of postmodern biblical criticism.

The Jesus Seminar—End of the Road?

This brings us to ask, Where does the Jesus Seminar fit into the scheme of the grand "quest"? Detailed information on the Jesus Seminar will be provided in the chapters that follow this one. At this juncture, the important thing to note is that the Seminar would *like* to claim intellectual membership in the so-called Third Quest. But as Jesus said of the good and bad trees, "You will know them by their fruits" (Matthew 7:16 NASB).

The Third Quest finds good reason to believe that "substantial" portions of the Synoptic Gospels are historically reliable. The Third Quest tells us that the sociocultural world that the Gospels present—the world of the Pharisees, Sadducees, zealots, tax-collectors, Herod, Pilate, Romans, John the Baptist, and Jesus—is a historically accurate one. This is, of course, what conservative scholars have said all along.

In contrast, the Seminar finds almost nothing about the Gospels to be historically reliable. To the Seminar, nothing is what it seems. Jesus is not a prophet, nor the Messiah. His followers forced these images upon Him because they couldn't fathom what He truly was: a secular Jewish cynic sage.[14] The Seminar has taken the Bultmannian "hermeneutic of suspicion" to its logical end. To the Seminar, everything is false until "proven" true—every narrative element evidence of a theological plot, every reference to the Old Testament Scriptures an obvious ploy for scriptural justification, every recorded miracle a mythic reinterpretation of natural events, or an outright hoax.

How did the fellows of the Seminar come to these conclusions? In theory, each of their methods of historical inquiry are potentially unique; and the results of the Seminar's votes reflect a consensus view over a wide range of potential hermeneutical and historical positions. *This is the theory.* In actual fact, the Seminar's "Rules of Evidence"* appear to be a kind of ideological screen through which all fellows must pass, albeit no doubt eagerly. The Seminar's lockstep pattern of compliance with these "rules" gives their claims to freedom from "ecclesiastical and religious control" a perverse irony. The "rules"—no doubt the product of mastermind Funk— determine a very specific, very liberal, and very skeptical hermeneutic.

The Seminar reflects the logical consummation of both the First and New (second) Quests. It has a thoroughgoing

---

* The next chapter contains a thorough discussion of these "rules."

paranoia about all motives: everyone in biblical times is bent to deceive, distort, commandeer, reshape. The methodology of the Seminar is more of a psychoanalysis of the ancient authors than a historical investigation. It hides behind the facade of standard historical inquiry, but in fact has largely lost confidence in the ability of such methods to find the truth. It has lost confidence in the nature of truth itself. The route to understanding chosen by the Seminar borrows heavily from the pliable tools of psychology, and it assumes spectacularly clear insights into the minds of those whom it is purporting to study. How were these insights derived? We aren't really told, because the Seminar hides most of its truly important "work" behind the facade of objective academic inquiry.

To be sure, there is at least one well understood psychological principle present in the Seminar's work: the principle of projection. The Seminar carves up the words of Jesus to fit into their own worldview, and behold, the earliest disciples have done the same thing. The Seminar doesn't believe in a coming kingdom of God, a final judgment, or a return of Jesus the Messiah; and *voila,* Jesus didn't believe in any of this stuff either. The fellows of the Seminar create a Jesus in their own image, but they are no doubt confident that this is just the latest chapter in the definition of the "real" Jesus, a process that has been ongoing since the foundation of the church.

In the final analysis, the "quest" of the Jesus Seminar is a-historical, because they have presupposed a reality that doesn't support historical reconstruction. The "reality" of the Jesus Seminar is the shifting, rational-irrational, semi-mystical reality of the postmodernists. And through it, they have found not the "historical Jesus" but an a-historical Jesus of their own projective imagination.

Year after year, at around Easter time, the all-powerful secular media wages an "objective" and "scholarly" assault on Jesus Christ, the founder and foundation of Christianity and the one whom countless millions attest as their Messiah. To those of faith, these media reports are thinly veiled assaults on their faith. For some reason, similar "objective reports" never seem to appear in the major media when Passover, Hanukkah, or Ramadan come in season. Since the media and all "thinking" people have decided it is politically correct to declare open season on Christianity, they still need "credible" witnesses for their attacks. Most recently they have pulled out from obscurity a very small group of self-proclaimed experts called the Jesus Seminar.

Without the media, this handful of doubters would not get any public hearing. Through them, in the words of Brad Scott, "Christianity is now besieged by one of the most powerful heresies it has faced in 2,000 years. This heresy is subtle because it assumes there can be no such thing as heresy." A room full of self-confessed theological judges play spin-the-bottle with Scripture, tilting back their heads, then proclaiming with ponderous tones, "I believe Jesus said this verse, but not that next one." And so they edit the Bible willy-nilly in their upper-story room in California wine country. And the unthinking public hasn't a clue as to what is going one. They read *Time* or *Newsweek* at Easter and suddenly discover the "scholars" have just destroyed the pillars of Christianity. Meanwhile, it is doubtful the media will turn its bright lights of attention on a good defense of the Christian faith. Nor is it likely that a majority of the public will ever be curious enough about the truth to really look beyond *Time* or *Newsweek.* In this chapter former New Ager turned Christian Brad Scott looks on with outrage as he reveals facts and insights concerning the Jesus Seminar.

10

JESUS ON THE RACK

THE JESUS SEMINAR
UNDER GLASS

Brad Scott

hristianity is now besieged by one of the most powerful heresies it has faced in 2000 years. This heresy is subtle because it assumes there can be no such thing as heresy. It deconstructs and reconstructs not only the church and the Bible, but Jesus Himself.

Of course, Gnostics, Docetists, Ebionites,* and others in the early church redefined the person and nature of Christ. More recently, higher critics, neoorthodox theologians, and New Agers have tried to do the same. The terrifying difference today is that the current heretics—a minority of radical

---

Ebionites: In the second and third centuries the Ebionites were a group of Jewish Christians who retained much of Judaism in their beliefs. They adopted a conservative Pharisaic creed at first, but after the second century, some of them espoused a mixture of Essenism, Gnosticism, and Christianity. According to the second-century Christian prelate and writer Irenaeus, they differed from orthodox Christians in denying the divinity of Christ and in considering the apostle Paul an apostate for having declared the supremacy of Christian teaching over the Mosaic law. The third-century Christian writer and theologian Origen classified the Ebionites into two groups—those who believed in the virgin birth and those who rejected it. Both the Sabbath and the (Christian) Lord's Day were holy to them, and they expected the establishment of a messianic kingdom in Jerusalem. Until the fifth century, remnants of the sect were known to have existed in Palestine and Syria.

scholars who call themselves the Jesus Seminar—receive unprecedented media coverage. Over the past decade, they have capitalized on the media's quest for controversy and the public's hunger for novelty to market their "findings" in popularized books and articles. In this postmodern, post-Christian world, most people are too biblically illiterate to discern the errors in the work of the Seminar's scholars.

Throughout the centuries, the faith of peasants in their isolated hamlets was safe from the vagaries of the intellectually elite. Today, however, the average person picks up a copy of *Time* magazine to learn that the Jesus of the Gospels is a fiction. At least that's what these scholars keep telling us in print, over the airwaves, and even on the Internet.[1]

Based on their "careful" examination of the primary documents of Christendom—the Gospels—these scholars now tell us that Jesus was a user-friendly sage in Birkenstocks who delivered pithy sayings but made no divine claims. He never intended to establish a church that would survive for 2000 years. In this post-Christian immorality play, the media have become Medea, devouring unwary Christian babes.

The watershed question of our day remains the one Jesus Himself asked: "Who do you say I am?" (Luke 9:20). On the answer to this question hangs the survival of our faith and our church. If we do not answer it firmly and immediately, believers and potential believers may suffer from the public dissection and deconstruction of Jesus and the gospel.

The Jesus Seminar has stretched our Lord on the rack, trying to prove Him merely human. Now is the time for all Christians, not just apologists and scholars, to rally to the Lord's side. Once they learn about the methods, motives, and implications of the Jesus Seminar, they will no doubt feel compelled to defend their Lord before an unsuspecting public, equipped to heed Peter's call: "Always be prepared to give an answer to everyone who asks you to give the reason for the hope that you have" (1 Peter 3:15).

The Jesus Seminar Under Glass

In the past, outside forces led the assault on Jesus and the authority of Scripture. Today, sabotage and high treason appear within the ranks of putative church members. At the forefront of the attack stands the media's latest religious phenomenon—the Jesus Seminar. For a decade, the Seminar in general and Seminar members in particular (in their own books) have touted a Jesus that is a warm, fuzzy counterculture guru, while exacerbating the breakdown in the authority of Scripture.

Background Information

Co-founded in 1985 by Robert W. Funk (former New Testament professor at the University of Montana and former secretary of the Society of Biblical Literature) and John Dominic Crossan (former Roman Catholic priest and New Testament professor at DePaul University), the Seminar is comprised of 74 fellows dedicated to identifying the "historical" or "true" Jesus. Their purpose, put in genteel academic terms by Seminar luminary Marcus Borg (professor of religion and culture at Oregon State University), is "to assess the degree of scholarly consensus about the historical authenticity of each of the sayings of Jesus."[2] Stated more bluntly by Crossan, "We want to liberate Jesus. The only Jesus most people know is the mythic one. They don't want the real Jesus, they want the one they can worship. The cultic Jesus."[3] This statement represents a bold program based on a naturalistic premise that Funk states clearly in *The Five Gospels* (1993):

> The Christ of creed and dogma, who had been firmly in place in the Middle Ages, can no longer command the assent of those who have seen the heavens through Galileo's telescope. The old deities and demons were swept from the skies by that remarkable glass. Copernicus, Kepler, and Galileo have dismantled the mythological abodes of the gods and Satan, and bequeathed us secular heavens.[4]

In other words, the Seminar wants to deconstruct and reconstruct Jesus.

Associated with Funk's Westar Institute, the Seminar was founded in the heady wine country of Sonoma, California. The Seminar's audacity, its inebriated leaps of logic, brand it as a kind of drunken Council of Sonoma. The "canon council," declares Funk, "will also want to consider whether any of the traditional books of the canon or parts of those books . . . should be dropped."[5]

To date, the Council of Sonoma has not only excluded the entire Gospel of John because it differs too much from the Synoptics and portrays Jesus as the world's only Savior, it has decimated the Synoptic Gospels themselves. Using colored beads—*red* ("That's Jesus"), *pink* ("Sure sounds like Jesus"), *gray* ("Well, maybe"), and *black* ("There has been some mistake")—the Jesus Seminar voted on over 1500 sayings of Jesus. When the beads had quit bouncing, the tallies showed that only 18 percent of the sayings of Jesus could be retained as authentic. In fact, of the 18 percent (the red and pink beads), only 2 percent (the red beads) were viewed by the scholars as representing the actual words of Jesus. This 2 percent figure rests on the agreement of a mere 83 percent of the voting members, a grade of "B" in any teacher's grade book.[6] According to the 74 fellows, there is a "good" chance that Jesus said what they think He said. A tally of the remaining beads—gray and black—"proved" that the Synoptic Gospels were mostly imaginary constructs of the overzealous postresurrection, postapostolic followers of the early church.

Conservative Christians will be comforted to learn that the Lord's Prayer at least retained its essential element: "Our Father." A troubling afterthought persists, however. Even Hindus can refer to Shiva as "father."

Ever More Startling Conclusions

Even bolder conclusions, published by various members of the Seminar, seem to bear the Seminar's official stamp of approval. Other pronouncements made by members to the media have a more idiosyncratic ring. Nevertheless, they *all* jibe with the Seminar's primary assumptions.

In *The Five Gospels* (the fifth is the questionable Gospel of Thomas), Robert Funk and Roy Hoover conclude that Jesus was nothing more than a laconic sage, "slow to speech, a person of few words," one who was "self-effacing, modest, and unostentatious." This type of holy man "does not initiate cures or exorcisms." Accordingly, the "real" Jesus who appears in the Gospels "is often reluctant to give help even when asked . . ." He "does not initiate debates or controversies." In fact, "the rare stories in which Jesus begins the argument are thought to be creations of the storyteller."[7]

In light of this image of Jesus, they say, "it is difficult to imagine Jesus making claims for himself—I am the son of God, I am the expected One, the Anointed—unless, of course, he thought that nothing he said applied to himself." Any divine claims that appear in the Gospels are "later and derivative developments" grafted onto the Gospel after Jesus' death: "The early Christian community allowed its own triumphant faith to explode in confessions that were retrospectively attributed to Jesus, its authority figure." Thus, "scholars [that is, the Jesus Seminar fellows] regard the fourth Gospel [John] as alien to the real Jesus, the carpenter from Nazareth."[8]

In *The Historical Jesus*, John Dominic Crossan asserts that Jesus was concerned less with ushering in the kingdom of God than with challenging "the standard political normalcies of power and privilege, hierarchy and oppression, debt foreclosure and land appropriation, imperial exploitation and colonial collaboration." In short, Jesus was a politically correct revolutionary, cast in the image of the late-twentieth-century radical. According to Crossan, Jesus' message was simple: "God says, 'Caesar sucks.'"[9] Among Crossan's unorthodox conclusions about Jesus in his statement that "Jesus lived on in the hearts of followers . . . but he did not physically rise from the dead. Taken down from the cross, his body was probably buried in a shallow grave and may have been eaten by dogs."[10]

Marcus Borg similarly believes that "the image of the historical Jesus as a divine or semi-divine figure, who saw himself as the divine savior whose purpose was to die for the sins of the world, and whose message consisted in preaching that, is simply not historically true."[11]

In *Jesus: A New Vision*, Borg portrays Jesus as a standard-bearer of a politics of compassion, freedom, equality, and inclusiveness.[12] Jesus, it appears, was ahead of His time politically and culturally. Had He been born in Liverpool in 1942, He could have sung with the Beatles in the 1960s, "Come together . . ." or "All you need is love, love. . . ."

Other conclusions of the Seminar fellows become even more incredible. Burton Mack, in his *Myth of Innocence*, argues that "Mark's making Jesus the founder of Christianity was the first step on the road to everything bad in Christianity and then in Western culture, down to the genocide of Native Americans, Star Wars, and Reaganomics . . ."[13]

Leif Vaage, New Testament professor at Emmanuel College, University of Toronto, goes so far as to say that Jesus was probably "*a party animal*, somewhat shiftless, and disrespectful of the fifth commandment: Honor your father and mother."[14]

Questionable Verbal Tactics

It is not my purpose here to analyze the scholarly technique of the Jesus Seminar members. More competent theologians have already done so.[15] I will focus my criticism on the words of Robert Funk and Roy Hoover in their Introduction to *The Five Gospels*, examining their *a priori* assumptions, faulty logic, and loaded rhetoric.

False Assumptions. The primary assumption underlying the work of the Jesus Seminar is a naturalistic—or an *antisupernaturalistic*—one. Identifying with the nineteenth century work of David Strauss, the fellows assume *a priori* that the Gospels are full of mythical elements. Their primary task, they believe, is to extract the historical truths from the myths (the virgin birth, the miracles, the resurrection, and so on). As noted in an earlier chapter, their first "pillar of scholarly wisdom" is "the distinction between the historical Jesus, to be uncovered by historical excavation, and the Christ of faith encapsulated in the creeds."[16] Related to this is their fifth pillar of "contemporary scholarship": "The liberation of the non-eschatological Jesus of the aphorisms and parables [the pithy little sayings of the laconic sage] from Schweitzer's eschatological Jesus . . ."[17]

Using this distinction between the mythic (fictional) Jesus and the real Jesus, they glibly undermine the abilities and motives of Jesus' apostles and followers:

> Jesus' followers did not grasp the subtleties of his posi-
> tion and reverted, once Jesus was not there to remind them,
> to the view they had learned from John the Baptist. As a
> consequence of this reversion, and in the aura of the
> emerging view of Jesus as a cult figure analogous to others
> in the Hellenistic mystery religions, the gospel writers over-
> laid the tradition of sayings and parables with their own
> "memories" of Jesus.[18]

Funk and Hoover go on to say, "The search for the authentic words of Jesus is a search for the forgotten Jesus."[19] I am sure the early Christian martyrs will be happy to know that they had "forgotten" Jesus before the flames licked their toes.

According to the Seminar fellows' presuppositions, Jesus couldn't have been divine, the Incarnate Son of God. The Jesus of the Gospels is an imaginative construction, they claim. Yet they remake Jesus in their own image, presupposing a politically correct, laid-back sage, tolerant of all lifestyles and religions.

Faulty Logic. In *The Five Gospels,* Funk and Hoover argue for their reading of the Gospels.[20] If the Gospels are inerrant and inspired, they reason, why can't conservative Christians agree on the picture of Jesus presented in them? Ignoring the exaggeration about the intensity of disagreement among Christians, let us examine the conclusion they draw: "The endless proliferation of views of Jesus on the part of those who claim infallibility for the documents erodes confidence in that theological point of view and in the devotion to the Bible it supports."[21]

Even if many views of Jesus existed among conservative Christians, faith in the infallibility of Scripture would not necessarily erode. We might more reasonably argue that such disagreement proves the fallibility *of men*, not the Gospels. (Fellows of the Jesus Seminar regard their own intellects as less fallible than the Gospels—and certainly less fallible than the intellects of faithful Christians.)

The Seminar fellows argue that "the two pictures painted by John and the Synoptic Gospels cannot both be historically accurate."[22] The Synoptics contain brief one-liners, couplets, and parables. John contains lengthy discourses and monologues, elaborate dialogues, and ambiguous statements. John's Gospel must be historically inaccurate, indeed, Jesus' words in the fourth Gospel must have been John's creations. (Apparently, John was a liar.) But other plausible explanations might better account for the differences: John wrote from firsthand experience; he had a better long-term memory and hence his late Gospel is reliable; he purposely set out to write a Gospel that drew on details that had been omitted by the Synoptic writers.[23]

Funk and Hoover justify including the Gospel of Thomas in the canon by arguing that "Thomas has forty-seven parallels to Mark, forty parallels to Q,* seventeen to Matthew, four to Luke, and five to John."[24] Seminar fellows maintain that Thomas, a Coptic and possibly Gnostic document, predates

---

* Q is an alleged source which the Gospel writers Matthew and Luke used to supplement the material in Mark's Gospel. "Q" is from the German word *Quell*, meaning "source."

Mark, which they accept as the earliest Gospel. However, as noted in an earlier chapter, if Thomas predates Mark why does it contain four parallels to John's Gospel, which was written last, between A.D. 80 and 90? Moreover, how could a Coptic document produced in Egypt predate the earliest biblical documents, most probably composed in Jerusalem, Judea, or Asia Minor? I know no evidence that Christianity appeared in Egypt as early as A.D. 40, 50, or 60. Isn't it more logical to say, as most scholars do, that Thomas was written after John, no earlier than the mid- to late-second century? Wouldn't it be more prudent to argue that the author of Thomas borrowed sayings from the other four Gospels?

Loaded Rhetoric. The Introduction to *The Five Gospels* defends the methods of the Jesus Seminar not by facts but by loaded rhetoric. We hear a "tragic and heroic story" of liberal scholars "who endeavored to break the church's stranglehold over learning."[25] "The church appears to smother the historical Jesus by superimposing this heavenly figure on him in the creed."[26] We are told that the new liberal version of Jesus "emerged from under the smothering cloud of the historic creeds."[27] We discover that Mark had ulterior motives: "To elicit the right confession, Mark has Jesus ask, 'What are people saying about me?' "[28] Apparently, overzealous Mark *puts* words into Jesus' mouth so that Christians will kowtow and genuflect in just the "right" fashion. Mark wants to "elicit" the "right confession"; he "has" Jesus ask the right question.

Finally, Funk and Hoover lament the attack on critical scholarship by conservative Christian groups—those benighted evangelicals and fundamentalists—who resort to devious tactics. Applying institutional pressure, "latter-day inquisitors among Southern Baptist and Lutheran groups have gone witch-hunting for scholars who did not pass their litmus tests." Using the straw man technique, the authors complain that those who usually attack the Seminar fellows (not their work, of course) are most often "those who lack academic credentials."[29] In other words, only the uneducated, marginally educated, or improperly educated could oppose the work of the Seminar.

Ulterior Motives

Obviously the Jesus Seminar has not only open but *hidden* agendas. Funk openly states, "Christianity as we have known it is anemic and wasting away." It is time to "reinvent Christianity," to give it new symbols, stories, and beliefs about Jesus. "I don't know whether the churches will wake up to this. Most church officials regard us as a threat. But then, the Roman church regarded Luther as a threat. That's the way it is with reformers."[30] This comparison to Luther shows how certain Funk is that his reformation will lead to a new and improved Christianity.

There *are* more subtle agendas, however. Certain Seminar fellows want to secularize biblical studies. In *The Five Gospels*, for example, the authors are careful to use the politically correct form for historical dating: C.E. (Common Era) instead of A.D. (Anno Domini). They see themselves as "critical scholars," skeptical empiricists committed to a postmodern "hermeneutics of suspicion"—namely, the belief that texts are inherently unreliable. They want to humanize and universalize Jesus so that He becomes palatable not only to secularists but to people of other religions.

To advance their radical agenda, the Seminar fellows resort to self-contradiction in *The Five Gospels* when they openly push the feminist agenda.[31] At the beginning of a paragraph they say, "The panel agreed at the outset not to translate out the social and cultural features of the text that are unfamiliar—*worse yet, distasteful*—to the modern reader."[32] At the end of the same paragraph, however, they say, "At the same time, the translators have avoided sexist language where not required by the original. Male singulars are occasionally turned into genderless plurals." Didn't they say they were going to retain even the "*distasteful*" elements?

Ominous Implications

The Jesus Seminar is dangerously anti-Christian for a variety of reasons. In its quest for the "true" Jesus it denies the validity of the historic Christian faith. It rejects 82 percent of the Gospels' witness. It rejects the testimony and theology of Paul, James, Peter, John, Jude, and the author of Hebrews. It dismisses the historical data provided by the early church fathers (though it does take seriously the "mythic" apocrypha, considered noncanonical by the church). It denies Christ's divinity, His miracles, His exclusive claim to Sonship, and His authority. Caught in the grip of naturalistic presuppositions, the Seminar fellows must conclude that Jesus was only a man, not a Savior. Finally, evincing a hostility toward evangelicals and "fundamentalists," the Jesus Seminar sets out to destroy the historic Christian faith by making Jesus generic and spirituality a universal, subjective experience.

By recasting Jesus as a generic, unhistorical Christ, the Jesus Seminar measures Him according to criteria outside of Christianity. What would a sage really say? If scholars judge Jesus to be a sage, ordinary people will expect Him to conform to their ideas of other religious teachers. Wise in their own conceit, they will accept general religious principles— love God, serve people, and do no harm to any living creature—and be satisfied that they have attained to wisdom. Effort, reason, and intuition become the path to "spiritual progress."

The Jesus Seminar offers what Western occultists and Eastern mystics have always offered: a private cornucopia of spiritual experiences and theological eisegetics.* We fall in step with the wisdom of the East: *Ekam sat vipra bahudda vadanti* ("As many faiths, so many paths"). All will be well, my former guru used to say, as long "as you don't disturb another's faith."

---

* *Eisegetics* refers to the subjective and self-styled interpretation of Scripture that goes against accepted principles of exegesis.

The Evisceration of Christianity

Relativism eviscerates the Christian faith. Thanks to the Jesus Seminar, we know that Jesus was just a sage. When its next book appears, *The Acts of Jesus* (1997), we will be told in more detail that Jesus performed no miracles and never left the tomb (remember the wild dogs?). The Seminar fellows are ripping apart the body of Christ. A merely human Jesus can be no one's Savior. The world of the Jesus Seminar is a world in which all paths, moral values, and truths are relative. The fellows deny the authority of Christ and His word, supplanting objective authority with subjective authority, by which no man can be judged. Salvation—or enlightenment—awaits all. As New Agers tell us, at the end of the tunnel on the way to the other side is only endless light. There, a universal "Christ," open-armed, waits for all, loving them "from where they're at." It's an old refrain, coming in the 1960s from New Age Christians and in the 1970s from Eastern mystics. Now liberal academe is coming round, as so many swivel chairs creak in unison.

Now, perhaps more than ever before, even Christians are seeking evidence of spiritual truth in private experiences. "Isn't it wonderful to know," a Roman Catholic woman said to me, "that there are now so many available spiritual traditions to be explored?" Aware of the spiritual smorgasbord, she was "hungering as never before, for spiritual experiences." During her vacation, she met in Oregon with her spiritual advisor, a Gaia-worshiping feminist ex-nun who is also "very in touch with Native-American spiritual traditions."

Forces crouch, purring for the moment, ready to pounce and eviscerate Christianity. In March of 1997 the Barna Research Group, a conservative organization in Glendale, California, . . . found that "30 percent of so-called 'born again' Christians do not believe that Jesus 'came back to physical life after he was crucified.' "[33] Such statistics are appalling.

The Remedy: A Return to a High View of Scripture

What leads committed Christians to such a broad-minded view of "spirituality" and to so much doubt? Chiefly, a breakdown in the authority of Holy Scripture. At the turn of the fifth century, Augustine foresaw the consequences of such a breakdown:

> It seems to me that the most disastrous consequences must follow upon our believing that anything false is found in the sacred books. [For] if you once admit into such a high sanctuary of authority one false statement, . . . there will not be left a single statement of those books which, . . . if appearing to anyone difficult in practice or hard to believe, may not by the same fatal rule be explained away.[34]

According to Augustine, criticism that undermines the veracity of any part of Scripture inevitably undermines the authority of Scripture as a whole. Some have contemptuously characterized this position (also held by Harold Lindsell and the late Francis Schaeffer) as a simpleminded "slippery slope" argument. Yet who better demonstrates the slippery slope than the Jesus Seminar?

The Question of Authority

The integrity of Scripture and the portrayal of Jesus depend on loyalty to an authority. How can we know Jesus and God's will? Do we "love" and do what "feels right"? Or do we have a reliable canon?

Merely believing in the risen Christ and the transforming power of the Holy Spirit, though essential to our faith, doesn't answer the question, "How shall we then live?" Where should we stand on the issues that face the church today: divorce, abortion, gay rights, premarital sex, the ordination of women, and so forth? To say that the Bible is true as long as we consider the "historical context" of each passage misses the mark. What if our interpretation of the historical context relativizes the words of Jesus, Paul, or Peter? An Episcopalian priest once explained to me, "Paul was conditioned by his age. Of course [in his ignorance] he relegated women to an inferior status in the church; of course he regarded homosexuality as a great sin. But we know better today." This approach gives us no authoritative answer to our most pressing question—"How shall we then live?" Shall our only authority be naturalistic reason aided by preference and sentiment?

In our time, reason and language have been deconstructed. The scholars know that words are unreliable. Every writer's motives are suspect. Sexism, racism, capitalism, and a thousand other ulterior motives supposedly underlie the "meaning" of any text. Once we realize the limiting nature of subjectivity, the postmodern scholars inform us, we understand that a text can mean anything or nothing.

If they are right, no written message can be authoritative. Suppose I read, "Love the Lord your God with all your heart and with all your soul and with all your mind" (Matthew 22:37). I can't be certain Jesus spoke these words. If I think the words *sound* like something Jesus would have said, I have already diluted my faith in them. Maybe He said them; maybe He didn't. If I think, "They *sound* like the words of a sage," I place them in the context of contradictory assumptions about the nature of God and my relationship with Him.[35] *How* shall I love God? And who is God? An impersonal cosmic force? If I approach these words the way the Jesus Seminar wants me to, the statement, "Love the Lord your God," could be a call to yogic self-effort, Buddhistic negation, or an occultic appeal to self-empowerment.

Even more problematic are these words: "I am the way and the truth and the life. No one comes to the Father except through me" (John 14:6). If Jesus really spoke these words—and, of course, the members of the Jesus Seminar unanimously declare that He didn't—then I can't accept that other religions represent "valid paths" to God. I can't accept the concept of universal salvation because Jesus claims that all must come through Him alone to get to the Father. One can't say, "Well, he means one must come to God through the Christ self." Jesus never spoke of some transcendental, universal "Christ self," nor did His apostles. What do I make of the words of Jesus, then, if I live in a postmodern world? All I can do is trust "my own experience" of the text and my "relationship" with the "living Christ." Or, I can argue that Jesus never said these words.

If I trust my own experiences, however, I can become skeptical of their authority and deconstruct them. With every change in a web site or the weather, I might wonder if I am deluding myself. Was that experience real? An individual who makes decisions on this basis has no moral compass, no absolutes; a country that adopts a subjectivistic authority has no moral consensus. In a context of moral chaos, the winners on issues like gay rights, multiculturalism, or the feminist agenda will be those with the most clout (money and media control).

Renewed Commitment

With such real threats to the faith before us, we must recommit ourselves to a belief in a revealed, fully authoritative Scripture. Such belief is indispensable to a Christian. Contrary to the "critical scholars," a high view of the Scriptures is based on a good deal of evidence as to their reliability. Unlike the Jesus Seminar scholars, who approach Scripture assuming it contains multitudinous "errors," orthodox Christian believers approach Scripture assuming two things. First, they presuppose the Scriptures to be the revealed Word of God. Second, they assume that "discrepancies" in the text can be resolved as scholarship progresses in the fields of textual criticism and hermeneutics.

If we persevere in seeking evidence, we will find plenty of good reasons to believe that Scripture is true and accurate.[36] If we can't accept this foundation, we have nothing left of our faith except ever-changing tradition or our own subjectivity.

Any faith without a corresponding faith in the authority of Scripture is a "blind faith." If Jesus exists as the one He claimed to be, He would still exist even if all scriptural records disappeared. But we wouldn't know Him without His revelation.

Christianity, like a woven tapestry, is of a piece. Handed only a pile of thread, we cannot pretend to see the overall design. If reality is only a pile of thread, we cannot pretend to know how to live, moment by moment, decision by decision. Without God's revelation of His design, we are all in deep trouble. We will succumb to the relativism of our age and do our own thing (as long as we don't hurt anyone). Some will change government and redefine morality for the rest of us as they insist, "We can't trust reason. We can't trust tradition. We can't trust Scripture." If they are right, then we certainly can't trust them!

An honest person must confront this dilemma: One must *believe* or *not believe* in the authority of Scripture. Not believing means, as Sartre claimed, that everything is meaningless, that we are alone, and that we can know only despair, for we are defined by ourselves without guidelines or reference points.

Gladius Dei

One person, after hearing the conclusions of the radical Jesus Seminar fellows, responded tellingly:

> I thought, "O-o-o-k-k-k-a-y. Well, that's interesting." I'm not in that academic, seminary-trained world, and I think my faith is strong enough that the debate going on in that world doesn't frighten me. In fact, I think it's good. Perhaps we will all learn something we haven't known.
>
> I trust in the staying power of Christianity. Some really goofy things have happened in the past 2,000 years, but somehow, the core, the essence, of the Christian religion has survived.[37]

The above quote typifies today's unwary believer, content to leave the thinking to someone else. He thinks it "good" that his historic faith is being sliced, diced, and skewered. He has faith that he will "learn something" from those who have no respect for his Lord's Word. Naively he thinks the Jesus Seminar is just another "goofy" thing that the church has to endure. Like many believers, this man thinks he can live in his own faith-world without realizing that the world of the Jesus Seminar is also his world. There is no dividing line. What the Jesus Seminar scholars say and write affects us all. It is simple trickle-down ideonomics.

We Christians must take our stand on the certain Word of God, advancing against the chaos and darkness, the swirling sea-foam whipped up by the Jesus Seminar and other radical scholars. We cannot afford to be so naive as to miss the danger.

The Jesus Seminar is a new heresy, worthy of the title "Funkism," with its own followers, the "Funkites." These shallow publicity-hungry scholars need to be driven back into their dens before they can further damage and smother the testimony of the faithful; before they can fully redefine Scripture as just one more document capable of a multitude of interpretations, devoid of historical fact, substance, and truth; and before they further mutilate our Lord. They are dwarfs before the Son of the living God, to whom they have become blind.

In 1986 the world was rocked by a stunning revelation that was widely reported throughout the United States, Europe, and beyond. The news: Jesus Christ had never promised to return, and, in fact, was not coming back. The long-awaited "second coming," the blessed hope of millions through the long centuries, was nothing more than a misunderstanding—a hoax.

Such was the finding of the so-called Jesus Seminar, a group of self-appointed experts who had taken it upon themselves to alert the world to the "true" facts about Jesus and the New Testament writings. Over the course of 12 years, the Seminar has proceeded to dismantle the "myth" surrounding the "historical Jesus," and present the "true" picture of who He was and what He said. This picture is vastly at odds with that preserved by the historic church—but it does agree with another tradition, almost as old: the ancient heresy of Gnosticism.

Who are these "experts," and how have they arrived at their momentous findings? In this chapter we will look at the methods and the makeup of the Jesus Seminar, whose impact on the public has been considerable.

11

THE JESUS SEMINAR

John Moore

During the Easter season of 1997, readers in North America and around the world were treated to a triple-barrel salute to the "quest for the historical Jesus" by the editors of *Time, Newsweek,* and *U.S. News and World Report.* Each of the three cover stories featured the work of the Jesus Seminar, a group of liberal New Testament scholars who banded together in the interest of bringing the popular understanding of Jesus out of the "dark ages" and into the light of modern liberal criticism.

The brainchild of Robert Funk, formerly of the University of Montana and now presiding over the Westar Institute in Sonoma, California, the Jesus Seminar's goal is to bring the "findings" of modern biblical criticism over the last two centuries out of the closet of the academy and into the public square—through the power of the mass media. In this, they appear to be succeeding wildly.

The result of this unprecedented experiment has been much confusion. The religious marketplace is already saturated with the feel-good pop-theologies of such luminaries as Oprah Winfrey and Bill Moyers, and fed the bulk of its "Christian" theological diet by televangelists. Now it is having to deal with the pronouncements by qualified "gospel experts" that Jesus never claimed to be God, that only 18 percent of the words attributed to Him in the New Testament are actually His, and that the rest was invented by overzealous disciples crazed at the agony of losing their Messiah and intent on continuing a movement that He never started. The *real* Jesus—the "historical Jesus"—says the Seminar, is a person who was the inspiration behind the mythical Jesus of the New Testament, but who bears little actual resemblance to the "Christ of creed and dogma" taught by the church today.

In its 1993 flagship publication, *The Five Gospels: The Search for the Authentic Words of Jesus,* the Seminar has simultaneously performed an ideological cleansing of the words of Jesus found in the Gospels and elevated the Gnostic Gospel of Thomas as a coequal in authority with the four canonical Gospels. Meeting since 1985 in a series of biennial voting sessions, the "fellows" of the Seminar have cast their now famous colored beads to determine the authenticity of virtually every saying of Jesus recorded in the Gospels and the Gospel of Thomas. Each saying is thereby assigned a color: *red*—Jesus said this; *pink*—Jesus probably said something like this; *gray*— Jesus did not say this but the ideas are close to His own; *black*—Jesus did not say this; it represents the perspective of a later or different tradition.

Through this "scientific" process, the Seminar has determined that only 18 percent of the words ascribed to Jesus are actually His or close to His (red or pink). In other words, using a red-letter edition of the Gospels as the basis, after the Seminar has applied its filtering process, only 18 percent of the red text remains red, or almost red. The entire Gospel of John is black! What is left of Jesus after the Seminar is through is a kind of secular Jewish sage, a theologically neutered Jesus who wouldn't cause much of a stir at a faculty get-together.

The Seminar's Jesus lived in a virtual theological vacuum: He never quoted a word of the Law or Prophets, or referred to any of the eschatological (end-time) ideas rampant in

Palestine in the first century. He certainly never referred to Himself as the Christ, or made any predictions about His death or resurrection. He never called any followers, and never talked about the coming kingdom of God or the final judgment.

Jesus' "philosophical" ideas were likely shaped more by His contact with the itinerant cynic sages who "probably" wandered through first century Palestine (unattested in any actual historical sources) than with the Judaism others have naively taken to be the foundation for His message.[1] Neither He nor His disciples (whom He hadn't called) ever had any arguments with the Pharisees. He had no institutional goals; it was His disciples who created the commandment to go into all the world carrying a gospel message that they had largely constructed themselves.

In short, Jesus never did much of anything, except spin out aphorisms and parables in unitized, laconic sound bites. His sayings do, the Seminar acknowledges, charitably "cut against the social and religious grain" and "characteristically call for a reversal of roles or frustrate ordinary, everyday expectations."[2] For these things He was crucified.

How, then, did the church arrive at such a wrongheaded picture of the man from Galilee? According to the Seminar, the blame can be laid at the feet of the earliest disciples:

> Jesus' followers did not grasp the subtleties of his position and reverted, once Jesus was not there to remind them, to the view they had learned from John the Baptist. As a consequence of this reversion . . . the gospel writers overlaid the tradition of sayings and parables with their own "memories" of Jesus.[3]

According to the Seminar, the disciples had very poor memories. So much so that 82 percent of their memories of Jesus, as recorded in the Gospels, constitute pure fiction. This claim seems hardly believable, absent other factors—such as a desire on the part of the disciples to "remember" sayings in accord with their own theology, which, we are told differed radically from Jesus' own. This, of course, is exactly what the Seminar is claiming. *The Five Gospels* is an effort to rescue the true picture of Jesus from the "firm grip of those whose faith overpowered their memories."[4]

This reconstruction circumvents C.S. Lewis's famous "Lunatic, Liar, or Lord" dilemma, because Jesus obviously never said any of the things that would force us to choose one of these options. Instead, it is the disciples who are either the lunatics or the liars; the "Lord" option is gone altogether, and Jesus becomes just the witty peasant sage of Galilee. Or better, He becomes Brian from the Monty Python film *Life of Brian*, a first-century Jew who, through no fault of His own, happens to fulfill the messianic hopes of a nation desperately seeking a Savior.

Strange Rules and Stranger Gospels

"Beware of finding a Jesus entirely congenial to you."
—Jesus Seminar's final "Rule of Evidence."[5]

Most of what the Jesus Seminar has to say is, by its own admission, not anything new. By presenting the various source theories (for example, theories about the oral traditions from which the written Gospels derive), information regarding the relationship and differences between the Synoptic Gospels, distinctions between the Synoptics and the Gospel of John, and so forth, the Seminar is introducing new ideas into the mainstream media, perhaps, but is adding nothing at all to scholarship about the historical Jesus.

Much of the impact the Seminar is having is due to the fact that the debate about the historical Jesus *has* been mainly hidden away in the academy for the past two centuries, although its effect has certainly been felt in the wider culture. The Seminar is presenting an extremely biased version of the debate. But compared to the dismal level of teachings about the Bible generally seen in the media, the Seminar's views seem in comparison to have the ring of academic truth-seeking.

What is distinctive about the Seminar's "scholarship" is its "authoritative" disqualification of so much of the Gospel record. The other distinctive feature is the Seminar's curious proclamation of the authority and early date of the Gospel of Thomas, a (by most accounts) second-century Gnostic document, of which a fourth-century copy was discovered just this century in a famous archaeological find at Nag Hammadi in Egypt. In what follows, we will examine the methodology the Seminar has used to reach its unique findings.

Pillars of Wisdom and Rules of Evidence

The Seminar credits several guidelines as the foundation for its search for truth.[6] These guidelines are broken into two main categories—the "Seven Pillars of Scholarly Wisdom" and a long list of "Rules of Evidence." The first four of the seven "pillars" are standard findings that liberal scholarship has drawn from the biblical criticism of the past two centuries. These are: (1) the belief in a "historical Jesus" as distinct from the Jesus of the Gospels; (2) the belief that the Synoptic Gospels (Matthew, Mark, and Luke) are closer to the historical Jesus than is the Gospel of John; (3) the view that Mark was written before Matthew and Luke; and (4) the identification of the hypothetical sayings-source called Q.[7] Actually, all but the first of these four "pillars" are assumed by most modern scholars, not just liberal scholars.

The next three pillars, however, are much more idiosyncratic in nature. These are: (5) liberation of the noneschatological Jesus from Albert Schweitzer's eschatological Jesus; (6) recognition of the fundamental difference between the oral culture and the print culture; and (7) reversal of the burden of proof—the Gospels are *presumed false* until proven true. To elaborate, the fifth pillar involves an attempt to "liberate" Jesus of His views that the end of the age would come, and with it the fiery day of God's wrath. The sixth pillar is true in a general sense, of course, but the Seminar has taken this theory to extremes in order to justify one of its main premises—the idea that Jesus' disciples had poor powers of recollection. The seventh pillar is simply a matter of presumption.

In addition to the seven pillars, the Jesus Seminar formulates certain "rules of evidence" and pledges to apply these purportedly objective standards to each phrase in the Gospels in order to arrive at a reliable chronicle of Jesus' sayings. These rules are laid out in a manner that gives a formalistic veneer to the Seminar's evaluatory process. Seminar fellows state that their rules are functionally the same as rules of evidence used in a court of law, and point out that they are derived from two centuries of biblical scholarship.[8] However, these rules of evidence are not so much criteria for evaluating the reliability of statements as they are foregone conclusions about the way the Gospels were written combined with unabashed assumptions about the Jesus they plan to reconstruct. The Seminar employs a methodology so obviously circular in its logic, so dependent on questionable presuppositions, that one observer writes:

> The structure of this "intellectual" process is pitifully simple: Assume that Jesus was not divine, and exclude from the historical record—the only one we have by the way—everything that suggests that He thought He was. What's left? Why the very thing you assumed in order to prove the thing you set out to find. I don't let freshmen get away with this in a bluebook examination.[9]

Rules of evidence used in a court of law are, primarily, rules used to exclude certain types of evidence from the decision-making process because they are deemed unreliable, tainted, or inherently prejudicial. For instance, "hearsay evidence" (any statement made out of court) is excluded because of the problems in verifying the truth of these sorts of statements. Of course, there are myriad exceptions to the hearsay rule. For example, admissions of guilt made out of court are deemed reliable and, therefore, admissible because people do not tend to lie when they make statements that hurt rather than help them. A similar rule that has been applied to the New Testament by certain biblical scholars is that the writers of the Gospels would not attribute a statement to Jesus that would make their lives more difficult unless it were an authentic saying and, therefore, we can conclude that the "hard" sayings of Jesus—such as His teachings on divorce—are authentic and reliable.

However, the rules used by the Jesus Seminar do not provide guidelines or criteria for evaluating the authenticity of statements. Instead, they are assumptions in the guise of truisms that Jesus never claimed to be the Messiah, could not possibly have been prophetic, and, *ad nauseam*, the Gospel authors simply must have made some things up. Included among the rules are the following:

> The evangelists frequently attribute their own statements to Jesus.[10]
>
> Sayings and parables expressed in "Christian" language are the creation of the evangelists or their Christian predecessors.[11]
>
> Sayings and narratives that reflect knowledge of events that took place after Jesus' death are the creation of the evangelists or the oral tradition before them.[12]
>
> Jesus makes no claim to be the Anointed, the Messiah.[13]

As an example of how the rules work, consider a passage from the "little apocalypse" of Mark 13 (the following text is from the Seminar's own "Scholars' Version," for the sake of argument):

> And Jesus would say to them, "Stay alert, otherwise someone might just delude you! You know, many will come using my name and claim, 'I'm the one!' and they will delude many people. When you hear of wars and rumors of

wars, don't be afraid. These are inevitable, but it is not yet the end. For nation will rise up against nation and empire against empire; there will be earthquakes everywhere; there will be famines. These things mark the beginning of the final agonies."—Mark 13:5-8, Scholars' Version (black)

This passage is *disallowed* on the basis that it has a "striking correspondence" to the writings of first-century Jewish historian Flavius Josephus describing events leading up to the Judean-Roman war of A.D. 66-70.[14] Having disqualified the passage on the basis of plagiarism, the Seminar goes on, curiously, to conclude that the sayings are either based on the "traditional apocalyptic materials" (oral tradition) or they may be "descriptions after the fact" (created by the evangelist Mark). In any case, the sayings didn't originate with Jesus.[15] The third rule of evidence listed above has obviously been a useful tool in reaching this conclusion. It is not possible, of course, that these were prophetic words spoken by Jesus because they speak of things that happen after His death.

What is going on here? These "rules" may represent *conclusions* or *findings* that someone might arrive at after studying the texts. But to represent these assumptions as "rules of evidence" is disingenuous in the extreme. Is it possible that the fellows of the Jesus Seminar are simply guilty of a semantic mistake, that they have confused rules of evidence with prior assumptions, or that they are unaware of the problems this creates for their methodology? This seems very unlikely; for whatever else one might say about the Jesus Seminar, it must be acknowledged that almost a dozen of the world's leading New Testament scholars are found in its ranks, including co-founders Robert Funk and J. Dominic Crossan (who authored *The Historical Jesus* in 1991) and Marcus Borg (who authored *Jesus: A New Vision* in 1987). These people are not unaware of what they are doing.

We must keep in mind that *The Five Gospels* was not written for a scholarly audience, but for a lay audience—an audience that presumably would not be keenly aware of the problem of stating what one is going to find, and then finding it. The battlefield that *The Five Gospels* is designed to win is not the minutiae-oriented world of biblical scholarship, but the wave-tossed world of popular perception. In the scholarly world of biblical criticism, *The Five Gospels* may be something of a joke. But in the winner-take-all struggle for the mind of the culture, it is a potent effector, a voice speaking "amazing things" that cannot easily be refuted by the same type of bite-sized media bombs that it uses to such effect. The Seminar has proved itself to be master of the media, and the media has proved itself to be peculiarly amenable to the message the Seminar brings.

Ultimately, the Seminar ignores its own "final general rule of evidence: "Beware of finding a Jesus that is entirely congenial to you."[16]

The Elevation of Thomas

The other distinctive of *The Five Gospels* is its curious elevation of the Gnostic Gospel of Thomas to the same status as that of the canonical Gospels. A fourth-century copy of the Gospel of Thomas was discovered shortly after World War II as part of a collection of mainly Gnostic documents found at Nag Hammadi in Egypt. Thomas is among those documents that were for centuries known only by their titles, due to the warnings against them found in writings of the early church fathers.

Gnosticism is an ancient philosophy—exact origins unknown—which was widespread in the Middle East in the early centuries of the first millennium A.D. Gnosticism was extremely mutagenic, adapting itself to belief systems of various kinds, and in the process creating multiple different strands of itself—all of which had in common a dualism between the material and immaterial worlds.

In the Gnostic conception, the material world was evil, and material existence an illusion that kept some of those living in the world from discovering their true natures as "sparks" of the divine flame. In this conception, the Gnostics had many interesting parallels with the Docetists, another ancient heretical faction that believed in the intrinsically evil nature of the material world, and therefore concluded that Jesus had only "appeared" (Greek: *dokein*) to take on a fleshly body.

Somehow, according to the "purest" strains of Gnosticism, some of those living in the material world had within themselves the divine nature of the true god, but had become trapped in the world of material illusion. The role of *gnosis* (Greek for "knowledge") was to awaken the sleepers and help them escape back to their home in the world of the spirit where they would reunite with the godhead.

Gnosticism—adaptable and mutagenic as it was—flourished like a weed in the fertile soil of the early Christian communities, and had to be stamped out repeatedly and forcefully over the course of several centuries. As a threat to Christianity, it probably reached its peak in the late second century. But traces of incipient Gnostic influence can already be seen in the heretical doctrines that Paul battled in his first letter to the Corinthians (circa A.D. 56). By the time of Paul's first letter to Timothy (circa A.D. 61-63), the threat had become fully manifest:

> O Timothy! Guard what was committed to your trust, avoiding the profane and idle babblings and contradictions of what is falsely called *knowledge*. . . . (1 Timothy 6:20 NKJV, Greek for "knowledge": *gnosis*)

The Gospel of Thomas represents an advanced state of Christian-Gnostic hybridization. Evangelical New Testament scholar Craig L. Blomberg notes that roughly one-third of the sayings in the Gospel of Thomas are clearly Gnostic in nature; between one-third and one-half are paralleled fairly closely in Matthew, Mark, Luke, or John; the remaining sayings are not demonstrably unorthodox but could lend themselves to Gnostic interpretations.[17] As an example, here is a "saying" from Thomas, apparently a corruption of Peter's confession of Jesus as the Messiah (see Matthew 16:13-20), in which the apostle Thomas receives a secret revelation:

> Jesus says to his disciples: "Compare me, and tell me whom I am like." Simon Peter says to him: "Thou art like a just angel." Matthew says to him: "Thou art like a wise man and a philosopher!" Thomas says to him: "Master, my tongue cannot find words to say whom thou art like." Jesus says: "I am no longer thy master; for thou hast drunk, thou art inebriated from the bubbling spring which is mine and which I sent forth." Then he took him aside; he said three words to him. And when Thomas came back to his companions, they asked him: "What did Jesus say to thee?" And Thomas answered them: "If I tell you (a single) one of the words he said to me, you will take up stones and throw them at me, and fire will come out of the stones and consume you!" (Gospel of Thomas, 14).[18]

Thomas, alone among the disciples, discerned correctly that the master is beyond description (beyond comprehension). For this, he was rewarded with recognition of his equal footing with Jesus, and with a secret word, for which the other disciples were not yet ready, or perhaps not capable of hearing. The elitism of Gnosticism, and its "secret" nature, are evident.

While it has been overshadowed by the furor that erupted over the Seminar's word-coloring scheme, the inclusion of the Gospel of Thomas in *The Five Gospels* was the Seminar's own stated primary reason for issuing the work:

> Foremost among the reasons for a fresh translation is the discovery of the Gospel of Thomas. The scholars responsible for the Scholars Version determined that *Thomas had to be included in any primary collection of gospels.*[19]

To justify this claim, the Seminar has come up with a unique dating scheme—largely or perhaps exclusively the work of J. Dominic Crossan—that asserts a hypothetical early version of Thomas appearing around A.D. 55. This puts the earliest "layer" of Thomas as a contemporary of Q, and about 15 or so years antecedent to the Gospel of Mark, which the Seminar assumes to have been written around A.D. 70. The implication of this dating scheme is that Thomas becomes the oldest existing Christian text, which gives it great claims to recording the earliest Christian beliefs, if not the purest form of Jesus' original teaching, that we have on record.[20]

This dating scheme "sets on its head" the rest of the academic world, which dates Thomas to the late second century, where it fits quite nicely into a general proliferation of Gnostic writing. Craig L. Blomberg lists several reasons why Thomas is generally given the later date. I will only list the first (which would seem to be enough)—and that is that Thomas contains parallels to material found in all four of the canonical Gospels, including every "layer" of the Gospel tradition.* That is to say, it has parallels to material found in common in all three of the Synoptic Gospels (the "triple tradition"), material found in Q (a hypothetical sayings source containing material common to Matthew and Luke but not found in Mark), and traditions unique to all four Gospels, including John. Under standard source theory, this would mean that the writer of Thomas would have to have had access to *all five* of the separate streams of the earliest tradition: Mark, Q, special Matthew, special Luke,** and some hypothetical source behind John.

This is *not* very probable, even if we allow the existence of all the hypothetical sources. What is much more probable is that the writer of Thomas simply had access to this material

---

** Layers of the Gospel tradition: Higher critics surmise that the Gospels were not works written by single authors, but were instead conglomerations of material written by different authors at different times. These critics believe they can detect different "layers" within the Gospels, like the strata of a rock that has been built up over the years by successive layers of mineral deposits.

** The higher critics speak of the material that is unique to Matthew (not found in Mark or Luke) as "special Matthew," and the material that is unique to Luke as "special Luke."

after it had already appeared in the canonical Gospels, which makes a second century date very plausible. It should be noted that there is no actual historical evidence of any kind that would allow pushing the date of Thomas to earlier than around A.D. 150.

Why does the Seminar go to such great lengths and contortions of logic on behalf of Thomas? Because the theory of an early Thomas would greatly support the Seminar's theological agenda. Consider the following:

- *Looks like Q:* Thomas looks a lot like the hypothetical Q—it is a collection of sayings without any narrative elements. An early Thomas adds credibility to the view that Q existed, and that it existed as a completed work as opposed to a simple collection of sayings that was never intended to circulate as an independent source.

- *Stripped-down Gospel:* Thomas contains no accounts of Jesus' birth, miracles, death, or resurrection. If Thomas is the earliest Gospel, then this is evidence that these elements of the Gospels were added later.

- *Non-historical:* Thomas contains only sayings; there is no historical context. An early Thomas would be evidence that the earliest tradition was not interested in recording factual historical details about Jesus and His ministry. Therefore, the supposed historical details of the canonical Gospels were tacked on later.

- *De-eschatologizing of the Gospel:* Thomas contains no eschatological (prophetic) sayings. If it is early, this is evidence that the eschatology in Jesus' message was tacked on later. This is perhaps the biggest theological axe the Seminar has to grind.

- *Multiple Gospel Types:* Crossan, co-founder of the Seminar, likes to promote the theory that there were orthodox and Gnostic Gospels vying for supremacy in the early church. As a result of the political clout it was able to command, the orthodox view prevailed, and thus became the "orthodox" position.[21] This position is unattested by any actual historical evidence. An early Thomas would be evidence that early Gnostic Gospels did, in fact, exist.

On the other hand, if the Gospel of Thomas is a second-century document, then it is simply additional evidence that the Gnostics were a heretical parasite of the early church, not interested in the historical details of Jesus' life, but only in the "gnosis" that they might wring out of His teaching.

The Oldest Quest

The Jesus Seminar is just the latest chapter in a tale of skeptical criticism known as the "quest for the historical Jesus." The quest was spawned out of the skeptical naturalism of the Enlightenment and its basic disbelief in the miraculous—the ability of God to intervene in the affairs of the material world. In my previous chapter, "The Quest for the Historical Jesus," I addressed the various stages of this quest.

As noted earlier, the Seminar's seventh "Pillar of Scholarly Wisdom" involved the idea that the Gospel records are presumed to be false until "proven" true. The Seminar has followed the twentieth-century "hermeneutic of suspicion" to its logical conclusion: nothing is true, and everything is true. Truth is something waiting to be defined.

The Jesus Seminar is not, however, the first group to undertake a search for Jesus on such premises. There is another group to whom "nothing is as it seems," for whom the supposed reality of the external world requires careful and complicated sifting in order to discern the threads of truth buried beneath the layers of illusion. Long before the Jesus Seminar appeared—indeed, long before the nineteenth-century "First Quest" or the Enlightenment even—this group embarked on a project to liberate the "true" Jesus from the distorting confines of orthodox belief. I am referring, of course, to the Gnostics. I could just as easily be talking about the Docetists or the Manicheans, or any one of many other virulently dualistic ancient heresies. But since it is the Gnostic

Gospel of Thomas that the Jesus Seminar is attempting to rehabilitate, it is the Gnostics who now take center stage.

During the second century in particular, the Gnostics produced a multitude of "gospels" in an effort to present the true picture of Jesus, a picture informed by the esoteric knowledge that was required to truly understand His life and mission. That these gospels were composed largely of imaginary (mythic) episodes in the lives of famous apostles was not of concern to Gnostic believers. Truth was spiritual in nature in the Gnostic conception, the material world an illusion; so liberties taken in the realm of the material were of little consequence or meaning.

What mattered to the Gnostics was not faith based on a historical figure, but knowledge delivered by a heavenly messenger. The actual historical details were mainly superfluous, as attested by the fairy-tale type nature of the bulk of the Gnostic gospels, such as the *Gospel of Peter,* or by the complete lack of historical detail in the *Gospel of Thomas.* The Gnostics arrived at the conclusion that it was Jesus' "true" words that mattered, not the supposed details of His life, long before the modern "quest" came to that same conclusion.

This "Oldest Quest" to redefine the true Jesus has been forced underground at various times through the long centuries, but it has never completely died out. Instead, like some spiritual virus directly coded into the human soul, it lies dormant for generations, only to spring up in diverse times and places, creating theological havoc and ruin.

One recent notorious example would be the Branch Davidians, whose secret teachings have survived the Waco inferno, and are now available for true seekers on the World Wide Web. Even a superficial perusal will show the telltale signs—the spaghetti-like logic twisting through yards and yards of Old and New Testament texts, all words and ideas being bent beyond recognition by the esoteric refraction of some hidden prism. Be careful, warns the web site: those who have had access to these teachings will be held eternally responsible for either responding to or ignoring its summons to deeper things.

These Things Are True

> Then God saw everything that He had made, and indeed it was very good. (Genesis 1:31 NKJV).

The Bible does not give us the option of dualism—not unless we are willing to stoop to the level of blasphemy of the ancient Gnostics, and split the godhead into the "gods" of the Old and New Testaments, making the Old Testament God Yahweh a bungling demiurge responsible for creating the material world. Unless we are willing to do this *and* discard about 82 percent of the statements made by and concerning Jesus in the New Testament, we cannot both believe in Jesus and believe that His physical, historical life was somehow unimportant, something less than absolutely, intrinsically essential.

When John recorded the words of Jesus in John 6, he was doing so, at least in part, to combat the Docetic and Gnostic dualism already infiltrating the church:

> I am the living bread which came down from heaven. If anyone eats of this bread, he will live forever; and the bread that I shall give is My flesh, which I shall give for the life of the world. (John 6:51 NKJV).
>
> Unless you eat the flesh of the Son of Man and drink His blood, you have no life in you. (John 6:53b NKJV).

The Greek word for "flesh" used here and throughout John 6 is *sarx*, which can mean both the literal "flesh" of "flesh and blood" material reality, and the totality of the makeup of a human being: body, soul, and spirit. John makes one implication of this teaching of Jesus clear in his first letter:

> This is how you can recognize the Spirit of God: Every spirit that acknowledges that Jesus Christ has come in the flesh is from God, but every spirit that does not acknowledge

Jesus is not from God. This is the spirit of the antichrist, which you have heard is coming and even now is already in the world. (1 John 4:2-3)

The belief of the church through the past two millennia has been that the Gospels are what they purport to be—eyewitness (Matthew, John) or second generation (Mark, Luke) accounts of the life, ministry, and teaching of Jesus of Nazareth, a real person, a flesh and blood Jew who lived in the first century. The Gospels have been regarded as accurate in their portrayal of His message, His healings and other miracles, and His actual physical victory over the death He suffered on a Roman cross. This view, which has survived the long centuries since Jesus walked the Earth, is the basis of Christian orthodoxy. To believe in the orthodox viewpoint, one must believe in God, and believe in a God who has the ability and inclination to enter into the affairs of man.

As Christians, we have nothing to fear from *valid* historical research into the person of Jesus. As N.T. Wright, former professor of New Testament at Oxford, put it: "It's hard work, but if you stick with the historical enterprise to the bitter end, not only can you preach from it, but it's more powerful than what . . . the liberal reductionists offer.[22]

We do, however, have plenty to be concerned about with regard to the kind of historical revisionism practiced by the Jesus Seminar. The Seminar's next major project will be to issue their findings as to what Jesus *did.* No one who is familiar with the Seminar's ideology and methodology is in any doubt concerning what the central finding of this work will be: the resurrection will be the first thing to go.

Of course, attacks on the central issues of the Christian faith are nothing new. To be sure, the champions of orthodoxy have been engaged in a constant struggle for the "purity of the faith" since the very beginning. Paul's letters, for example, reflect his efforts to inoculate the earliest congregations against the doctrines of "Judaizers" and Gnostic/Docetic influences. Paul's defense is part of what allows us to confidently assert that the teaching of Jesus' bodily resurrection has been the historic teaching of the church from its earliest point. In Paul's first letter to the Corinthians, he spells out the tradition he received, the very early creedal statement of the church:

> For I delivered to you first of all that which I also received: that Christ died for our sins according to the Scriptures, and that He was buried, and that He rose again the third day according to the Scriptures, and that He was seen by Cephas, then by the twelve. (1 Corinthians 15:3-5 NKJV).

Moreover, Paul warns the Corinthians that this gospel is the basis of their salvation:

> Moreover, brethren, I declare to you the gospel which I preached to you, which also you received and in which you stand, by which also you are saved, if you hold fast that word which I preached to you—unless you believed in vain. (1 Corinthians 15:1-2 NKJV).

Biblical scholar Gordon D. Fee suggests that Paul is writing to the Corinthians to correct their *dis*belief in the resurrection from the dead, and their overemphasis of the charismatic, or "pneumatic," aspects of the faith.[23] Evidently a false theology, rooted in a radical pneumatism, had invaded the church which denied the value and significance of the physical body. This false theology was being expressed in a "spiritualized" eschatology which denied the physical resurrection of the dead. In answering this heresy, Paul makes it clear that the resurrection of Jesus is the central event of the gospel:

> We preach: Christ has been raised from the dead,
>   Some of you say: there is no resurrection of the dead.
> But if there is no resurrection of the dead, neither has Christ been raised.

If Christ has not been raised, then both our preaching and your believing are to no avail.

More than that, we are found to be false witnesses of God, because we bore witness about God, that he raised Christ, whom he did not raise, if indeed the dead are not raised, for if the dead are not raised, not even Christ has been raised. (1 Corinthians 15:12-16)[24]

Paul then makes it clear in 1 Corinthians 15:51 that we, likewise, will be resurrected in the same manner as our Lord—with "spiritual bodies" (Greek: *soma pneumatikon*). What is a *soma pneumatika*? This is a mystery, but it involves physicality—a "soma" (body). As Fee puts it:

If for Paul, and therefore for us, there is an element of mystery to the concept of a "spiritual body" (verse 51), there can be little question that for him Christ's resurrection is central to everything. It is the ultimate eschatological event.[25]

Years ago I sat in a hotel room in South India on the day I had my initial encounter with Christ. I had just left the most powerful self-proclaimed godman in India and was surrounded by a number of fellow-disciples who were having doubts of their own. The fact that I, Tal Brooke, had just left him added to their growing list of doubts. I had once been touted by this godman as a chief disciple whom he had called to India. I had once seemed a bastion of unlimited faith. Now I was voicing my doubts aloud. I was emerging from a powerful deception. This "avatar" in India was not who he said he was. He had a terrible dark side. Evil had disguised itself as divinity and I knew it.

Someone from the group asked in so many words, "Well, who *is* the real Christ?" And suddenly it became extraordinarily clear to me. *"Christ,"* I responded. *"He* is the real one, the true Savior of the world." I realized I had just survived a real-life drama that was in reality a huge chess game involving my soul. I had come from the brink of losing the whole thing. At stake was my eternal destiny. And God had to intervene. I knew I had been deceived by a false Christ. I realized that the real Christ had already appeared in the world. He had already stood up to announce Himself, His nature, and His mission. It is to Him that we turn in this chapter to learn the extent to which He already "stood up," providing evidence piled upon evidence as to His true identity.

12

THE REAL JESUS ALREADY STOOD UP

Brooks Alexander

O ther chapters in this book reveal clearly enough who Jesus is not. He is not the cosmic guide and guru of the New Age. He is not the illegitimate black magician of the Talmud. He is not the failed (and uncrucified) prophet of the Koran. He is not the rustic Palestinian preacher of the Jesus Seminar. But after we reject all the false teachings about Him, we still face the question the false teachers tried to answer in the first place—namely, "Who is this man?"

The answer to that question is both simpler and deeper than most people care to imagine. It is easy to state but hard to grasp, because Christ's sacrifice embodies the ultimate paradox of the Christian faith. That is, in Christ God conquers evil by allowing it to triumph on its own terms. In Christ, God makes evil serve His purposes in its very rejection of Him. In Christ, God lets evil do its worst against Him, then makes the worst itself a part of His salvation. By letting evil express its nature without restraint, God turns it into its opposite—*good*. It is God's alchemy. It is His ultimate trump. If that paradoxical "mystery of the faith" is not understood—or at least *acknowledged*—there is no way that Jesus Himself can be understood, a fact that goes far to explain the many current misunderstandings about Him.

The Short Answer

The question, "Who is Jesus?" has both a short answer and a long one. The short answer is that Jesus represents the presence of God Himself, injected into fallen human history. In Jesus, God deliberately intruded into a world that had already rejected Him—knowing full well that His coming would create turmoil and conflict. In Jesus, God personally faced the hostility and hatred of fallen man—armed with enough love to neutralize our murderous rejection of Him by accepting it without resistance. And finally, Jesus reversed the meaning of His death by rising from the dead. In that way, the sacrifice of Christ nullified the barrier between God and man that our fallenness created. His resurrection is proof of His conquest of evil, and demonstrates the completeness and finality of His victory.

The resurrection is the climactic message of the gospel. The word "gospel" means "good news." The death and resurrection of Christ are "news" because they happened in history—just like other reportable events. The news is "good" because those particular events overthrew evil fundamentally and forever. Jesus brought eternity into history and made death release its grip on Him. When He rose from the dead to share His victory with us, the rule of death ended. The power of Christ's resurrection sets us free in this world and makes us whole in the world to come. "Christ is risen!" is the core of the Christian proclamation to the world.

In abbreviated terms, the real Jesus is the one who "stood up" to death and evil, and who "stood up" again in triumph after they had laid Him low. But the ultimate short answer to the question, "Who is Jesus?" is given by the apostle Paul. In his first letter to the Corinthians, he distills the essence of Christianity's good news into a four-step definition that is a model of clarity and brevity:

> For I delivered to you as of first importance what I also received, that Christ died for our sins according to the Scriptures, and that He was buried, and that He was raised on the third day according to the Scriptures, and that He appeared to Cephas, then to the twelve (1 Corinthians 15:3-5 NASB).

Those few lines are full of information and are rich with implication. The message, however, is too deep for shallow minds, which turn its insights into clichés of disdain: "Christ died for your sins," "Jesus is the Light of the world," "You must be born again." For many, those are words without content, empty phrases, relics of an antiquated way of thought. Few are aware that they describe the mystery of God's presence in our fallen world—the Eternal enters history, the Infinite becomes particular, the Boundless takes on form, judgment becomes mercy, and evil is turned to good. It is a paradox deep enough to change the universe and powerful enough to transform human affairs.

The Long Answer

There is also a long answer to the question, "Who is Jesus?" and it properly starts with a look at the human condition. The gospel (good news) of Jesus is really God's precise response to the human predicament—though that fact is only clear when we understand what the human predicament is.

The human race has always and everywhere understood that it *is* in a predicament. In every age and every culture, man has not only *known* he is in cosmically deep trouble, he has enshrined that knowledge in his religions. Religion is as universal as any human behavior can be, and religions universally claim to solve some fundamental human problem. As William James pointed out, religion's defining feature is that it claims to cure or overcome some basic lack or flaw in human nature by appealing to something beyond the human. At the end of his monumental inquiry into *The Varieties of Religious Experience,* James summed up his insight into the root of man's religious impulse, and demonstrated that the real unity of human religion lies in its insistence on humanity's spiritual *need:*

> The warring gods and formulas of the various religions do indeed cancel each other, but there is a certain uniform deliverance in which religions all appear to meet. It consists of two parts:
>
> 1) An uneasiness; and
> 2) Its solution.
> 1) The uneasiness, reduced to its simplest terms, is a sense that there is *something wrong about us* as we naturally stand.
> 2) The solution is a sense that *we are saved from the wrongness* by making proper connections with the higher powers.[1]

James showed that the basic function of religion is to "put the wrongness of human nature right," and to do so by contacting something "beyond" the human. Obviously, *how* you call on the "higher powers," and *how* you expect them to help with the human condition, depends very much on how you understand the original problem. But as James observed, all religions agree that we do have a problem.

As we ourselves can observe, the different religions define the problem in different ways, and offer their answers accordingly. In the midst of this transcendental traffic jam, inquiring minds want to know: "Is there any real reason to embrace one solution, one answer, one religion over another—aside from accidents of birth and circumstance, or whims of personal preference? Are all religions equally effective in dealing with our problem? Or are all of them equally *in*effective?"

Such inquiries lead directly to the one question James refused to answer, namely, "What really *is* our problem?" James bypassed the issue because his psychological approach wouldn't let him assess the validity of religious beliefs or deal with existential truth-claims.

However, as people who live in the real world, we don't have that luxury. We are not theorizing about the abstract patterns of human behavior, we are struggling with the concrete patterns of our own behavior. In that context, we need to know, before anything else, what the "problem" of human nature really is—because *whatever* it is, it is our problem too. And the way we understand the human predicament will determine how we think thereafter about the purpose of life and the priorities we pursue.

What Is the Problem?

So, what *is* the problem? The Bible offers a clear and concrete answer to that question. But even without appealing to Scripture, we can find some important clues in the patterns of human religion.

One of the first patterns we notice is that religion's most universal things are also its most ancient things. The themes of religion that occur most widely are also its oldest themes. There are beliefs running through our religions that seem to be a reverberation of some primal knowledge, hints of a spiritual consensus once shared by the whole human race but now consigned to obscure myths and distant recollections.

A case in point is the concept of "the absent Creator-God." In the oldest forms of religion and folklore worldwide, we find the story of a universe torn apart by the departure of the "One High God" from our presence, taking sky and heaven with Him. The prevalence of that belief across barriers of space and time precludes any possibility of "cultural transmission." This isn't a belief that has "spread" or "developed," it's a *knowledge* that has been passed down from the past in all parts of the world.

The clearest examples of belief in the "supreme God who becomes remote" can be found among the most isolated and primitive people. Some, like the pygmies of central Africa, experienced virtually no contact with the outside world until recently. Amazingly, the pygmies have neither animism nor ancestor worship in their culture (though both are staples of primitive religion worldwide), but they do believe in a supreme being to whom all things are subjected. The pygmies plainly didn't import that belief from other cultures. They got it from their tradition, which passed it on as a package from their ancestors.

G. K. Chesterton spoke of a missionary who stumbled on a tribal version of that tradition without even realizing he had done so. The missionary was

> preaching to a very wild tribe of polytheists, who had told him all of their polytheistic tales, and telling them in return of the existence of the one good God who is a spirit and who judges men by spiritual standards. And there was a sudden buzz of excitement among these stolid barbarians, as at somebody who was letting out a secret, and they cried to each other, "Atahocan! He is speaking of Atahocan!"
>
> Probably it was a point of politeness and even decency among those polytheists not to speak of Atahocan . . . social forces are always covering up and confusing such simple ideas. Possibly the old god stood for an old morality found irksome in more expansive moments; possibly intercourse with demons was more fashionable among the best people, as in the modern fashion of Spiritualism.[2]

Chesterton commented in conclusion that such beliefs all "testify to the unmistakable psychology of a thing taken for granted, as opposed to a thing talked about . . . something assumed and forgotten and remembered by accident."[3]

Wilhelm Schmidt, a Jesuit professor at the University of Vienna, spent over 40 years (1912-1955) documenting and compiling evidence for what he called "primitive monotheism." In 1931 he published his findings as *The Origin and Growth of Religion,* a book that revolutionized the study of religious anthropology.

Schmidt thought that such beliefs were the residue of a primal revelation of God to man, the surviving forms of a once common knowledge of the one God, which through human fallenness and error has been overlaid by magic, animism, ancestor worship, spiritism, polytheism, and other forms of spiritual delusion. Schmidt continued to validate his thesis with relentless research over the years. By 1955 he had published over 4000 pages of evidence in 12 large volumes.

Chesterton summed up the import of Schmidt's ground-breaking studies:

> There is very good ground for guessing that religion did not originally come from some detail that was forgotten because it was too small to be traced. Much more probably it was an idea that was abandoned because it was too large to be managed. There is very good reason to suppose that many people did begin with the simple but overwhelming idea of one God who governs all; and afterwards fell away into such things as demon-worship almost as a sort of secret dissipation.[4]

God's Goodbye

Primitive theologies of the one God always include some explanation of why He is no longer present. His departure is routinely regarded as a cosmic disaster—a rupture in the natural fabric of things brought on by some fault or failure on the part of human beings. In some myths, the fault seems almost trivial, involving a technical error in the performance of some (now) obscure ritual, thus causing the universe to unravel and leave man spiritually marooned. In other forms of primitive monotheism, the failure is more morally serious, involving man's betrayal of his duty to his creator, thus causing God to depart in sorrow and judgment.

The details differ, but all the myths tell a common story, and the story is clearly a part of our common heritage. Ironically, the evidence of anthropology indicates that ancient man was more in agreement concerning the nature of our spiritual problem than we have agreed about anything since that time. The reason is doubtless that their consensus was one of memory and not of opinion.

Schmidt's work uncovered one momentous fact for all to see—namely, that humanity's most ancient and universal assessment of its own condition is simply this: "God is not with us." For whatever reason, God's personal presence has been withdrawn from us. *God's absence is our problem.*

The curious thing is that many modern theologies of unbelief also affirm the absence of God, usually as a rationale for urging man to fill the gap. "Man's coming of age" always seems to involve filling the void of God's absence with our own expansive spiritual pride. The "death of God" theologians took God's "departure" literally (in the mortician's sense) and wrote His obituary, declaring His absence to be an irreversible condition. Those who deny the gospel, it seems, sentence themselves to struggling anew with the problem the gospel so pointedly solves—the problem of the absence of God.

The Bible, of course, provides a rich and detailed account of how and why God went missing to begin with. It also tells us what God did to heal the separation. The Bible as a whole is a history of the acts God performed among us to arrange our restoration—a history that culminates in the coming of Jesus Christ.

The beginnings of that history are familiar enough. The episode in the Garden of Eden—the serpent, the forbidden fruit, the temptation, the fall, and the exile from paradise— all of that is still part of the cultural baggage of many people. Unfortunately, few have more than a cartoonish view of the story, or sense the real depth of its message to us.

For our purposes (that is, understanding who Jesus is), we need to emphasize two aspects of the fall: (1) the change in our nature that the fall produced, and (2) why that change made God distance Himself from us—an estrangement ordained both in judgment and in mercy.

Without going into the *causes* of the fall, the immediate and enduring *effect* of the fall is that "the center does not hold, and things fall apart." God our Creator is the lynchpin of reality. When we reject Him, we reject our integrating core, and our reality begins to disintegrate in every way. The visible symptom of that breakdown is a relentless, unstoppable process of *division*, on every level—spiritually, mentally, socially, physically, and otherwise. Adam and Eve found themselves divided from God, from nature, from their own selves, and from one another—and so do we, their children.

Both Scripture and personal experience give us the same message. Genesis 3 tells us that the whole human race is caught in an out-of-control cycle of inner division, outer conflict, cosmic alienation, physical decay, and final death. The history of humanity tells us the same thing—and so does our own daily struggle with life.

Adam and Eve chose their way into a new, inferior state of being, and we, their descendants, are powerless to choose our way back out again (the children of exiles are born into exile by definition). Worst of all, our fallen condition has had an abrupt and disastrous impact on our relationship with God.

By any measure, we are now severely out of harmony with Him. His very nature stands against what we have tragically become. God and man now find themselves in opposition—a condition far removed from the harmony in which we were created.

That new state raises a critical problem. The full-bore presence of God simply blows away anything not in harmony with Him. In the face of God's infinite power and force of will, only those things in complete accord with His purposes can even hope to exist. The intensity of His identity disintegrates dissonance instantly.

Merciful Judgment and the Paradox of Love

Once the fall has taken place, Adam and Eve must be hustled out of God's presence at once if they and their descendants (that is, *us*) are to have any hope of living beyond the next fragment of time. *God's separation from us is His first act of mercy to us.* Adam and Eve's exile from Eden is commonly taken as a sign of God's judgment—and so it is—but it is also a sign of His mercy and a promise of His grace to come.

By evicting us from paradise and pushing us into a fallen world apart from Him, God insulated us from the purifying power of His presence, thus "saving" us from the immediate threat to our own existence that our fallenness created. He also thereby took the first step in His plan to redeem His fallen creatures, and indeed to reverse the meaning of the fall itself.

God created "history" as we know it for three necessary and sufficient reasons: (1) as an asylum of exile from His presence (that is, for our own protection); (2) as a dimensional ghetto to contain and restrict the results of the fall; and (3) as a stage on which He could act out His redemptive love for us in a way that could not be changed but could be recorded, so that the whole world could thereby hear about it and understand it.

The dilemma for God is how to enter "history" and bring His presence back to us without destroying us in the process. When God enters our alienated world to face His fallen creatures, He confronts the same problem that forced our exile from Eden to begin with—namely our fundamental dissonance with Him. That is the spiritual conflict that logically ends with eradicating fallen man from the fabric of the universe.

That is the grim reality we have to face before we can understand who Jesus really is. *That* is the "bad news" that makes the "good news" good. Here is the fatal equation:

(1) We are in conflict with God.
(2) God is omnipotent.
(3) We are not.

End of story, end of conflict, end of us. The facts are indisputable and their meaning is inescapable: we are out of sync with God, and things that are out of sync with God don't survive—period. That transparently *is* the human predicament—according to Scripture, according to tradition, and according to personal experience.

Fortunately, God does not let sheer power determine the outcome of our conflict with Him. Because He loves us—and for no other reason—our Creator approaches the problem creatively, and arranges a truly astonishing solution. God finds an option for "saving" man in the fact that there are *two* possible outcomes to our conflict with Him, not just one.

The first possible outcome is the obvious one—we, the fallen human race, will absorb the results of the conflict in our own being, in which case we will be instantly obliterated, extinguished, consumed, blown out like a candle. Humankind will simply cease to exist, and that will be the end of that.

Amazing Grace

The second possible outcome is the unexpected one. It is the so-called (and *well*-called) "amazing grace"—in the form of *reverse* judgment. God elects to absorb the results of our conflict with Him in His *own* being.

If God opts for that outcome, it means that whenever and however He chooses to show up among us in history, He will be the focus of all the accumulated antagonism from our side of the discord. If God doesn't obliterate us with the sheer force of His presence when He arrives, then we will reflexively try to obliterate Him with whatever force we can muster. When that happens, we will get God's sacrificial death in history by definition, because our ultimate form of force is killing, and we will not fail to bring it against Him. In other words, we *will* get a crucifixion—in one form or another—because God's decision to "save" us rather than destroy us involves submitting to our murderous rejection of Him as part of the bargain.

The crux of the matter is this: If Christ *isn't* crucified, then humankind goes the way of the dodo bird—period—no options, no exceptions. If you are alive and reading this, then you *already* owe Jesus Christ a debt of gratitude. If God had *not* come to us in history as a willing sacrifice, none of us would even be here today to discuss whether we "believe" that He did so or not.

The logic of that conclusion is inescapable. Between God and fallen, sinful man is dissonance and conflict. That conflict must be discharged somehow. For God to come and be present to us in love and not in judgment, He must come prepared to let the full force of that discharge fall upon Himself rather than on us. He must come, in other words, prepared to endure our rejection of Him without resisting, even to the point of His (inevitable) death.

In Christ, God does exactly that. In Christ, God accepts the discharge of that conflict on Himself, instead of letting it discharge on us. In Christ, God comes to us as the Almighty, able to extinguish us in an instant, but prepared—because of His love—to let Himself be extinguished as a sacrifice instead, slowly, and by painful degrees.

Christ acted as the lightning rod for the cosmic tension between God and the whole fallen human race. Christ put His body and His being forward to receive the discharge of that conflict so that we wouldn't have to. He didn't deserve it . . . we did. He took it anyway, however, so that God could come to us in our alienated state *without* blowing us away. His act of sacrifice neutralized the barrier to God that our fallenness imposed. With that barrier gone, God could establish His presence among us in an entirely new way—which, in fact, He proceeded to do, as described in the book of Acts.

He did it all in history. He was willing, out of love, to endure the constraints of our fallen world in order to free us from it. His conception and birth occurred in history, His conflict with our fallenness occurred in history, and the discharge of that conflict on His own innocent shoulders occurred in history as well. The unjust execution of Jesus by torture occurred at a time and a place that are specified in great detail. "Christ died for your sins" is not a metaphor, it is a brutal and bloody *event* that took place on a hill outside Jerusalem.

Christ's crucifixion opened wide the door for God to bring His personal presence back to fallen man. And His resurrection demonstrates that God did indeed come through that open door. Because Christ died, God was *able* to come among us. Because Christ rose from the dead, we know that He *did* come among us. And because He gave us the Holy Spirit, we know that He is *still* among us—"even to the end of the age" (Matthew 28:18-20).

The Difference It Makes

It is important to realize that the gospel is not just another spiritual ideology—another abstract way of talking about the human condition. The gospel isn't a bright idea that came to someone as a spiritual insight. It is a brute fact that came to all of us as a shocking historical event. It happened in real life. And because it happened in real life, it makes real things happen in our lives when we believe it.

One of the first things that happens when we believe the good news is that we come into a new relationship with the fallen world system. That happens automatically, because the gospel exposes the system's bluff and bluster as an empty threat. The gospel shows us clearly what is important and what is not. For that reason, it exposes the masquerade when trivial things are dressed up to *look* important. When it comes to the world-system, with all of its lies and empty delusions, the gospel lets us understand that "the emperor isn't wearing any clothes."

Let me explain. As Christians, we believe in a definite future. We have it on the best authority that the kingdoms of this world will pass away. Therefore we know that the current world system has a limited lifespan (whether long or short by our clock is beside the point) because the kingdom of God is coming to replace it. God's kingdom has not only been promised, it has already been planted, in full view of everyone. The cornerstone of God's kingdom is the conquest of death. Christ already did that. The coming kingdom of

God is already rooted in history, and its final arrival won't be delayed or deflected.

As part of that coming kingdom, Christians believe in the resurrection. That belief, as a practical hope, revolutionizes our relation to the fallen world system. The resurrection negates the finality of death, and nullifies the final sanction behind all forms of earthly rule—namely, "Do what I say or I'll kill you."

This, then, is the formula of our liberation—the syllogism of our freedom from the fear of earthly powers:

(1) If there is a resurrection, then death isn't final;

(2) if death isn't final, then it isn't a final threat;

(3) if it isn't a final threat, then the fear of death can't coerce your conscience in final things;

(4) if your conscience can't be coerced by the fear of death, then the grip of the world-system is broken; and the Truth has set you free.

In light of the resurrection, the world system's "big stick" turns out to be a limp baton. Jesus made the same point to His disciples when He said that they should not "fear those who kill the body but cannot kill the soul; but rather fear Him who can destroy both soul and body in hell." (Matthew 10:28) To be properly in fear of God is automatically to be fearless in the face of His enemies. That is one of the great gifts we have because of the fact that the gospel is real and historically true. Because He really rose from the dead, we can rely on Him to really raise us from the dead as well.

Beyond Merit: Healing Our Divisions

The gospel not only frees us in our conflicts with earthly powers, it frees us in our conflicts with one another. Authentic Christian faith will transform human relations in a way that nothing else can.

People today are searching for solutions to human conflicts at every level. But because we are in denial about the fall, the only "answers" we are willing to try are those that ignore our fallen condition. "Political correctness" is just the most recent example of a "humanistic" effort to wrestle with the outward symptoms of the fall without acknowledging their real source or accepting their real solution. Political correctness tries to enforce right attitudes with legal sanctions and encourage right attitudes with peer pressure and media manipulation. "Diversity" is turned into a federal mandate, "multiculturalism" is made the mission of public education at all levels, and "tolerance" becomes the standard for acceptance into polite society.

None of it will work, of course. If we don't understand (or won't admit) where our conflicts really come from, we don't have a prayer of resolving them. But we try anyway—attempting, by force, to do the essentially undoable.

The bogus "tolerance" and "diversity" of the political correctness movement can never deliver on its advertised purposes because political correctness refuses to come to grips with the real source of human conflict. Only Christianity reaches to the root of the problem and turns it into a solution. To understand how that happens, we need to understand how and why our fallenness makes us fight with one another to begin with.

One of the most insidious effects of the fall is to divide human beings and turn them against one another. Adam and Eve's first response when confronted with their own sin was to pass the fault and point the finger at someone else (Genesis 3:11-13). That reflex of separation and blaming has only intensified among their children. Cain set the pace for us by dividing himself first from God, then from his brother, and finally from the whole human race by his act of murder (4:4-12). Those who came after him have not only followed his example but improved on it. Fallen human beings can be counted on to divide themselves from (and against) one another over any point of "otherness" they can find—from obvious differences such as race and gender, all the way to trivial distinctions of dialect and personal appearance.

Not surprisingly, our most obvious differences have produced our most vicious and enduring conflicts. Race, sex, religion, and nation, to name just a few of the largest and plainest examples, seem to have been our battlegrounds forever. Whites against blacks and blacks against whites; men against women and women against men; rich against poor and poor against rich; nation against nation and vice versa—all are dreadfully familiar struggles that seem to never go away.

Only the Christian faith holds the key to resolving those tensions and hostilities—not one of them, or some of them, but *all* of them—from the ground up and the inside out. Over thousands of years, the self-divisions of fallen man have grown into an insoluble knot of social problems—a tangle of interconnected conflicts that is impossible to unravel. But Christ brings a sword that cuts that gordian knot to its core.

The cutting edge of that sword is His universal relevance and accessibility. Christ's universality is both radical and revolutionary, which is to say that it goes to the root of our problem and turns it upside down. Fallen human nature seeks any kind of difference to fight over, and builds bigotries on all of them. The gospel, in contrast, stands for the complete demolition of all merely human distinctions. The gospel explodes every prejudice and levels every claim to superiority. It utterly negates our most basic fallen tendency, which is to distinguish ourselves from others by pointing the finger and pretending that we're "better" than they are.

The gospel declares that God has come to make Himself available to everyone—not on the basis of spiritual merit, but completely and pointedly *apart* from spiritual merit. Based on merit, no one qualifies and everyone has already fallen short (Romans 3:23). Because of the Fall, it is already too late for any of us to measure up.

Since everyone is in that condition, everyone is equal in spiritual need. Whatever our status in life may otherwise be, all of us are equally candidates for redemption—king and beggar, slave and master, cop and criminal alike. All of us stand before God without rank, degree, or distinction. The scholar and the dunce stand on equal footing in His presence. The publican and the Pharisee are reduced to a common predicament—to which Christ is the common solution.

In the light of Christ, all the levels and distinctions that people depend on to set themselves apart from one another disappear. Differences of race, religion, culture, gender, intelligence, ethnicity, class, status, wealth, power—all the standard excuses for snobbery and discrimination—are rendered irrelevant. None of those petty distinctions count for anything before the enormity of our universal need. Those who believe the gospel are united invisibly in Christ far more than they are divided by their visible differences.

That is the genius, the universality, and the spiritual leveling power of the Christian faith. The single Savior Jesus can speak redemptively to every one of us because He *is* one of us. He shares the basic human experiences that unite us all—namely, birth in travail, life in a fallen world, and death under judgment. Having identified with us in our mortality, He attained a stunning victory over death on our behalf. Christ identified with us by sharing our experience of life and death. If we identify with Him, we can share His experience of resurrection to glory.

The real Jesus is the one who already stood up and left the empty grave behind Him. The Orthodox liturgy puts the mystery in its simplest form: "Christ has risen from the dead, trampling down death by death."

The real Jesus offers that victory to us personally as well. The reconciliation with God that He achieved is available to every one of us—for free. He already paid the price of our return to God. The only "price" we have to pay is the cost that repentance requires of our egos. That's not just the deal of the century, it's the deal of eternity—and all at the cost of a simple decision. No wonder they call it amazing grace.

Is God powerful enough to speak into history and in so doing, choose the method of revealing Himself? If He is God, He can. Scripture claims to be uniquely that revelation from God to man. In a book dealing with counterfeit Christs and false revelations, it is only appropriate to have a chapter focusing on the inspiration and inerrancy of Scripture. This chapter demonstrates that the Scriptures are indeed the only legitimate source for reliable information about the person and work of Jesus Christ.

The fundamental theological battle as we approach the new millennium will continue to be fought round the fortress of the worth and authority of holy Scripture. Let us not forget that forging a new version of Christ, as many have done today, necessarily involves first dismissing the authority of Scripture. Can this be done so easily?

Holy Scripture has the support of history and archaeology, and enjoys massive manuscript support as well—like no other antiquarian document in history, not by a long shot. False gospels, such as the *Gospel of Thomas* or *The Aquarian Gospel of Jesus the Christ*, face an uphill battle against the incumbent. If such false gospels wish to truly compete with holy writ, let them marshal their historical merits and stand them up against the massive historical support that undergirds Scripture. Until then, it has to be *sola scriptura*.

13

HAS GOD REALLY SPOKEN?

Ron Rhodes

There is no demilitarized zone when it comes to attacks against the Bible. The inspiration and authority of Scripture has been and continues to be relentlessly undermined by humanists, liberal Christians, cultists, and critics from a variety of intellectual disciplines. Truly the fundamental theological battle as we approach the new millennium will continue to be fought round the fortress of the worth and authority of holy Scripture.[1]

The stakes are high in this battle. If the authority of the Bible is successfully toppled, then all the essential doctrines of Christianity—including the deity of Christ, the resurrection, salvation by grace, and, indeed, the very uniqueness of Christianity—topple right along with it.

In a single chapter, we can do little more than present the briefest of summaries on one of the most important of doctrines. I strongly urge the reader to consult some of the resources cited in the bibliography for further, more thorough research.

For our purposes, we begin with the recognition that at the creation God made Adam in His own rational image (Genesis 1:26). When He did so, He gave Adam the gift of intelligible speech, thus enabling him to communicate objectively with his creator (and with other human beings) by way of sharable linguistic symbols called words. Indeed, God sovereignly chose to use human language as a medium of revelational communication.[2]

The Bible as a body of literature exists because human beings need to know certain spiritual truths to which they cannot attain by themselves. Thus these truths must come to them from without—that is, through objective, special revelation from God (Deuteronomy 29:29). God has communicated this revelation *through words*, and these words are found in the pages of holy Scripture.

It is truly amazing to contemplate that the human authors of Scripture were from all walks of life—kings, peasants, philosophers, fishermen, physicians, statesmen, scholars, poets, and farmers. These individuals lived in different cultures, had vastly different experiences, and often were quite different in character. Yet, despite these differences, the Bible has a remarkable continuity that can be observed from Genesis to Revelation.

How could this be? How did God accomplish this? It's related to a process we call *inspiration*.

The Inspiration of Scripture

Today many liberal Christians say the Bible is inspired in the same sense that Shakespeare's writings are inspired—that is, *they are inspiring to read*. But this is not the biblical concept of inspiration. Inspiration doesn't mean the writer just felt enthusiastic, like the composer of the "Star Spangled Banner." Nor does it mean the writings are necessarily inspiring to read, like an uplifting poem.

The biblical Greek word for *inspiration* literally means "God-breathed" (see 2 Timothy 3:16). Because Scripture is breathed out by God—because it *originates* from Him—it is true and inerrant.

Biblical inspiration may be defined as God's superintending of the human authors so that, using their own individual personalities—and even their writing styles—they composed and recorded *without error* His revelation to humankind in the words of the original autographs. Benjamin B. Warfield, the prince of theologians, explains that

> the original documents of the Bible were written by men, who, though permitted to exercise their own personalities and literary talents, yet wrote under the control and guidance of the Spirit of God, the result being in every word of the original documents a perfect and errorless recording of the exact message which God desired to give to man.[3]

Hence, the writers of Scripture were not mere writing machines. God did not use them like keys on a typewriter to mechanically reproduce His message. Nor did He dictate the words, page by page. The biblical evidence makes it clear that each writer had a style of his own:

> One need only compare the powerful style of Isaiah with the mournful tone of Jeremiah in the Old Testament. In the New Testament, Luke manifests a marked medical interest, James is distinctly practical, Paul is theological and polemical, and John has an obvious simplicity. God has communicated through a multiplicity of human personalities, with their respective literary characteristics.[4]

The Human-Divine Interchange

Second Peter 1:21 provides us a key insight regarding the human-divine interchange in the process of inspiration. This verse informs us that "prophecy [or Scripture] never had its origin in the will of man, but men spoke from God as they were carried along by the Holy Spirit." The phrase *carried along* in this verse literally means "forcefully borne along."

Though human beings were used in the process of writing down God's Word, they were all literally "borne along" by the Holy Spirit. The human wills of the authors were not the originators of God's message. God did not permit the will of sinful human beings to misdirect or erroneously record His message. Rather, as Norman Geisler and William Nix put it, "God *moved* and the prophet *mouthed* these truths; God *revealed* and man *recorded* His word."[5]

Interestingly, the Greek word for "carried along" in 2 Peter 1:21 is the same as that found in Acts 27:15-17. In this passage the experienced sailors could not navigate the ship because the wind was so strong. The ship was being *driven*, *directed*, and *carried along* by the wind. This is similar to the Spirit's driving, directing, and carrying the human authors of the Bible as He wished. The word is a strong one, indicating the Spirit's complete superintendence of the human authors. Yet, just as the sailors were active on the ship (though the wind, not the sailors, ultimately controlled the ship's final destiny), so the human authors were active in writing as the Spirit directed. Theologian John F. Walvoord comments:

> A passenger is borne by a ship to his ultimate destination with utmost certainty. The passenger, however, loses none of his human characteristics and can move within the ship with great freedom. Thus holy men spake, whether orally or in writing, within the limits of their own vocabulary and cultural environment, and yet were "borne" along by God so that what they wrote was the infallible Word of God.[6]

Building on this biblical theme, theologian Charles C. Ryrie tells us that God's work of inspiration meant using the human authors

> in research (Luke 1:1-4), permitting them to express intense feeling (Romans 9:1-3), transmitting direct revelation (Deuteronomy 9:10), giving authoritative commands (1 Corinthians 7:10), expressing opinions (1 Corinthians 7:40), but always guided and guarded by the Holy Spirit (2 Peter 1:21) so that the product can be said to have been breathed out by God (2 Timothy 3:16).[7]

The Holy Spirit is thus the ultimate author of Scripture. Though He used erring humans as penmen, He superintended them as they wrote, keeping them from all error and omission.[8] The Scriptures, in the original autographs, possess the quality of freedom from error. In all their teachings they are in perfect accord with the truth.

The International Council of Biblical Inerrancy affirmed that

> inspiration involves a divine superintendence which preserved the writers in their word choices from using words that would falsify or distort the message of Scripture. . . . Evangelical Christians have wanted to avoid the notion that biblical writers were passive instruments like pens in the hands of God, yet at the same time they affirm that the net result of the process of inspiration would be the same. . . . Inspiration, however God brought it about, results in the *net effect* that every word of Scripture carries with it the weight of God's authority.[9]

Old and New Testaments Inspired

It is fascinating to observe that many Old Testament passages quoted in the New Testament are said to have the Holy Spirit or God as their author, even though a human prophet actually uttered the words in the Old. The words spoken by the human prophets thus carried divine authority.

Acts 1:16 is highly significant in this regard, for we read: "Brothers, the Scripture had to be fulfilled which *the Holy Spirit spoke long ago through the mouth of David* concerning Judas, who served as guide for those who arrested Jesus" (emphasis added). Though God used David (and other biblical writers) in the process of communicating His words, the Holy Spirit was in charge of the process so that no human error entered into the picture (Acts 4:24,25; Jeremiah 1:9; Zechariah 7:12).

We noted earlier that Scripture is "God-breathed." In 2 Timothy 3:16 we read, "All Scripture is God-breathed and is useful for teaching, rebuking, correcting and training in righteousness." The Greek form of "God-breathed" (or "inspired") in this verse is passive. This means the Bible is the *result* of the "breath of God." If the form were active, the verse would be saying that all the Bible breathes or exudes God. But here we are told that God *breathed out* something, namely, the Scriptures. The origin of the Bible—both Old and New Testaments—is thus seen to be God.

It is highly revealing that in 1 Timothy 5:18, the apostle Paul joins an Old Testament reference and a New Testament reference and calls them *both* (collectively) Scripture (Deuteronomy 25:4 and Luke 10:7).[10] It would not have been unusual in the context of first-century Judaism for an Old Testament passage to be called "Scripture." But for a New Testament book to be called "Scripture" so soon after it was written says volumes about Paul's view of the authority of New Testament books.

To be more specific, only three years or so had elapsed between the writing of the Gospel of Luke and the writing of 1 Timothy (Luke was written around A.D. 60; 1 Timothy was written around A.D. 63). Yet, despite this, Paul (himself a Jew—a "Hebrew of Hebrews") does not hesitate to place Luke on the same level of authority as the Old Testament Book of Deuteronomy.[11] He recognized that Luke's Gospel was "God-breathed," as was Deuteronomy.

Moreover, Paul understood that his own writings were inspired by God and therefore authoritative. The Synod of the Christian Reformed Church in 1961 summarized the scriptural evidence this way:

> Paul, while holding to the view of a canon of God-breathed writings which constitute "the oracles of God," claims for his own teaching, either oral or written, equal status. The word that he preached was not "the word of men" but "the word of God" (1 Thessalonians 2:13). That which he wrote was "the commandment of the Lord" (1 Corinthians 14:37). He that does not obey the writing of the apostle is to be disciplined (2 Thessalonians 3:14). If any

man preach or teach any other gospel than that which Paul proclaimed, he is to be accursed (Galatians 1:8-9). When Paul speaks as an apostle of Jesus Christ to the churches it is "Christ that speaketh" in him (2 Corinthians 13:3). Paul did not learn his gospel at the feet of men but rather received it "through revelations of Jesus Christ," Galatians 1:12, some of which were "exceeding great" (2 Corinthians 12:7).[12]

Objections to Inspiration

Down through the centuries, numerous critics have objected to the idea that the Bible is really God's Word. For those who have already made up their minds against the Bible—those who really don't want to be confused by the evidence—it seems that no amount of argumentation is enough to change their hardened viewpoint. It is nevertheless instructive to briefly respond to a few of these objections.

There are critics, to begin with, who have questioned the reliability of the Bible by arguing that the four Gospel writers were biased. They had theological "motives." Their intent was to convince readers of Jesus' deity, we are told, and hence their historical testimony is untrustworthy.

The fallacy here, as New Testament scholar Craig Blomberg put it so well, is

to imagine that telling a story for a purpose, even in the service of a cause one believes in passionately, necessarily forces one to distort history. In our modern era, some of the most reliable reporters of the Nazi Holocaust were Jews passionately committed to seeing such genocide never repeated.[13]

The New Testament is made up not of fairytales but rather eyewitness testimony (which was, as we have seen, superintended by the Holy Spirit). In 2 Peter 1:16 we read, "We did not follow cleverly invented stories when we told you about the power and coming of our Lord Jesus Christ, but we were eye-witnesses of his majesty." First John 1:1 affirms, "That which was from the beginning, which we have heard, which we have seen with our eyes, which we have looked at and our hands have touched—this we proclaim concerning the Word of life."

There are other critics today who argue against the Bible's validity by saying it is full of miraculous events. And since science disproves such miracles, the Bible is not to be trusted. This line of argumentation is flawed to the core.

To begin, science depends upon observation and replication. Miracles—such as the Incarnation and the resurrection—are by their very nature unprecedented events. No one can replicate these events in a laboratory. Hence, science simply cannot be the judge and jury as to whether or not these events occurred. The scientific method is useful for studying nature but not *super*-nature.

Besides, there is good historical reason to believe in the biblical accounts of miraculous events. One highly pertinent factor is the brief time that elapsed between Jesus' miraculous public ministry and the publication of the Gospels. *It was insufficient for the development of miracle legends.* Many eyewitnesses to Jesus' miracles would have still been alive to refute any untrue miracle accounts (see 1 Corinthians 15:6). Further, the men who witnessed these miracles (for example, Peter, James, and John) were of noble character, and were not prone to misrepresentation. They were even willing to give up their lives rather than deny their beliefs.

One often overlooked factor is that there were *hostile* witnesses to the miracles of Christ. When Jesus raised Lazarus from the dead, for example, none of the chief priests or Pharisees disputed the miracle (John 11:45-48). (If they could have disputed it, they would have.) Rather, their goal was simply to stop Jesus (verses 47-48). Because there were so many hostile witnesses who observed and scrutinized Christ's life, a successful fabrication of miracle stories during the time of His ministry would have been impossible.

Still other critics have attacked the validity of the Bible by arguing that the miracles recorded in the Bible are the fantasies of ignorant people in biblical times who did not understand the laws of nature. Such a claim is preposterous. People in biblical times *did* know enough of the laws of nature to recognize bona fide miracles. As C.S. Lewis put it,

> When St. Joseph discovered that his bride was pregnant, he was "minded to put her away." He knew enough biology for that. Otherwise, of course, he would not have regarded pregnancy as a proof of infidelity. When he accepted the Christian explanation, he regarded it as a miracle precisely because he knew enough of the laws of nature to know that this was a suspension of them.[14]

Moreover, Lewis observed,

> When the disciples saw Christ walking on the water they were frightened: they would not have been frightened unless they had known the laws of nature and known that this was an exception. If a man had no conception of a regular order in nature, then of course he could not notice departures from that order.[15]

Nothing can be viewed as "abnormal" until one has first grasped the "norm."

From time to time, I hear critics question the reliability of the Bible because of its "utterly unbelievable" account of the resurrection of Jesus Christ. Many critics have suggested that Jesus' followers simply *made up* the resurrection story.

Such a claim makes little sense when you think about it. It is very hard to believe that these followers of Jesus—predominantly Jewish and therefore aware of God's stern commandments against lying and bearing false witness—would make up such a lie, and then suffer and *give up their own lives* in defense of it. Moreover (as noted earlier), if Jesus' followers concocted events like the resurrection, wouldn't Jesus' critics have then immediately come forward to debunk these lies and put an end to Christianity once and for all?

The apostle Paul noted that the resurrected Christ appeared to more than 500 people at a single time, "most of whom are still alive" (1 Corinthians 15:6). If Paul had misrepresented the facts, wouldn't one of these 500 have come forward to dispute his claims?

There are also critics who allege that the Bible is not scientifically accurate in view of its frequent use of phenomenological language. Ecclesiastes 1:5, for example, refers to the sun "rising and setting." From a scientific perspective, the sun does not actually rise or set. But let's be fair. This is the same kind of language weather forecasters use. "Rising" and "setting" are accepted ways of describing what the sun appears to be doing from an earthly perspective. So, the Bible's use of such language does not prove there are scientific errors in it.

Finally, there are critics who argue against the Bible in view of the "many" contradictions in the Gospel accounts. These critics have failed to distinguish between *differences* and *contradictions*.

Although it is not my purpose in this chapter to respond to individual alleged contradictions (this has been done capably in several books that are readily available to Christians[16]), it is nevertheless important to note that "most of the ones who cry out about the 'millions of contradictions' in the Bible can't list more than three or four at the most of which they have any personal knowledge. The old adage that 'many put down the Bible before they pick it up' is sadly too true."[17] Bob Passantino gives us an important insight on this issue:

> If the gospels . . . were exactly the same, the critics would immediately cry, "Scheme! Collusion!" And yet, if the gospels did in reality contradict each other, the critics would cry even louder, "Fraud! How can a true God lie?" God has chosen the perfect road between these two positions. He has directed the minds and hearts of the Scripture writers to write exactly what He wanted but in their own styles. This allows for differences without contradictions.[18]

Archaeological Support for the Bible

Unlike other alleged holy books (the Book of Mormon, for example), the Bible's accuracy and reliability has been repeatedly proved and verified by archaeological finds produced by both believing *and* nonbelieving scholars and scientists. This includes verification for numerous customs, places, names, and events mentioned in the Bible.[19]

One among many examples is the fact that for many years the existence of the Hittites (a powerful people who lived during the time of Abraham) was questioned because no archaeological digs had uncovered anything about them. Critics claimed the Hittites were pure myth. Today, however, the critics are silenced. *Abundant* archaeological evidence for the existence of the Hittites during the time of Abraham has been uncovered.

Nelson Glueck, a specialist in ancient literature, did an exhaustive study of archaeology and concluded: "It can be stated categorically that no archaeological discovery has ever controverted a biblical reference."[20] Bible scholar Donald J. Wiseman has similarly concluded, "The geography of Bible lands and visible remains of antiquity were gradually recorded until today more than 25,000 sites within this region and dating to Old Testament times, in their broadest sense, have been located."[21] Well-known Bible scholar William F. Albright, following his comprehensive study, concluded: "Discovery after discovery has established the accuracy of innumerable details, and has brought increased recognition of the value of the Bible as a source of history."[22] Archaeological studies have been a true friend to the Christian Bible.

Manuscript Support for the New Testament

There are more than 24,800 partial and complete manuscript copies of the New Testament. There are also some 86,000 quotations from the early church fathers and several thousand lectionaries (church service books containing Scripture quotations used in the early centuries of Christianity).[23]

There are enough quotations from the early church fathers alone that even if we didn't have a single copy of the Bible, we could still reconstruct all but 11 verses of the entire New Testament. And this material was written within 150 to 200 years from the time of Christ.[24] Can any other ancient document boast of such widespread and reliable support?

In the many thousands of manuscript copies of the New Testament, scholars have discovered that there are some 200,000 "variants."[25] This may seem like a staggering figure to the uninformed mind. Critics like to cite such numbers to make it appear that the Bible is untrustworthy. To those who study the issue, however, the numbers are not so damning as it may initially appear. Indeed, a look at the hard evidence shows that the New Testament manuscripts are amazingly accurate and trustworthy.

Scholars have noted that out of the 200,000 variants, 99.9 percent hold virtually no significance whatsoever.[26] Many of these simply involve a missing letter in a word; some involve reversing the order of two words (such as "Christ Jesus" instead of "Jesus Christ"); some involve the absence of one or more insignificant words. When all the facts are put on the table, only about 40 of the variants have any *real* significance—and even then, not a single doctrine of the Christian faith or any moral commandment is affected by them.[27]

Now, it is very important to understand precisely what qualifies as a "variant" in textual studies, and how a "variant" differs from an "error." Norman Geisler and Ronald Brooks explain it this way:

> With all those manuscripts, there are a lot of little differences. It is easy for someone to leave the wrong impression by saying that there are 200,000 "errors" that have crept into the Bible when the word should be "variants." A variant is counted any time one copy is different from any other copy and it is counted again in every copy where it appears. So when a single word is spelled differently in 3,000 copies, that is counted as 3,000 variants. In fact, there

are only 10,000 places where variants occur and most of those are matters of spelling and word order. There are less than 40 places in the New Testament where we are really not certain which reading is original, but not one of these has any effect on a central doctrine of the faith.[28]

It must also be stressed that the sheer volume of manuscripts we have in our possession greatly narrows the margin of doubt regarding what the original biblical document said. The number of biblical manuscripts increases proportionately our means of correcting minor errors, so that the margin of doubt left in the process of recovering the exact original wording is remarkably small.[29]

Manuscript Evidence for the Old Testament

The Dead Sea Scrolls prove the accuracy of the transmission of the Old Testament books of the Bible. In fact, in these scrolls discovered at Qumran in 1947, we have Old Testament manuscripts that date about a thousand years earlier (150 B.C.) than the other Old Testament manuscripts previously in our possession (which dated to A.D. 980).[30] The significant thing is that when one compares the two sets of manuscripts, it is clear that they are essentially the same, with very few changes. The fact that manuscripts separated by a thousand years are essentially the same indicates the incredible accuracy of the Old Testament's manuscript transmission.

The copy of the book of Isaiah discovered at Qumran illustrates this accuracy. Dr. Gleason Archer comments:

> Even though the two copies of Isaiah discovered in Qumran Cave 1 near the Dead Sea in 1947 were a thousand years earlier than the oldest dated manuscript previously known (A.D. 980), they proved to be *word for word identical* with our standard Hebrew Bible in more than 95 percent of the text. The 5 percent of variation consisted chiefly of obvious slips of the pen and variations in spelling.[31]

The Dead Sea Scrolls *prove* that the copyists of biblical manuscripts took great care in going about their work. These copyists knew they were duplicating God's Word. Hence they went to incredible lengths to insure that no error crept into their work. The scribes carefully counted every line, word, syllable, and letter to guarantee accuracy.[32]

From manuscript discoveries like the Dead Sea Scrolls, we have concrete evidence that today's Old Testament Scripture, for all practical purposes, is essentially the same as it was when originally inspired by God and recorded in the Bible.[33] Combine this with the massive amount of manuscript evidence we have for the New Testament, and it is clear that the Christian Bible is a trustworthy and reliable book.

God's Preservation of the Bible Through the Ages

The Westminster Confession declares:

> The Old Testament in Hebrew and the New Testament in Greek, being immediately inspired by God and, by His singular care and providence *kept pure in all ages*, are therefore authentic; so in all controversies of religion, the Church is finally to appeal unto them.[34]

This confession makes a very important point here. The fact is, the God who had the sovereign power to *inspire* the Scriptures in the first place is surely going to continue exercising His power and sovereign control in the *preservation* of Scripture.

God's preservational work is illustrated in the text of the Bible itself. By examining how Christ viewed the Old Testament, we see that He had full confidence that the Scriptures He used (*which were manuscript copies of Old Testament books*) had been faithfully preserved through the centuries. Apologist Greg L. Bahnsen summarizes this point as follows:

> Because Christ raised no doubts about the adequacy of the Scripture as His contemporaries knew them, we can safely assume that the first-century text of the Old Testament

was a wholly adequate representation of the divine Word originally given. Jesus regarded the extant copies of His day as so approximate to the originals in their message that He appealed to those copies as authoritative. The respect that Jesus and His apostles held for the extant Old Testament text is, at base, an expression of the confidence in God's providential preservation of the copies and translations as substantially identical with the inspired originals.[35]

King Solomon possessed what was obviously a copy of the original Mosaic law (see Deuteronomy 17:18), yet it was considered by him to contain God's "decrees and commands, his laws and requirements" (1 Kings 2:3). Ezra clearly had only a copy of God's law, yet he considered it authoritative in his ministry (Ezra 7:14). As Bahnsen sums up, "the Bible itself indicates that copies can faithfully reflect the original text and therefore function authoritatively."[36]

I'm Convinced

There is more that needs to be said, but space forbids. Suffice it to say, I believe that anyone who objectively looks at the evidence can only come to the conclusion that the Bible is the Word of God. The Scriptures are

> God preaching, God talking, God telling, God instructing, God setting before us the right way to think and speak about him. The Scriptures are God showing us himself: God communicating to us who he is and what he has done so that in the response of faith we may truly know him and live our lives in fellowship with him.[37]
> *Selah!*

Conclusion

THE TRUE GOD

Tal Brooke

"The grass withers, the flower fades; but the word of our God shall stand for ever" (Isaiah 40:8, *Revised Berkeley*).

As we saw in the previous chapter, the Bible stands at the apex of all books ever written in history. There are enough amazing facts about it to fill a *Guinness Book of World Records,* yet few people are aware of them. Indeed, few have bothered to do more than flip through the Bible once or twice in a lifetime. For most people, the Bible is merely a book filling a space in a bookcase collecting dust. Such people often have a smooth array of pat answers which they can summon up when questioned about the Bible, but the truth is that public ignorance about the Bible is staggering. This is not as it should be, for the Bible refers to itself as the Word of God, unlike any other book in existence.

Aldous Huxley once said that he never really had an intellectual problem with Christianity; he had a *moral* one, for he did not deny the facts or the inevitable sense they made. Likewise, there may be a thousand synods whose aim it is to change the simple truth and evolve some new insight; there may be a new papal bull or some inner echelon that claims special revelation. But the fact remains, "The word of our God endures forever" (Isaiah 40:8). And the pages of Scripture are open, plain for all to see.

Is the Bible's ultimate author *really* God and not the amazingly harmonious lineage of prophets and scribes who did the actual speaking and recording? Have God's communications been coming through clearly? Or, to look at the problem from another angle, if there really is a God who created the universe, then is it not within His power to actually enter history and reveal Himself? And would He not seek to do so if His creation of man had a purpose after all, and was not some random event? If man indeed does have a purpose, then God would be *negligent* if man were left alone to grope in the dark and puzzle things out for himself, especially if it were beyond man's capacities to arrive at ultimate solutions.

From our human perspective, we could say that the complex creation around us plus our innate abilities seem to testify to the fact that man has significance. We are more than just a bag of chemicals. Man, through all his faculties, can receive and understand communications about the meaning and purpose of the whys and wherefores of existence itself. It therefore stands to reason that God could and would reach from the infinite down to the finite, cross the gulf that none of us could ever cross, and directly intervene in our world.

That is exactly what the Bible claims has happened. God intervened in history, and the Bible is the record of that intervention. Man did not just perform some religious rite and summon so great a one as God into speaking. Rather, God Himself purposed His communications in His own way and on His own terms, which has always been a problem to many.

God chose people of incredible integrity through whom He would give His Word. His prophets were utterly different from the mediums and psychics of Babylon and the East, both in simple, humble, human character, and in morals. Rather than receiving subjective inner experiences, His prophets were enlivened with active and not passive minds. They felt the awesome power of their living God, and they were 100-percent accurate in what they said and predicted, with miracles occurring time and time again to support and verify the truth of their words. Above all, they testified that their revelations were from a transcendent, holy God, before whom all they could do was to fall upon their faces. They never even hinted at a divine-within experience or a higher-self experience.

Why the need for revelation? Because even if the human race had a billion years of uninterrupted laboratory investigation, and had broken down all the material and mechanical facts behind the physical universe, we would still be ignorant of the much higher qualities of spiritual reality. Not that there is not a clear continuum tying the physical to the spiritual, but simply, from our point of view, we lack the resources to tie them together. Something lesser cannot transcend itself to understand the greater. An idiot will never understand cybernetics or James Joyce. And certainly man's billion-year-old laboratory would never go beyond the universe to peer into the character of an infinite God. We must understand this in order to comprehend the need for revelation.

Consider that in America today we all stand upon a foundation of prior events in history—civilizations have come and gone; wars, eras, fashions, inventions, and great men have preceded us, all of them directly affecting where we are right now. America did not just spring out of nowhere; it emerged from a historical progression of events, and there is plenty of evidence today that they took place. The same historical argument holds true for Christ's appearance.

The book of Acts records the fact that at one point 500 people saw the resurrected Christ in full view. J.N.D. Anderson, a professor of law, says:

> Think of the number of witnesses, over 500. Think of the character of the witnesses, men and women who gave the world the highest ethical teaching it has ever known, and who even on the testimony of enemies lived it out in their lives. Think of the psychological absurdity of picturing a little band of defeated cowards cowering in an upper room one day and a few days later transformed into a company

that no persecution could silence—and then attempting to attribute this dramatic change to nothing more convincing than a miserable fabrication they were trying to foist upon the world. That simply would not make sense.[1]

No one will proceed with a willful deception when it involves his life, and hosts of the early Christians were painfully martyred. This makes it clearer why the contemporaries of the New Testament writers did not refute their writings, and how these eyewitness accounts could be written in their day and stand.

These eyewitnesses were further emboldened by their understanding of prophecy. Written in great detail centuries before Christ's birth, they state where and when He would be born; of what lineage; and His purpose, mission, death, and ascent. The staggering fact is that 332 specific Old Testament prophecies center on Christ.

Moreover, in every Gospel, in chapter after chapter, Christ is found claiming incredible things for Himself, unlike anyone who ever existed. Christ claimed the power to forgive sins (Mark 2:5), He controlled the forces of nature (Mark 4:39), He claimed authority over venerable tradition (Matthew 15:1-7), and He boldly predicted His own resurrection and return to judge the world (John 2:19). As many have observed, eventually the authorities had enough of it and put Him to death for blasphemy. Jesus was not unwilling to die, for He saw death as part of His redeeming mission (Matthew 26:28). But He reiterated time and again that death would not hold Him, and that His resurrection would decisively prove His claims.

The one nation that would not take a man's claim to deity lightly was the Jewish nation, which feared and venerated the names of their God (Jehovah and Elohim, for example). If a man were to try to set himself up and pretend the role, Israel was not the place to do it; Greece, Rome, Egypt, or Persia, perhaps, but not Israel. As He led an utterly sober and blameless life, Christ would describe Himself in the identical Old Testament language used for Jehovah alone: "Before Abraham was,

I am" (John 8:58); "He who has seen Me has seen the Father" (John 14:9 NASB); and, like Jehovah, He was referred to as the Creator (John 1:3), the Savior (Titus 2:13), the Judge (John 5:22), the Light of the world (John 8:12), the Glory of God (Matthew 17:1-21), the Redeemer (Acts 20:28), the Forgiver of sins (Mark 2:1-12), and the Alpha and Omega (Revelation 1:17-18). All of these are attributed to God in the Old Testament. The Jews knew that only one was deserving of worship—God. And Christ received worship from a leper, from Thomas, and others. The epistle to the Hebrews says that even the angels adored and worshiped Christ (Hebrews 1:6), an honor that was out of the question for a mere mortal. When Stephen the martyr was stoned to death, he *prayed* to Christ (as God) to receive his spirit (Acts 7:59).

It seems evident that Christ's claim to deity was very real, and the implications of what this means have never been put better than in the words of C.S. Lewis:

> I am trying here to prevent anyone saying the really foolish thing that people often say about Him: "I'm ready to accept Jesus as a great moral teacher, but I don't accept His claim to be God." That is the one thing we must not say. A man who was merely a man and said the sort of things Jesus said would not be a great moral teacher. He would either be a lunatic—on a level with the man who says he is a poached egg—or else he would be the Devil of Hell. You must make your choice. Either this man was, and is, the Son of God: or else a madman or something worse.[2]

The counterfeit cannot exist without the real. It is parasitic upon the real. And the counterfeit Christs and their gospels in no way could gain the hearing they do without hearers wanting to hear their messages, often filled with false promises. Nor could they gain a hearing as counterfeits without the reality of the genuine Christ. *He* is the cornerstone of history—and not them—as time and eternity will show.

Appendix A

GNOSTICISM AND MODERNISM: IS THERE A CONNECTION?

Modernism, as Phillip Johnson likes to point out, is the reigning belief system of our age. It is a combination of what Johnson calls atheistic naturalism and liberal rationalism, both of which came out of the Enlightenment's exaltation of human reason as the final measure of all things?[1]

Gnosticism and modernism would appear to be at the two ends of the worldview spectrum. Gnosticism posits a material world that is illusion, while the true world is the world of the spirit. Naturalistic modernism, on the other hand, concerns itself with knowing only those things that can be known within the confines of material reality; nature is "all there is." Gnosticism looks for a hidden truth that can only be discerned by the elite few. Modernism, at least the nineteenth-century variety, looks for an *open* truth that is equally revealed to all in the natural world.

Beyond these and other very substantial differences, however, there is at least one very interesting way in which modernism and Gnosticism are not so grossly incompatible. Both lead to a radical dualism between the material and the immaterial. Gnosticism, of course, views the material world as evil and inferior. Naturalism views the material world as "all there is," and regards everything else as "immaterial." These dualisms cut in opposite directions, of course. But the essential nature of a divided universe is established in both. It is only a matter of switching the priorities of modernism from

269

the material to the immaterial, as we see happening in post-modernism, to bring it into essential alignment with the Gnostic worldview.

The modernism we know today is not the naively confident rationalist modernism of the nineteenth century, however. It is a bruised and battered modernism that is not nearly so sure about reality as it used to be. Those in the halls of science cling to the old view of things. But outside the halls, and even within (chaos theorists, for example), there are many who are not sure about the nature of objective reality, or that there is such a thing.

The intellectual worldview of the late twentieth-century is a curious mix of the definite and the amorphous, the iron and the clay. We have come too far and rely too heavily on technology to deny that science is a wonderful tool. But we are no longer confident enough in the absolutism on which it is based to declare right and wrong, truth and error, beauty and perversity. Modernism has painted itself into an epistemological corner, and the only way out is to jump from the rational into . . . *the irrational.*

Deeper Knowledge

Jesus Seminar luminary Marcus Borg writes:

> I have argued against the kind of "historical reductionism" that says that something must be historically true to be true. To use an example, I regularly say, "I don't think the virgin birth happened, but I think the stories of the virgin birth are powerfully true."[2]

Enter irrationality! As a backdrop, the "death of God" proclaimed in the nineteenth century was perhaps an inevitable end-product of the Enlightenment. It represents the uncontrolled desire of man to be bound by nothing outside his own reason. Ironically, as Phillip Johnson shows in his book *Reason in the Balance*,[3] this desperate attempt to liberate reason from the shackles of superstition leads inexorably to the end of reason itself.

Some of the early outer workings of this death of reason were noted by Albert Schweitzer, who pointed out the essential flaws in the modernist criticism of the nineteenth-century "First Quest." Schweitzer observed that the supposedly "objective" scholarship of the First Quest was producing pictures of the "historical Jesus" that were remarkably conformed to the ideologies of the scholars who were doing the work.

Rudolph Bultmann, who presided over the cleanup of this embarrassment to modernist criticism, came up with the reason: the true historical Jesus was beyond recovery because the earliest chroniclers were not interested in preserving true historical records. Bultmann said the earliest Christians had created myths according to their own messianic desires. Bultmann was far from done, however. As his crowning achievement, he provided the true interpretation of Jesus: the true Christ—the Christ *of faith*—was the Christ that the church had invented and canonized in its officially sanctioned book of myths, the New Testament.

The epistemological crisis of twentieth-century biblical criticism is part of, or perhaps the precipitator of, the larger crisis of modernism in this century. As a result of this crisis, the modernist concept of truth has been disfigured beyond recognition. The classical beliefs about truth have been declared dead, along with God. In their place are a set of assumptions that define a kind of relativistic truth: all truth is conditioned by its source; all truth is a function of the one who believes it to be true. We can therefore be skeptical, the modernists tell us, about any claims of an objective or universal truth (such as the claim that "Jesus is Lord").

If these things are *assumed* to be true, the question is how to go on from here. The conundrum of postmodernism is how to get beyond reason. Increasingly, it seems, the intellectual elite of the West believe they have found answers that supersede the boundaries of rationalistic reason—answers that have interesting parallels in the belief systems of the East, such as Hinduism and Buddhism. These beliefs have long-standing traditions of viewing reason as inferior to man's spiritual nature in its ability to discern true reality.

This exaltation of the intuitive/spiritual and devaluation of the rational/material is a trait shared by the Gnostics as well. According to Marcus Borg, and the Gnostics before him, it is not the flesh and blood drama that is played out in the hours, minutes, and seconds of our material existence that determines reality. It is some "spiritual" truth, independent of such material mundanities, that determines what is true.

ABOUT THE
CONTRIBUTORS

▼*Brooks Alexander* is the founder and research director of SCP (Spiritual Counterfeits Project), a Berkeley-based conservative think tank that researches and critiques new religions, cults, and cultural trends. He earned a degree in political science from Texas Christian University, and did five years of graduate work in international politics (at Texas Christian) and law (at the University of Texas) before he "turned on, tuned in, and dropped out" in 1963 to become part of the emerging drug and occult counterculture. He migrated to New York City, then to California, arriving in Los Angeles the day the Watts riots started. He later became part of the Haight-Ashbury scene in 1967. Alexander became a Christian in 1969 in Berkeley and founded SCP in 1973 to help Christians and others understand the changes our culture is undergoing.

▼*Tal Brooke,* quoted in *Newsweek* and numerous other media, is a recognized expert on the wave of new spiritual trends inundating the West, from New Age to the occult. He is the president and chairman of SCP, and has authored eight books, including the bestseller *When the World Will Be As One.* His book *Lord of the Air* chronicles his years in India as Sai Baba's top Western disciple. His work has been recognized in *Marquis Who's Who in the World, Contemporary Authors,* and *The International Who's Who of Authors.* As editor of the *SCP Journal,*

Brooke received an Evangelical Press Association first-place award in the critical review category in the touted annual national contest. Brooke grew up in an American diplomatic family, spending the majority of his childhood in England, Europe, and the Middle East. He graduated from the University of Virginia and Princeton. He has also been a guest lecturer at Cambridge, Oxford, Princeton, Sorbonne, Berkeley, the University of Virginia, and the University of Edinburgh.

▼*Peter Jones* has a growing reputation as an expert on Gnosticism and its connections to the New Age and neopagan movements. He is a professor of theology at Westminster Theological Seminary in California, having obtained a ThM from Harvard Divinity School and a PhD from Princeton. He is the author of *The Gnostic Empire Strikes Back* and *Spirit Wars*. His wife Rebecca, when not keeping an eye on their "remaining" seven children (several have finished university), edits and writes—often assisting Peter in his research and publishing tasks. Their son Julian was one of SCP's most gifted interns when he was a student at UC Berkeley! (SCP is now eyeing other members of the family.)

▼*John Moore,* SCP associate editor, is a writer and computer consultant living in Oakland with his wife and two daughters. When not working on SCP articles, John serves as a consultant for the Disabled Students Program at UC Berkeley. Prior to that, John was a doctoral student in the UC Berkeley school of law, but felt called by God into other work. He presently oversees the SCP web page among numerous other SCP responsibilities (including SCP's database).

▼*Ron Rhodes,* formerly of Christian Research Institute (a "regular" on the national *Bible Answer Man* broadcast), is president of Reasoning from the Scriptures Ministries. He holds a doctorate from Dallas Theological Seminary and he is well known in the field of apologetics through his numerous books (over a dozen, two of them becoming Gold Medallion

Award finalists) and frequent appearances in the media. His books include *Christ Before the Manger, The Heart of Christianity, The Complete Book of Bible Answers, Angels Among Us, Reasoning from the Scriptures with the Jehovah's Witnesses,* and *When Cultists Ask* (co-authored with Dr. Norman Geisler). He lectures extensively across the United States. He resides in Southern California with his wife Kerri and their two children.

▼*Brad Scott* is author of *Embraced by the Darkness,* an analysis and refutation of the root beliefs of New Age thought. The book includes Brad's long pilgrimage through Western occultism and Eastern mysticism leading to his conversion to Christ. Currently he is working on a new book, *Progress Without Reason.* He teaches at Golden Gate University where he is an adjunct associate professor of English and communication.

NOTES

The Conspiracy to Silence the Son of God

1. Thanks to such forerunners as Jesuit scholar Teilhard de Chardin, who pursued a global planetary faith using the seductive pragmatic arugument to syncretize the religions into one. Of course, the Gnostics almost 2000 years ago tried to infiltrate the church with similar beliefs, but were thwarted by a robust church (via the Council of Nicea) that saw the writing on the wall.

Chapter 1: Jesus and the Den of Thieves

1. See Julius Wellhausen, *Prolegomena to the History of Israel* (Atlanta, GA: Scholars Press, 1994).

Chapter 2: Preparing for a Global Religion

1. Teilhard de Chardin, *Human Energy* (New York: Harcourt, Brace, Jovanovich, 1970), pp. 37-38.
2. Teilhard de Chardin, *The Heart of Matter* (New York: Harcourt, Brace, Jovanovich, 1979), p. 53.
3. R. C. Zaehner, *Zen, Drugs, and Mysticism* (New York: Vintage Books, 1974), p. 179.
4. Ibid., p. 188.
5. Teilhard de Chardin, *The Phenomenon of Man* (New York: Harper Colophon Books, 1975), p. 272.
6. Teilhard de Chardin, *Letters to Two Friends* (New York: New American Library, 1968), p. 187.
7. Zaehner, p. 179.
8. Ibid., p. 180.
9. Ibid.
10. Ursula King, *Towards a New Mysticism: Teilhard de Chardin and Eastern Religions* (London: Collins, 1980), p. 98.
11. Ibid., p. 172.
12. Teilhard de Chardin, *How I Believe* (New York: Harper & Row, 1969), pp. 81-82.
13. Ibid., p. 80.
14. Ibid., p. 85.
15. King, p. 92.
16. Zaehner, p. 181.

Chapter 3: Apostasy and the Descent into Paganism

1. Donna Steichen, *Ungodly Rage* (San Francisco: Ignatius Press, 1993), p. 71.
2. Ibid., p. 21.
3. Ibid., p. 13.
4. Ibid., p. 21.
5. Ibid., p. 32.
6. This phrase is from a public lecture by Rosemary Radford Ruether, reported in

Donna Steichen, *Ungodly Rage* (San Francisco: Ignatius Press, 1993), p. 32.

7. Rosemary Radford Ruether, *Women-Church: Theology and Practice of Feminist Liturgical Communities* (San Francisco: Harper and Row, 1985), p. 223. The very phrase, "Women-Church," is at odds with the biblical notion of a community that is inclusive of people from every nation and tongue—both males and females.

8. Ibid.

9. Miriam Starhawk, *Yoga Journal*, May-June 1986, p. 59, cited in Ruth Tucker, *Another Gospel: Alternative Religions and the New Age Movement* (Grand Rapids: Zondervan, 1989), p. 340.

10. Ruether, p. 171.

11. Steichen, p. 55.

12. Ruether, p. 175.

13. Ibid., p. 145.

14. Ibid, pp. 220, 229.

15. Matthew Fox, *The Coming of the Cosmic Christ* (San Francisco: Harper and Row, 1988), pp. 170, 180.

16. Transcript from tapes of the addresses given at the RE-Imagining Conference in Minneapolis, 1993, published by Good News: A Forum for Scriptural Christianity Within the United Methodist Church, January 1994, p. 13, insert added.

17. In particular, *The Presbyterian Layman* (PCUSA) and *Good News* (United Methodist).

18. Steichen, pp. 295-370.

19. Berit Kjos, "An Unholy Renaissance of Sacred Sexuality," *Southern California Christian Times*, July 1994, p. 9.

20. James R. Edwards, "Earthquake in the Mainline," *Christianity Today*, 14 November 1994, p. 39. This is a profound analysis of the heretical opinions voiced at the conference.

21. Peter Berger, "The Other Face of Gaia," *First Things*, August-September 1994, pp. 15-17.

22. See *World*, September 1993.

23. See Nancy Wilson, *A Lesbian Ecu-Terrorist Outs the Bible for the Queer Millennium* (San Francisco: HarperSanFrancisco, 1996).

24. *Books for the Nineties* [Catalog] (San Francisco: HarperSanFrancisco, 1996), p. 10.

25. Virginia Mollenkott, *Sensuous Spirituality: Out from Fundamentalism* (New York: Crossroads, 1992), p. 16.

26. Ibid., p. 16.

27. Ibid., p. 27.

28. Ibid., p. 42.

29. Ibid., p. 49.

30. Ibid., p. 118.

31. Ibid., p. 139.

32. Ibid., p. 100. By "easy" Mollenkott clearly means what most would call "casual sex."

33. Ibid., p. 167.

34. Transcript of tapes of the RE-Imagining Conference, p. 11.

35. Robert W. Funk, Roy W. Hoover, and the Jesus Seminar, *The Five Gospels: The Search*

for the Authentic Words of Jesus (New York: Macmillan, 1993).

36. Ibid., dedication page.
37. The following information is drawn from Horton Harris, *David Friedrich Strauss and His Theology* (Cambridge: The University Press, 1973), p. 16.
38. Ibid., p. 2.
39. Ibid., p. 13.
40. *Strauss's Gesammelte Schriften*, ed. Zeller, 1876-78; cited in Harris, p. 16, inserts added.
41. Marcus Borg, *Meeting Jesus Again for the First Time* (San Francisco: HarperSanFrancisco, 1993).
42. Marcus J. Borg, "Me and Jesus: The Journey Home," *The Fourth R,* July-August 1993, p. 9.
43. Scott McKnight, "Who Is Jesus: An Introduction to Jesus Studies," *Jesus Under Fire: Modern Scholarship Re-invents the Historical Jesus,* eds. Michael J. Wilkin and J. P. Moreland (Grand Rapids: Zondervan, 1995), p. 70, n. 22. Professor McKnight here mentions a master's thesis written under his direction at Trinity Evangelical Divinity School by Dana K. Ostby, "The Historical Jesus and the Supernatural World: A Shift in the Modern Critical Worldview with Special Emphasis on the Writings of Marcus Borg" (1991), which traces Borg's theological development.
44. Alan Morrison, *The Serpent and the Cross: Religious Corruption in an Evil Age* (Birmingham, UK: K&M Books, 1994), p. 568. Huston Smith has published with the Theosophical Publishing House of Wheaton, Illinois [Huston Smith, *Beyond the Post-Modern Mind* (Wheaton, IL: Theosophical Publishing House, 1989)]. Readers will recall that the Theosophical Society was founded toward the end of the nineteenth century by the spiritualist Helena Petrovna Blavatsky, and later headed by Annie Besant. Both women are now considered foremothers of the New Age movement. An authority on the history of the occult calls the Theosophical Society "the very pillar of the late nineteenth century revival of the occult." See James Webb, *The Occult Establishment* (La Salle, IL: Open Court, 1976), pp. 25, 553.
45. Ibid.
46. Borg, "Me and Jesus," p. 9.
47. See Herbert J. Pollitt, *The Inter-Faith Movement: The New Age Enters the Church* (Edinburgh: Banner of Truth, 1996). See also Peter Jones, *The Gnostic Empire Strikes Back* (Phillipsburg, NJ: Presbyterian and Reformed, 1992), and my book *Spirit Wars: Pagan Revival in Christian America* (Escondido, CA: Main Entry Editions, 1996).
48. Hippolytus, *The Refutation of All Heresies*, 4.45.

Chapter 4: The New Christ of Paganism

1. "Jesus Christ, the same yesterday, today and forever" (Hebrews 13:8).
2. Shirley MacLaine, *Going Within* (New York: Bantam, 1989), p. 218.
3. Madeleine L'Engle, *A Stone for a Pillow* (Wheaton, IL: Harold Shaw Publishing, 1986), p. 201, cited in Samantha Scott and Brenda Smith, *Trojan Horse: How the New Age Infiltrates the Church* (Lafayette, LA: Huntingdon House, 1993), p. 190.
4. Cited in William Oddie, *What Will Happen to God? Feminism and the Reconstruction of Christian Belief* (San Francisco: Ignatius Press, 1988), p. 12.
5. Matthew Fox, *The Coming of the Cosmic Christ:* (San Francisco: Harper and Row, 1988), pp. 129-55. Donna Steichen makes the same judgment of Fox's "Cosmic

Christ": "closer to the monist 'oversoul' of Eastern Religions, New Agers and Starhawk's 'imminent goddess' than to Jesus Christ," *Ungodly Rage* (San Francisco: Ignatius Press, 1993), p. 232.

6. Rosemary Radford Ruether, *Gaia and God: An Ecofeminist Theology of Earth Healing* (San Francisco: HarperSanFrancisco, 1992), p. 242.

7. Scott and Smith, p. x. Note that L'Engle has been published and promoted by numerous Christian magazines and lectured on Christian college campuses.

8. Ibid., p. 54, citing Madeleine L'Engle, *The Irrational Season* (New York: Seabury Press, 1979), 169.

9. Scott and Smith, p. xi. Note the following facts about L'Engle:

    'Engle repeatedly claims, "I know nothing about the New Age movement, nor do I care to." Yet she is author-in-residence and assistant librarian at the Cathedral of St. John the Divine in New York City, where she also serves as a lay preacher. The Cathedral was credited in the *New Age Journal* as being the "Miracle on 112th Street." It houses Shinto and Native American shrines, has displayed a female figure of Christ called "Christa," and performs T'ai Chi rituals and Earth Masses. David Spangler, one of the world's most admired New Age teachers, goes there frequently to perform Eucharist. David Spangler believes that Christ is the same force as Lucifer. . . . Omega, a New Age Institute for holistic studies, lists Madeleine L'Engle as a faculty member, along with her close friend, "New Age" psychologist, M. Scott Peck. . . . Other leading New Age figures she endorses, quotes, and promotes include: Marilyn Ferguson, author of "the watershed New Age classic," *The Aquarian Conspiracy*; physicist Fritjof Capra, author of a Bantam New Age book *The Tao of Physics*; and Lawrence LeShan, author of *The Medium, the Mystic and the Physicist* and New Age-labeled book, *How to Meditate.*

10. Ibid., p. 47.

11. Ibid.

12. M. S. Sjoo and B. Mor, *The Ancient Religion of the Great Cosmic Mother of All* (United Kingdom: Rainbow Press, 1981), p. 289.

13. Chris Griscom, *Ecstasy Is a New Frequency* (Santa Fe, NM: Bear and Company, 1987), p. 137.

14. Ibid., p. 138.

15. Ibid., pp. 141-43.

16. Interestingly, in Hinduism, meditation on the self is associated with the serpent. See Tal Brooke, *Lord of the Air* (Eugene, OR: Harvest House, 1990), p. 143.

17. Carol Christ, "Why Women Need the Goddess: Phenomenological, Psychological and Political Reflections," in Carol Christ and Judith Plaskow, *WomanSpirit Rising: A Feminist Reader in Religion* (San Francisco: Harper and Row, 1979), p. 277.

18. This is a subtle reference to meditation similar to that proposed by Chris Griscom and Shirley MacLaine. Its origin is paganism and not Christianity.

19. Ninian Smart and Steven Konstantine, *Christian Systematic Theology* (Minneapolis: Fortress Press, 1991), p. 441.

20. Romans 1:25.

21. Miriam Starhawk, *The Spiritual Dance* (San Francisco: Harper, 1979).

22. Obliquely, Timothy C. Morgan in his essay "RE-Imagining Labeled 'Reckless,' "

Christianity Today, 18 July 1994, p. 49, admits to this when he says: "it has been the PCUSA's inattention to the women's movement and feminism that, in part, placed the denominational leaders in hot water with local congregations." This could be said for many churches and organizations as well.

23. Oddie, p. 11.
24. Ibid., p. 4.
25. Naomi Goldenberg, *Changing the Gods: Feminism and the End of Traditional Religions* (Boston: Beacon Press, 1979), p. 41. See also Sjoo and Mor, p. 197:

> The very religions that have turned human sexuality into pathology and nightmare should not be allowed to determine how public school children should learn about sex! Most of our American misogyny, especially ideas about menstrual "uncleanness," comes from the Bible; for this reason alone the Bible should be kept from public schools, as a major source of the cultural defamation of women. Surely the First Amendment should protect young girls from being told "God" made them to be "unclean . . ."

26. Goldenberg, p. 5.
27. Sjoo and Mor, p. 344.
28. Peter Jones, *The Gnostic Empire Strikes Back* (Phillipsburg, NJ: Presbyterian and Reformed Publishing, 1992), p. 48.
29. See Carol P. Christ, "Symbols of Goddess and God in Feminist Theology," *The Book of the Goddess: An Introduction to Her Religion*, ed. Carl Olson (New York: Crossroads, 1983), p. 241.
30. Mary Daly, *Beyond God the Father: Towards a Philosophy of Women's Liberation* (Boston: Beacon Press, 1985), cited by Oddie, p. 19. See also Emily Culpepper, "The Spiritual, Political Journey of a Feminist Freethinker," *After Patriarchy: Feminist Transformations of the World Religions*, eds. Paula M. Cooey et al. (Maryknoll, NY: Orbis Books, 1991), p. 154. Culpepper believes in the second coming of a female Christ. Oddie notes: "Though the extract from Mary Daly which I have just quoted is by no means the most immoderate or the most anti-Christian that could have been found in the book from which it is taken, it remains immovably on Christian feminist lists of recommended reading." As an example of this influence, Roman Catholic theologian Katherine Zappone, in *The Hope for Wholeness: A Spirituality for Feminists* (Mystic, CN: Twenty Third Publications, 1991), p. vii, acknowledges that "Mary Daly's sensitivity, generosity, and amazing breadth and depth of vision provided a wellspring for this book." On the following page she acknowledges the support of "Alan Connors of the Aquinas Academy in Sydney, the Dominican Sisters of Adelaide, and Women and the Australian Church (W.A.T.A.C.), Pauline Smoothy and Greg Riely of the Catholic Education Office in Brisbane." Though Daly (who, as we have noted, identifies the second coming with the coming of Antichrist) formally left the Roman church, her work is still widely read and greatly appreciated within it.
31. MacLaine, p. 189.
32. Sjoo and Mor, p. 51.
33. Tal Brooke, *When the World Will Be As One* (Eugene, OR: Harvest House, 1989), p. 210.
34. Madame Blavatsky—who died in 1891 but whose writings are still held in high esteem in the New Age movement—attributed redemption to Satan.
35. Marcus J. Borg, *Jesus: A New Vision: Spirit, Culture and the Life of Discipleship* (San

Francisco: Harper, 1987), p. 8. With slightly more nuance, Stephen J. Patterson, *The Gospel of Thomas and Jesus* (Sonoma, CA: Polebridge Press, 1993), p. 231, states: "It is becoming ever more difficult to imagine a Jesus who reflected upon his own death, and preached an imminent apocalyptic judgment to be visited upon the world."

36. Heinz O. Guenther, "The Sayings Gospel Q and the Quest For Aramaic Sources: Rethinking Christian Origins," *Semeia* 55 (1991), p. 41.

37. Elizabeth Schüssler Fiorenza, *Miriam's Child, Sophia's Prophet* (New York: Continuum, 1994).

38. This is Robinson's proposal in 1988, through an exegesis of "Q 13:34." See "Very Goddess and Very Man: Jesus' Better Self," *Images of the Feminine in Gnosticism,* ed. Karen L. King (Philadelphia: Fortress, 1988), pp. 113-27.

39. Borg, pp. 190-91. Borg is the associate professor of religious studies at Oregon State University and a frequent contributor to *The Christian Century.*

40. Ibid., p. 184.

41. Ibid., p. 199.

42. Francis Watson, "Is John's Christology Adoptionist?" *The Glory of Christ in the New Testament: Studies in Christology,* eds. L.D. Hurst and N.T. Wright (Oxford: Clarendon Press, 1987), p. 114.

43. Ibid., p. 117.

44. 7.51.20–52.10, cited in ibid., p. 120.

45. Davies, "Christology and Protology," p. 663. See also George J. Riley, associate professor of New Testament at the School of Theology at Claremont, CA. In his book *Resurrection Reconsidered: Thomas and John in Controversy* (Minneapolis: Fortress Press, 1994), he argued that the Gospel of Thomas's view of the resurrection of Jesus as a spiritual event reflects the authentic Christian view.

46. Ibid., p. 679.

47. Ibid., p. 675.

48. Borg, p. 8. See also Patterson, p. 231.

49. This is the same notion found in the Gnostic Secret Book of James which is included among the "Complete Gospels." "Heaven's domain is discovered through knowledge . . . [and the major concern of the document] . . . lies in Jesus' teaching and the furnishing of a foundational revelation for a community of Gnostic Christians." Ibid., 324-25.

50. Burton L. Mack, *The Lost Gospel* (San Francisco: HarperSanFrancisco, 1993), p. 1.

51. Patterson, p. 234.

52. Ibid., p. 235.

53. See Elizabeth Schüssler Fiorenza, *In Memory of Her* (New York: Crossroad, 1994), pp. 124, 130ff; see also Louise Schottroff, "Itinerant Prophetesses: A Feminist Analysis of the Sayings Source Q," *Institute for Antiquity and Christianity, Occasional Papers* 21 (Claremont, CA: Institute for Antiquity and Christianity, 1991).

54. Ibid., pp. 4-5.

55. See Quality Paperback Bookclub flyer.

56. 1 Corinthians 15:1-3.

57. Cited in Brooke, *When the World Will Be As One,* p. 127.

58. Marianne Williamson, *A Return To Love* (New York: Harper, 1994), p. 4.

59. Cited in Douglas Groothuis, "The Shamanized Jesus," *Christianity Today,* April 1991, p. 20.

60. Ibid.

61. John White, *The Meeting of Science and Spirit* (New York: Paragon House, 1990).
62. Transcript of tapes of the RE-Imagining Conference, published by GoodNews, January 1994, p. 11.
63. Presbyterian Layman, 27:1, January-February 1994, p. 3.
64. Scott and Smith, pp. 53, 174, 175.
65. Guenther, p. 41.
66. Ibid., p. 97.
67. This is the same notion found in the Gnostic Secret Book of James which is included among the "Complete Gospels." "Heaven's domain is discovered through knowledge . . . [and the major concern of the document] . . . lies in Jesus' teaching and the furnishing of a foundational revelation for a community of Gnostic Christians." Ibid., 324-25.
68. Ibid., p. 199. This original community doubtless included gays and lesbians. See Robert Goss, *Jesus Acted Up: A Gay and Lesbian Manifesto* (San Francisco: Harper, 1994).
69. MacLaine, p. vi.
70. Rita Gross, "Hindu Female Deities as a Resource for the Contemporary Discovery of the Goddess," in Olson, pp. 217-18. In effect, in Hindu Saktism the goddess is the savior. See K. Klaus, "Sakti: Hindu Images and Concepts of the Goddess," in L. Hurtado, ed., *Goddesses in Religions and Modern Debate* (Atlanta, GA: Scholars Press, 1990), p. 149.
71. "Co-creating Heaven on Earth," *The Light Connection*, April 1993, p. 11.

Chapter 5: The Cosmic Christ of Matthew Fox

1. Matthew Fox, *The Coming of the Cosmic Christ* (San Francisco: Harper and Row, 1988), p. 15.
2. Ibid., pp. 148.
3. Ibid., p. 38.
4. Ibid., p. 19.
5. Ibid., pp. 52, 18, 69.
6. Ibid., pp. 2,3.
7. Ibid., p. 17. Cf. Matthew Fox, *Original Blessing: A Primer in Creation Spirituality* (Santa Fe, NM; Bear Publications, 1983), p. 50.
8. Ibid., p. 50. Cf. David L. Smith, *A Handbook of Contemporary Theology: Tracing trends and Discerning Directions in Today's Theological Landscape* (Wheaton, IL: Bridge-Point, 1992), p.298.
9. Ibid., p. 57.
10. Ibid., p. 70.
11. Ibid., p. 139.
12. See Mitchell Pacwa, "Catholicism for the New Age: Matthew Fox and Creation Centered Spirituality," *Christian Research Journal*, Fall 1992, electronic on-line version, CRI Internet Site.
13. Fox, *The Coming of the Cosmic Christ*, p. 6.
14. Ibid., pp. 153, 134, 7, 8, 135.
15. Ibid., p. 235. Cf. Matthew Fox, *Creation Spirituality* (San Francisco: Harper and Row, 1991), p.14.
16. Ibid., p. 241.
17. Ibid., pp. 154, 209, 142, 109.

18. Pacwa.
19. Fox, *The Coming of the Cosmic Christ*, p. 7.
20. Ibid., p. 65.
21. Ibid., p. 228.
22. Matthew Fox, *On Becoming a Musical, Mystical Bear* (New York: Paulist Press, 1972), pp. 136-37.
23. Fox, *The Coming of the Cosmic Christ*, p. 164. Cf. Matthew Fox, *Whee! We, Wee All the Way Home* (Santa Fe, NM: Bear Publications, 1981), p.76.
24. Ibid., p. 151.
25. Pacwa.
26. Ibid.
27. Ibid.
28. Cited in ibid.
29. Cited in ibid.
30. See Ron Rhodes, *The Counterfeit Christ of the New Age Movement* (Grand Rapids: Baker Book House, 1990) for a full refutaiton of New Age Christology. See also Ron Rhodes, *The New Age Movement* (Grand Rapids: Zondervan Publishing House, 1995).

Chapter 6: The Cosmic Christ of Channeled Revelation

1. Robert Skutch, "The Incredible Story Behind *A Course In Miracles*," *New Realities*, July-August 1984, p. 17.
2. Ibid., pp. 18-19.
3. Ibid., p. 19.
4. *SCP Journal*, vol. 7, No. 1, 1987.
5. Skutch, p. 21.
6. Ibid., p. 23.
7. Ibid., p.11.
8. Ibid.
9. Ibid., p. 12.
10. *A Course In Miracles* (New York: Viking, 1996), p. 165.
11. Ibid., p. 150.
12. Thomas Sugrue, *There Is a River* (New York: Holt, Rinehart, and Winston, 1942), p. 361.

Chapter 7: Between Isaac and Ishmael:
Jewish and Islamic Animosity Toward Christ

1. William Dalrymple, "If I Forget Thee, O Jerusalem," *The Spectator,* 22 October 1994, p. 107.
2. See Geoffry Parrinder, *Jesus in the Qur'an* (New York, NY: Oxford University Press, 1977), pp. 152-66.
3. Ibid., p. 160.
4. Gregory M. Livingston, *The Comparative Status of Christianity and Islam in North Africa,* in Don McCurry, ed., *The Gospel and Islam* (Monrovia, CA: MARC/World Vision International, 1978), p. 257.
5. George Otis, Jr., *The Last of the Giants: Lifting the Veil on Islam and the End Times* (Tarrytown, NY: Chosen Books, 1991). p. 68.

6. Robert Morey, "Somalia and Saudi Arabia Top Persecution List," *The Truth Seeker,* December 1996, p. 4.

7. Israel Shahak, *Jewish History, Jewish Religion: The Weight of Three Thousand Years* (London: Pluto Press, 1994), p. 97.

8. Ibid., pp. 97-98.

9. Sanhedrin 67a.

10. Toldoth Jeschu.

11. Sanhedrin 107b.

12. Shahak, p. 97.

13. Gittin 57a.

14. Shahak, p. 98.

15. Ibid.

16. Ibid., p. 21.

17. Phil Roberts, "To the Jew First," *Interfaith Focus,* Winter 1996, p. 2.

18. Shahak, p. 99.

19. Kathryn Casa, "Ethnic Cleansing in Jerusalem: Block by Block and Day by Day," *The Washington Report on Middle Eastern Affairs,* April-May 1995, p. 110.

20. Mohammed Hallaj, "Palestinians: Second Class Citizens in the Territories," *Christian Science Monitor,* 9 March 1992, pp. 64-65.

21. Matthew Engel, "A House Divided: Can Israel Make Peace With Itself?" *The Guardian,* 19 November 1996.

22. Israel Shahak, "From the Hebrew Press: Israel's State-Assisted Terrorism," *The Washington Report on Middle East Affairs,* February-March 1994, p. 16.

23. Katherine Metres, "Israeli Ethnic Cleansing Undiminished in Jerusalem," *The Washington Report on Middle East Affairs,* September-October 1994, p. 85.

24. Sheldon L. Richman, "Zionism Mandates Official Discrimination Against Non-Jews," *The Washington Report on Middle East Affairs,* December-January 1991/1992, p. 22.

25. Dalrymple, p. 108.

26. Ibid.

27. Ibid., p. 109.

28. Israel Shahak, "From the Hebrew Press: Israeli Discriminatory Practices Are Rooted in Jewish Religious Law," *The Washington Report on Middle East Affairs,* July-August 1995, p. 180.

29. Ibid., pp. 118-19.

30. Ibid., pp. 23-24.

31. Issa Nakhleh, *Encyclopedia of the Palestine Problem,* 2 vols. (New York, NY: Intercontinental Books, 1991), p. 397.

32. Quoted in Nakhleh, pp. 403-4.

33. Dalrymple, pp. 108-9.

Chapter 8: The Jesus of the Watchtower Society

1. Marian Bodine, *Christian Research Newsletter,* May-June 1992, p. 3.

2. Ibid.

3. *Reasoning from the Scriptures* (Brooklyn, NY: Watchtower Bible and Tract Society, 1989), p. 150.

4. *The Watchtower*, 15 March 1975, p. 174.
5. *The Watchtower*, 15 May 1969, p. 307, inserts added.
6. *Aid to Bible Understanding* (Brooklyn: Watchtower Bible and Tract Society, 1971), p. 391.
7. *The Watchtower*, 1 November 1964, p. 671.
8. *Reasoning from the Scriptures*, p. 308.
9. *Studies in the Scriptures*, vol. 7 (Brooklyn: Watchtower Bible and Tract Society, 1917), p. 57.
10. *You Can Live Forever in Paradise on Earth* (Brooklyn: Watchtower Bible and Tract Society, 1982), p. 143.
11. *"The Kingdom Is at Hand"* (Brooklyn: Watchtower Bible and Tract Society, 1944), p. 259.
12. *You Can Live Forever in Paradise on Earth*, p. 145.
13. *The Watchtower*, 1 September 1953, p. 518.
14. *"Things in Which It Is Impossible for God to Lie"* (Brooklyn: Watchtower Bible and Tract Society, 1965), p. 354.
15. Norman Geisler, *Christian Apologetics* (Grand Rapids: Baker Book House, 1976), p. 338.
16. *The Watchtower*, 7 December 1995, p. 4.
17. *Reasoning from the Scriptures*, p. 212.
18. Robert L. Reymond, *Jesus, Divine Messiah: The New Testament Witness* (Phillipsburg, NJ: Presbyterian and Reformed, 1990), p. 247.
19. Leon Morris, *The Gospel According to John* (Grand Rapids: Eerdmans Publishing Co., 1971), p. 658.
20. Robert M. Bowman, *Why You Should Believe in the Trinity* (Grand Rapids, MI: Baker Book House, 1989), pp. 14-15.
21. *The Watchtower*, March 1880, p. 83.
22. *The Watchtower*, 15 May 1892, p. 1410.
23. *The Watchtower*, 1 November 1964, p. 671.
24. *The Watchtower*, 15 July 1959, p. 421.
25. Robert Gundry, *Soma in Biblical Theology* (Cambridge: Cambridge University Press, 1976), p. 168.
26. Robert L. Reymond, *Jesus, Divine Messiah: The Old Testament Witness* (Scotland, Great Britain: Christian Focus Publications, 1990), pp. 78-84.
27. Jon A. Buell and O. Quentin Hyder, *Jesus: God, Ghost or Guru?* (Grand Rapids: Zondervan Publishing House, 1978), p. 27.
28. Reymond, *Jesus, Divine Messiah: The New Testament Witness*, pp. 92-94.
29. Millard J. Erickson, *The Word Became Flesh: A Contemporary Incarnational Christology* (Grand Rapids: Baker Book House, 1991), pp. 28-29.

Chapter 9: The Quest for the Historical Jesus

1. This overview of the history of the "quest" is indebted to the treatment found in Howard Clark Kee, *Jesus in History: An Approach to the Study of the Gospels* (New York: Harcourt Brace Jovanovich Publishers, 1977). Additional material was derived from Scott McKnight, "Who Is Jesus? An Introduction to Jesus Studies," in Michael J. Wilkins and J. P. Moreland, eds., *Jesus Under Fire* (Grand Rapids: Zondervan Publishing House, 1995). Kee, p. 12.

2. This is what John Stott calls the "scandal of particularity," a mystery which nevertheless has the full weight of Scripture—both Old and New Testaments—to back it up.

3. Strauss's work was no doubt influenced by the Romantic movement, an eighteenth-century backlash against the neoclassicism of the Enlightenment. The Romantics were interested in the myths of primitive and common man, believing that they offered insight into reality that was being lost in the rush to neoclassicism.

4. Kee, p. 24, insert added.

5. Birger A. Pearson, "The Gospel According to the Jesus Seminar," *Religion*, 1995, p. 319.

6. McKnight, p. 54.

7. This idea is expressed in Rudolph Bultmann, *Kerygma and Myth* (New York: Harper and Row, 1961), pp. 1-44.

8. Kee, p. 34, emphasis added.

9. As quoted in David Van Biema, "The Gospel Truth?" *Time*, 8 April 1996, p. 58.

10. Wilkins and Moreland, p. 3, insert added.

11. Quoted in Wilkins and Moreland, p. 26.

12. See Craig Blomberg's discussion of the Third Quest in Wilkins and Moreland, pp. 25-27, for a concise overview of this scholarship.

13. Blomberg, in Wilkins and Moreland, p. 27.

14. See Pearson for an analysis of how the "Jesus as sage" construction grew out of a "throw-away" analogy made by Gerd Theissen.

Chapter 10: Jesus on the Rack: The Jesus Seminar Under Glass

1. To eavesdrop on the continuing, though now degenerating, on-line debate first started by J. D. Crossan, Marcus Borg, and L. T. Johnson, subscribe to Crosstalk: lists@info.harpercollins.com.

2. Marcus Borg. "The Jesus Seminar and the Church." *Jesus in Contemporary Scholarship* (Valley Forge, PA: Trinity Press, 1994), p. 162.

3. Interview by Mary Rourke, "Cross Examination," *Los Angeles Times*, 24 February 1994, pp. E1, E5; as cited by Michael J. Wilkins and J. P. Moreland, *Jesus Under Fire* (Grand Rapids: Zondervan, 1995), "Introduction."

4. Robert W. Funk, Roy W. Hoover, and the Jesus Seminar, *The Five Gospels: the Search for the Authentic Words of Jesus* (New York: Macmillan, 1993), p. 2.

5. Robert Funk, "Call for Canon Council," *The Fourth R.*, May/June 1992, p. 7; as quoted in Gregory A. Boyd, *Jesus Under Siege* (Wheaton, IL: Victor Books, 1995), p. 24.

6. For a detailed breakdown of the voting from which I derived the figure of 83 percent, refer to Paul Harvey's work on-line at the following e-mail address: pharvey@quack.kfu.com.

7. Funk, Hoover et al., pp. 32-33.

8. David Van Biema, "The Gospel Truth?" *Time*, 8 April 1996, p. 3.

9. R. Watson, "A Lesser Child of God," *Newsweek*, 4 April 1994, p. 53.

10. Luke Timothy Johnson, *The Real Jesus: The Misguided Quest for the Historical Jesus and the Truth of the Traditional Gospels* (San Francisco: HarperCollins, 1996), pp. 39-44.

11. Johnson, pp. 39-44.

12. Johnson, p. 53.

13. Atlanta Constitution, 30 September 1989, as quoted in Johnson, p. 15, emphasis added.

14. Though the Fellows employ standard criteria of New Testament scholarship (the oral tradition behind the Gospel texts, and the principles of dissimilarity, multiple attestation and coherence) they apply these principles in peculiar ways. They assume, for example, that in the oral culture of Jesus' day people were incapable of remembering anything more than short pithy sayings; therefore, they conclude, Jesus couldn't have uttered the long speeches attributed to him in the Gospels. See the following discussions of the Jesus Seminar's work: Darrel L. Bock of Dallas Theological Seminary and R. Douglas Geivett of Talbot School of Theology in *Jesus Under Fire*; Gregory Boyd, Professor of Theology at Bethel College in St. Paul, in *Jesus Under Siege*; and Luke Timothy Johnson, Professor of New Testament and Christian Origins at the Candler School of Theology, Emory University, in *The Real Jesus*.

15. Funk, Hoover et al., p. 2-3.

16. Funk, Hoover et al., p. 4.

17. Funk, Hoover et al., p. 4.

18. Funk, Hoover et al., p. 4.

19. Funk, Hoover et al., p. 5.

20. Funk, Hoover et al., p. 6.

21. Funk, Hoover et al., p. 10.

22. This latter theory accords with tradition. According to the early church father Clement of Alexandria, "John, perceiving that what had reference to the bodily things of Jesus' ministry had been sufficiently related, and encouraged by his friends, and inspired by the Holy Spirit, wrote a spiritual gospel."

23. Funk, Hoover et al., p. 15.

24. Funk, Hoover et al., p. 3.

25. Funk, Hoover et al., p. 7.

26. Funk, Hoover et al., p. 7.

27. Funk, Hoover et al., p. 30.

27. Jeffrey L. Shaler, Mike Tharp, and Jill Jordan Seider, "In Search of Jesus," *U. S. News and World Report*, 8 April 1996, p. 49.

29. Funk, Hoover et al., p. xvi- xvii.

30. Emphasis added.

31. Matthew Fox, *The Coming of the Cosmic Christ: The Healing of Mother Earth and the Birth of a Global Renaissance* (San Francisco: HarperCollins, 1988).

32. According to "Rethinking the Resurrection: A New Debate about the Risen Christ," *Newsweek*, 8 April 1996.

33. Augustine, Letters, XXVIII, quoted in Norman Geisler, ed., *Inerrancy* (Grand Rapids: Zondervan, 1980), p. 309.

34. For a detailed discussion of these contradictions, see Brad Scott, *Embraced by the Darkness: Exposing New Age Theology from the Inside Out* (Wheaton, IL: Crossway, 1996).

35. See Harvie Conn, ed., *Inerrancy and Hermeneutics* (1988); Norman Geisler, ed., *Inerrancy* (1980); James Montgomery Boice, ed. *The Foundation of Biblical Authority* 1978); and *Jesus Under Fire* (1995).

36. Biema, p. 7.

Chapter 11: The Jesus Seminar

1. See, for example, Robert W. Funk, Roy W. Hoover, and the Jesus Seminar, *The Five Gospels: The Search for the Authentic Words of Jesus* (New York, NY: Macmillian Publishing Company, 1993), p. 287. In a commentary on the parable of the unshrunk cloth, Funk describes why "so many of the Fellows are inclined to regard Jesus as a secular sage who perhaps acquired his knowledge of common lore from itinerant philosophers who visited Galilee while he was growing up." Coincidentally, cofounder J. Dominic Crossan posited the Cynic-sage theory in book-length form in his 1991 bestseller, *The Historical Jesus* (San Francisco: HarperSanFrancisco, 1991).

2. Funk, Hoover, et al., p. 31.

3. Ibid., p. 4.

4. Ibid.

5. Ibid., p. 5.

6. I am indebted, in this analysis, to the treatment offered by Birger A. Pearson, "The Gospel According to the Jesus Seminar," *Religion*, 1995, p. 322 and ff.

7. Q, short for the German "Quelle," or "source," is a hypothetical "sayings source"—a document (or perhaps an oral tradition) containing sayings of Jesus that is theorized to be the basis for sayings common to both Matthew and Luke that are not found in Mark. This document, if it existed, is not known in any form. It has disappeared from the historical record.

8. Funk, Hoover, et al., p. 16.

9. Adam Brooke Davis, "The Ineffectual Jesus of the Jesus Seminar," *New Oxford Review*, July-August 1996. See John Moore, "The Jesus Seminar," *Spiritual Counterfeits Journal*, vol. 20:3-4, 1996, p. 48.

10. Funk, Hoover, et al., p. 23.

11. Ibid., p. 24.

12. Ibid., p. 25.

13. Ibid., p. 32.

14. Ibid., p. 109.

15. Ibid., p. 110.

16. Ibid., p. 5.

17. Craig L. Blomberg, "Where Do We Start Studying Jesus," in Michael J. Wilkins and J. P. Moreland, eds., *Jesus Under Fire* (Grand Rapids: Zondervan Publishing House, 1995), p. 23.

18. As found in Howard Clark Kee, *The Origins of Christianity: Sources and Texts* (New York, NY: Prentice Hall, 1973), p. 250. According to the Seminar's translation in *The Five Gospels*, this is saying 13. I have used this older translation as opposed to the Seminar's translation because the Seminar's translation downplays the elevated status that Thomas is accorded due to his "confession." This passage is unique in Thomas in that it contains even a semblance of narrative action.

19. Funk, Hoover, et al., p. xiii, emphasis added.

20. Cofounder Crossan, in his recent work *The Historical Jesus,* lays the groundwork for this dating of Thomas. As summarized by Pearson (p. 321):

> Trickster like, Crossan deftly sets standard critical scholarship on its head by assigning to the earliest stratum (30-60 C.E.) such sources as the Gospel of Thomas (that is, a supposed "first layer"), Papyrus Egerton 2, and other papyrus fragments, and the Gospel of the Hebrews, writings usually assigned to the 2nd century. He even invents a new gospel of his own which he assigns to this period, the "Cross Gospel," which he reconstructs out of the 2nd-century Gospel of Peter.

21. See J. Dominic Crossan, Reply—Week 2, in Borg, Crossan, Johnson (1996), http://www.harpercol.com/sanfran/2c.htm.
22. David Van Biema, "The Gospel Truth?" *Time,* 8 April 1996, p. 58.
23. Gordon D. Fee, *The First Epistle to the Corinthians* (Grand Rapids, MI: Eerdmans, 1987), pp. 716ff.
24. Ibid., p. 739.
25. Ibid., p. 91.

Chapter 12: The Real Jesus Already Stood Up

1. William James, *The Varieties of Religious Experience* (New York: Longmans, Green and Co., 1902), emphasis in the original, p. 389.
2. G. K. Chesterton, *The Everlasting Man* (New York: Dodd, Mead and Co., 1925), pp. 87-88.
3. Ibid., p. 88.
4. Ibid., p. 87.

Chapter 13: Has God Really Spoken?

1. N.A. Woychuk, *The Infallible Word* (St. Louis, MO: Miracle Press, 1970), p. 7.
2. Charles Ryrie, *Basic Theology* (Wheaton, IL: Victor Books, 1986), p. 113.
3. B. B. Warfield, *The Inspiration and Authority of the Bible* (Phillipsburg, NJ: Presbyterian and Reformed, 1948), p. 173.
4. Norman Geisler and William Nix, *A General Introduction to the Bible* (Chicago, IL: Moody Press, 1978), p. 55.
5. Geisler and Nix, p. 28.
6. John F. Walvoord, "Contemporary Problems: Is the Bible the Inspired Word of God?" *Bibliotheca Sacra,* vol. 116 #461, January 1959, electronic on-line version. Downloaded from Dallas Theological Seminary Web site.
7. Charles Ryrie, *Bibliotheca Sacra,* January-March 1979, electronic on-line version. Downloaded from the Dallas Theological Seminary Web site. See also Robert P. Lightner, *Evangelical Theology: A Survey and Review* (Grand Rapids: Baker Book House, 1986), p. 13.
8. *Explaining Inerrancy: A Commentary* (Oakland, CA: International Council on Biblical Inerrancy, 1980), pp. 17-18.
9. I am indebted to Geisler and Nix for this.
10. This is not circular reasoning, arguing *for* the Bible *from* the Bible. These books, at the time Luke was alive, had not yet been collected into a single volume but rather circulated as distinct documents.

11. An important issue that we are forced to neglect because of lack of space involves the canonicity of individual Bible books. Those interested in studying this important issue should consult Geisler and Nix.

12. Decision of the Synod of 1961.

13. Craig Blomberg, "The Seventy-Four 'Scholars': Who Does the Jesus Seminar Really Speak For?" *Christian Research Journal,* Fall 1994, p. 36.

14. C. S. Lewis, *God In the Dock* (Grand Rapids: Eerdmans, 1972), p. 26.

15. Ibid., p 26.

16. For example, Norman Geisler and Thomas Howe, *When Critics Ask: A Popular Handbook on Bible Difficulties* (Wheaton, IL: Victor Books, 1992).

17. Bob Passantino, "Contend Earnestly for the Faith: How Far Can We Trust the Bible?" Downloaded from Answers In Action Web site. Answers In Action, P.O. Box 2067, Costa Mesa, CA 92628.

18. Ibid.

19. Dan Story, *Defend the* Faith (Nashville: Thomas Nelson Publishing, 1995), p. 47.

20. Nelson Glueck, *Rivers in the Desert* (Philadelphia, PA: Jewish Publications Society of America, 1969), p. 31.

21. Donald J. Wiseman, "Archaeological Confirmation of the Old Testament"; in Norman L. Geisler, *Christian Apologetics* (Grand Rapids: Baker Book House, 1976), p. 322.

22. William F. Albright; cited in Josh McDowell, *Evidence that Demands a Verdict* (San Bernardino, CA: Campus Crusade for Christ, 1972), p. 68.

23. See Geisler and Nix for a thorough discussion of this.

24. Story, pp. 38-39.

25. Rene Pache, *The Inspiration and Authority of Scripture* (Chicago: Moody Press, 1978), p. 193.

26. Geisler and Nix, p. 49.

27. Pache, p. 193.

28. Norman Geisler and Ronald Brooks, *When Skeptics Ask* (Wheaton, IL: Victor Books, 1989), p. 159-60.

29. See F.F. Bruce, *The New Testament Documents: Are They Reliable?* (Downers Grove, IL: InterVarsity Press, 1984), p. 19.

30. Story, p. 35.

31. Gleason Archer, *A Survey of Old Testament Introduction* (Chicago: Moody Press, 1964), p. 19, italics added.

32. Story, p. 35; cf. McDowell, p. 22.

33. Story, p. 35.

34. The Westminster Confession.

35. Greg L. Bahnsen, "The Inerrancy of the Autographa," in *Inerrancy,* ed. Norman L. Geisler (Grand Rapids: Zondervan Publishing House, 1980), p. 161.

36. Ibid.

37. J. I. Packer, *Knowing Christianity* (Wheaton, IL: Harold Shaw Publishers, 1995), p. 16.

The True God

1. J.N.D. Anderson, "The Resurrection of Jesus Christ," *Christianity Today,* 29 March 1968.

2. C.S. Lewis, *Mere Christianity* (New York: Macmillan, 1952), p. 40.

Appendix A: Gnosticism and Modernism: Is There a Connection?

1. See Philip Johnson, *Reason in the Balance* (Downers Grove: InterVarsity Press, 1995).

2. Marcus Borg, Reply—Week 2, in Borg, Crossan, Johnson (1996), http://www.harpercollins.com/sanfran/2b.htm.

3. Johnson.

4. Richard N. Ostling, "Jesus Christ, Plain and Simple," *Time*, 10 January 1994, pp. 32-33; as cited William Lane Craig, "Did Jesus Rise from the Dead?" in Wilkins and Moreland.

GLOSSARY

A Course in Miracles—A New Age textbook written by Helen Schucman via "automatic writing." The course teaches that man's basic problem is his faulty belief in being separate from God. The solution is a rediscovery of one's Christhood.

adept—Often used to refer to an occult initiate progressing in esoteric wisdom.

Age of Aquarius—Astrologers believe man's evolution goes through progressive cycles corresponding to the signs of the zodiac. Each of these allegedly lasts between 2000 and 2400 years. It is believed that humanity is now moving from the Piscean Age (the age of *intellectual* man) into the Aquarian Age (the age of *spiritual* man and consciousness expansion).

ahistorical—Refers to that which is outside the context of history. It is therefore not attested, authentic, chronicled, documented, or factual.

Akashic records—Occultists believe the physical earth is surrounded by an immense spiritual field known as "Akasha" in which is impressed—like a celestial tape recording—every impulse of human thought, will, and emotion. It is therefore believed to constitute a complete record of human history. Some New Age seers and occultists, such as Edgar Cayce, claim to have the ability to "read" the Akashic records.

animism—A part of shamanism, animism is the doctrine that all objects in the world possess an inner or psychological being. Primitive peoples, defined as those without written traditions, believe that spirits or souls are the cause of life in human beings; they picture souls as phantoms, resembling vapors or shadows, which can transmigrate from person to person, from the dead to the living, and from and into plants, animals, and lifeless objects.

apocryphal writings—Late Jewish writings of dubious authenticity that all scholars consider extracanonical. These writings are ascribed to canonical worthies of the Old Testament period, date from intertestamental times, and have not been preserved in their original Hebrew or Aramaic.

Arianism—A fourth-century Christian heresy named for Arius (c. 250-336), a priest in Alexandria. Arius denied the full deity of the pre-existent Son of God, saying He was of a different (lesser) "substance" than that of God the Father.

automatic handwriting—A process in which a spirit entity guides a person's hand in writing, thereby communicating paranormal information. Many occultic "revelations" have been received by this means.

avatar—One who "descends" into human form from above, never having gone through incarnation. Such a one is considered a manifestation of divinity and seeks to reveal divine truths especially important to a particular age.

canon of Scripture—*Canon* comes from a Greek word meaning "measuring stick." The word eventually came to be used metaphorically of books that were "measured" (by rules of canonization) and thereby recognized as being God's Word. When we talk about the canon of Scripture today, we are referring to all the biblical books that collectively constitute God's Word.

channeling—Sometimes described as voluntary possession, channeling is a New Age form of mediumship or spiritism. The channeler voluntarily yields control of his capacities (both cognitive and perceptual) to a spiritual entity with the intent of receiving paranormal information.

cosmic Christ—In esoteric schools of thought, the Christ is variously defined, but always divine, and is considered to be a universal spirit or cosmic force. The primary goal of this impersonal spirit or force is to guide the spiritual evolution of humankind.

cosmic consciousness—A spiritual and mystical perception that all in the universe is "one"—including oneness between God and man.

divination—The attempt to acquire hidden knowledge and insight into events—past, present, and future—through the direct or indirect contact of human intelligence with supernatural or paranormal entities. Forms of divination best known today include astrology, crystal gazing, bibliomancy (the interpretation of secret messages from books, especially the Bible); numerology, and the reading of palms, tea leaves, and cards.

Docetism—An early heresy concerning the person of Jesus Christ. Derived from the Greek *dokeo*, meaning "to seem" or "to appear," Docetism taught that the eternal Son of God did not really become human or suffer on the cross; He only *appeared* to do so. The heresy arose in a Hellenistic milieu and was based on a dualism which held that the material world is either unreal or positively evil.

Ebionites—A second-century group of Jewish Christians who retained much of Judaism in their beliefs. They adopted a conservative Pharisaic creed at first, but after the second century some of them espoused a mixture of Essenism, Gnosticism, and Christianity. According to the second-century Christian prelate and writer Irenaeus, they differed from orthodox Christians in denying the divinity of Christ and in considering Paul an apostate for having declared the supremacy of Christian teaching over the Mosaic law. Until the fifth century, remnants of the sect were known to have existed in Palestine and Syria.

eco-feminism—A blending of feminism and pagan earth worship.

epistemology—The study of the nature and grounds of knowledge, especially with respect to its limitations and validity.

eschatology—Literally "discourse about the last things," this word refers on the popular level to the study of prophecy. Eschatology has traditionally included the second advent of Christ, the resurrection of the dead, the last judgment, the immortality of the soul, the doctrines of heaven and hell, and the consummation of the kingdom of God.

esoteric—A word used to describe knowledge that is possessed or understood only by a few—the specially initiated.

evangelical—A Christian who emphasizes orthodoxy on cardinal doctrines, morals, and especially on the authority of the Bible—namely, the Bible's inerrancy (freedom from error in history as well as in faith and morals). Evangelicals believe each individual has a need for spiritual rebirth and personal commitment to Jesus Christ as Savior.

exegesis—From the Greek words *ex*, out, and *hegeisthai*, to guide, exegesis involves drawing the meaning of a biblical text *out of* the text itself, as opposed to reading a meaning *into* the text (which is eisogesis). The student of Scripture must study the word meanings and grammar of the text to discern the intended meaning of the passage.

existentialism—A philosophical movement emphasizing individual existence, freedom, and choice that influenced many diverse writers in the nineteenth and twentieth centuries. Jean-Paul Sartre used the term in regard to his own philosophy, which was explicitly atheistic and pessimistic. Indeed, he declared that human beings require a rational basis for their lives but are unable to achieve one, and thus human life is a "futile passion."

form criticism—A method of textual criticism that seeks to trace the origin and history of biblical passages through systematic study in terms of conventional literary forms, such as parables, proverbs, and love poems. It seeks to "get behind" the written sources to determine what was actually said and done.

Fundamentalism—A movement originating in the United States in 1920 in opposition to theological liberalism and secularism and their eroding effect on orthodoxy and morality.

gnosis—Esoteric knowledge of spiritual truth held by the ancient Gnostics to be essential to salvation.

Gnosticism—A movement existing from the first through the third centuries which (1) emphasized a higher truth (gnosis) that only the more enlightened could receive from God; (2) held to dualism—the idea that spirit is good but matter is evil; and (3) denied the humanity of Jesus Christ (since a human body composed of matter would be evil).

hermeneutics—From the Greek word *hermeneutikos*, meaning "interpretation," hermeneutics is the branch of theology that prescribes rules by which the Bible should be interpreted.

higher criticism—A method of interpreting the Bible from the standpoint of literature. It seeks to determine the authorship, date, and underlying literary documents of books of the Bible, as well as their historical dependability.

hypostatic union—Refers to the union of Jesus' divine and human natures in one person. In the Incarnation Jesus' divine nature was forever and inseparably united with His human nature, yet the two natures remain distinct and whole without mixture.

I AM presence—Said to be in each person, the "I AM presence" allegedly represents a point of contact with divine reality. One can reportedly attune to this presence by chanting I AM decrees. This concept is rooted in the I AM movement, founded in the 1930s by Guy and Edna Ballard. A modern promoter of this idea is Elizabeth Clare Prophet of the Church Universal and Triumphant.

I Ching—A Chinese book of ancient origin consisting of 64 interrelated hexagrams along with commentaries. The hexagrams embody

Taoist philosophy by describing all nature and human endeavor in terms of the interaction of yin and yang. (See "Taoism" and "Yin and yang.")

JEDP hypothesis—A theory of higher criticism which holds that the five books of Moses (Genesis, Exodus, Leviticus, Numbers, and Deuteronomy) are not the works of one author. Rather, the contributions of several anonymous authors can allegedly be identified by the names they used for God and other factors. These hypothetical authors came to be known as the Yahwist (J), the Elohimist (E), the Deuteronomist (D), and the Priestly Source (P).

karma—Refers to the debt a soul allegedly accumulates because of good or bad actions committed during one's life (or past lives). If one accumulates good karma, it is believed he or she will be reincarnated in a desirable state. If one accumulates bad karma, he or she will be reincarnated in a less desirable state.

Koran—The holy book of Islam containing the revelations of Mohammed.

layers of tradition—Higher critics surmise that the Gospels were not works written by single authors, but were instead conglomerations of material written by different authors at different times. These critics believe they can see different "layers" within the Gospels, like the strata of a rock that has been built up over the years by successive layers of mineral deposits.

medium—Traditionally refers to an occultist through whom disembodied spirit entities communicate. New Agers often use the word in reference to (the human) Jesus acting as a bodily vehicle for the cosmic Christ.

modernism—A liberal theological movement that involves the attempt to "update" biblical doctrines to make them acceptable to the modern mind. This school of thought assumes that only the modern scientific mind can truly know reality since it alone possesses advances in technology and understanding. Therefore, biblical teaching needs to be rewritten in terms tolerable to current ways of thinking.

monism—A metaphysical theory that sees all reality as a unified whole. Everything in the universe is seen as being composed of the same substance.

monotheism—From the Greek words *monos*, one, and *theos*, God, monotheism is the belief that there is one God and only one God.

Montanism—A Christian apocalyptic movement that arose in the second century preaching the imminent end of the world, austere morality, and severe penitential discipline. It took its name from Montanus, a Phrygian, who, shortly after his baptism as a Christian (A.D. 156), claimed to have received a revelation from the Holy Spirit to the effect that he would lead the Christian church into its final stage.

mother goddess—Popular in pagan and neopagan circles, mother goddess worship is a female-centered spirituality over and against patriarchal religion, which is alleged to be a male-exalting religion evidenced by such phrases as "God the Father." Neopagans often say the goddess *is* the world, and can be mystically manifest within every person.

naturalism—A worldview that completely dismisses God from the picture and denies anything having to do with the supernatural. Naturalism attempts to explain all phenomena by means of strictly natural categories.

neoorthodoxy—A twentieth-century theological school of thought that broke with nineteenth-century liberal theology, yet did not fully embrace orthodoxy because of its perceived conflict with science. Key tenets of neoorthodoxy include God's transcendence, the reality of sin, and revelation as a personal encounter with God through the Scriptures. (The text of Scripture is not considered to be propositionally true, but rather "becomes" the Word of God as it transforms the individual.)

neopaganism—A movement involving a revival of paganism. Neopagans reject Western distinctives such as organized religion, male-dominated society (including patriarchal, "male-exalting" religion), and man's abuse of the world of nature. Instead, neopagans share a feminist perspective and seek to reharmonize themselves with the mother goddess.

Newtonian worldview—Sir Isaac Newton understood the universe in terms of predictable mechanical laws set in the context of absolute space and time. When Albert Einstein set forth his theory of relativity, Newton's mechanical theories soon fell from favor. Relativity ushered Newton's view of time and space out the scientific backdoor. Space and time were no longer viewed as distinct and absolute.

panentheism—The worldview that all is in God and God is in all. God is to the world as a soul is to a body. God's being is said to include the being of the universe, but also transcends it. God is allegedly *in* everything that exists, but is viewed as being *more* than the world.

pantheism—Pantheism is the view that God is all and all is God (based on the Greek words *pan*, all, and *theos*, God). All reality is viewed as being infused with divinity. The New Age pantheistic God is an impersonal, amoral *it* as opposed to the personal, moral *He* of Christianity. The distinction between the Creator and the creation is completely obliterated in this school of thought.

paradigm shift—A paradigm is a set of basic assumptions about something. A paradigm shift thus refers to a shift in one's basic assumptions. It involves a shift in worldviews.

patriarchal religion—A term used by feminists to refer to alleged male-exalting religion that is evidenced by such phrases as "God the Father." Worship of the mother goddess is preferred by such feminists.

polytheism—Belief in many different gods or deities.

post-Christian era—Refers to the present day, in which a host of religions, cults, and occultic systems are vying continuously for people's commitments.

Q—A designation taken from the German word *quelle*, meaning "source." It is the symbol for the hypothetical document that purportedly was a common source for writing the Gospels.

Radical Q scholarship—Shorthand reference to the radical wing of New Testament studies, strongly represented in the Jesus Seminar, which sees in the common material between Matthew and Luke evidence of a document, Q. From this hypothetical document is extracted "evidence" of the earliest community around Jesus, who allegedly did not believe in the gospel of cross and resurrection theology.

rationalism—The philosophical theory that knowledge is primarily gained by intellectual and deductive means, as opposed to sensory and inductive means. This school of thought holds to the primacy of reason, before experience, as the preferred criterion of truth.

redaction criticism—Seeks to identify the sources the biblical writer used and the editorial work that was done on them. It views the writers of the Gospels not as mere compilers of material but as editors who creatively shaped their materials in keeping with their own understanding of the events and claims.

re-imagining—Christian feminists seek to "re-imagine" Christianity by infusing new female-friendly notions of goddess worship and sexual liberation into biblical faith.

Romantic era—In the late eighteenth and nineteenth centuries, the romantics—spearheaded by influential writers and artists—revolted against classicism and philosophical rationalism with its emphasis on reason. They idealized man's return to nature while believing in the innate goodness of man. If man was innately good, and therefore not tainted by sin, he did not need a Savior. Thus Christ's central role as Savior was jettisoned so that He could now be cast into various other roles—teacher, higher master, even the "Christ consciousness" of the various occult groups that emerged in the late 1800s.

shaman—A visionary believed to be capable of communicating directly with spirit entities, often while in ecstatic states or trances. By controlling such spirit entities, shamans can allegedly ward off evil, heal, and tell the future.

Sophia—A goddess worshiped by many radical religious feminists.

special Matthew and special Luke—The higher critics speak of the material that is unique to Matthew (not found in Mark or Luke) as "special Matthew," and the material that is unique to Luke as "special Luke."

Synoptic Gospels—Matthew, Mark, and Luke. These Gospels can be "seen together"—that is, they present the details of Jesus' life and ministry using a consistent timeline.

Taoism—Refers to a Chinese philosophy based on the teachings of Lao-tse and Chuang Tzu in the sixth to fourth centuries B.C. The central theme of Taoism has to do with harmony with the natural flow of the universe. Letting nature take its course is believed to be the key to happiness and fulfillment. To Taoists, nature is synonymous with the Tao which makes up the entire universe; it is elusive, hidden, mysterious. The Tao, in turn, is divided into two forces called the yin and yang. Taoist philosophy sees the universe as a balance between these two inseparable, opposing forces. All manifestations of the Tao, and all changes in nature, are believed to be generated by the dynamic interplay of these two polar forces. (See "yin and yang.")

Targum—Jewish simplified paraphrases of the Old Testament Scriptures. The Targumists tried to give the sense of the passage being read, and not simply to translate mechanically.

Theosophy—A term that literally means "divine wisdom." The Theosophical Society, founded by Helena P. Blavatsky in 1875, sets forth several distinctive doctrines: (1) There are said to be "ascended masters" who guide man's spiritual evolution. (2) Religious truth has been communicated by many other holy men besides Jesus (for example, Buddha, Hermes, Zoroaster, and Orpheus). (3) Jesus was just a human being who embodied the Christ spirit. Many modern New Age ideas are rooted in Theosophy.

Wellhausen's Documentary hypothesis—See "JEDP Theory."

Yin and yang—The "Tao" is divided into two forces called the yin and yang. These represent the negative and positive aspects of the universe, each flowing into one another in a continuous cycle of change. Yin is characterized as the negative force of darkness, coldness, and emptiness. Yang stands for the positive energy that produces light, warmth, and fullness. These alternating forces are indestructible and inexhaustible. They contradict as well as complement each other. Taoist philosophy sees the universe as a balance between these two inseparable, opposing forces. All manifestations of the Tao, and all changes in nature, are believed to be generated by the dynamic interplay of these two polar forces.

BIBLIOGRAPHY

Aid to Bible Understanding. Brooklyn: Watchtower Bible and Tract Society, 1971.

Archer, Gleason. *A Survey of Old Testament Introduction*. Chicago: Moody Press, 1964.

Borg, Marcus J. *Jesus: A New Vision: Spirit, Culture and the Life of Discipleship*. San Francisco: Harper, 1987.

Borg, Marcus J. *Jesus in Contemporary Scholarship*. Valley Forge: Trinity Press, 1994.

Borg, Marcus J. *Meeting Jesus Again for the First Time*. San Francisco: Harper San Francisco, 1993.

Bowman, Robert M. *Why You Should Believe in the Trinity*. Grand Rapids: Baker Book House, 1989.

Brooke, Tal. *Lord of the Air*. Eugene: Harvest House, 1990.

Brooke, Tal. *When the World Will Be As One*. Eugene: Harvest House, 1989.

Bruce, F F. *The New Testament Documents: Are They Reliable?* Downers Grove: InterVarsity Press, 1984.

Buell, Jon A. and O. Quentin Hyder. *Jesus: God, Ghost or Guru?* Grand Rapids: Zondervan Publishing House, 1978.

Chesterton, G.K. *The Everlasting Man*. New York: Dodd, Mead & Company, 1925.

Daly, Mary. *Beyond God the Father: Towards a Philosophy of Women's Liberation*. Boston: Beacon Press, 1985.

Epstein, Rabbi Dr. I., ed. *The Babylonian Talmud*. London: Soncino Press, 1936.

Erickson, Millard J. *The Word Became Flesh: A Contemporary Incarnational Christology*. Grand Rapids: Baker Book House, 1991.

Explaining Inerrancy: A Commentary. Oakland: International Council on Biblical Inerrancy, 1980.

Fee, Gordon D. *The First Epistle to the Corinthians*. Grand Rapids: Eerdmans, 1987.

Fox, Matthew. *Creation Spirituality*. San Francisco: Harper and Row, 1991.

Fox, Matthew. *On Becoming a Musical, Mystical Bear*. New York: Paulist Press, 1972.

Fox, Matthew. *Original Blessing: A Primer in Creation Spirituality*. Santa Fe: Bear Publications, 1983.

Fox, Matthew. *The Coming of the Cosmic Christ*. San Francisco: Harper and Row, 1988.

Fox, Matthew. *Whee! We, Wee All the Way Home*. Santa Fe: Bear Publications, 1981.

Funk, Robert W. and Roy W. Hoover et al., *The Five Gospels: the Search for the Authentic Words of Jesus*. New York: Macmillan, 1993.

Geisler, Norman. *Christian Apologetics*. Grand Rapids: Baker Book House, 1976.

Geisler, Norman. *Inerrancy*. Grand Rapids: Zondervan, 1980.

Geisler, Norman and Ron Rhodes. *When Cultists Ask*. Grand Rapids: Baker Book House, 1997.

Geisler, Norman and Ronald Brooks. *When Skeptics Ask.* Wheaton: Victor Books, 1989.

Geisler, Norman and Thomas Howe. *When Critics Ask: A Popular Handbook on Bible Difficulties.* Wheaton: Victor Books, 1992.

Geisler, Norman and William Nix. *A General Introduction to the Bible.* Chicago: Moody Press, 1978.

Glueck, Nelson. *Rivers in the Desert.* Philadelphia: Jewish Publications Society of America, 1969.

Goldenberg, Naomi. *Changing the Gods: Feminism and the End of Traditional Religions.* Boston: Beacon Press, 1979.

Goss, Robert. *Jesus Acted Up: A Gay and Lesbian Manifesto.* San Francisco: Harper, 1994.

Griscom, Chris. *Ecstasy Is a New Frequency.* Santa Fe: Bear and Company, 1987.

Gundry, Robert. *Soma in Biblical Theology.* Cambridge: Cambridge University Press, 1976.

James, William. *The Varieties of Religious Experience.* New York: Longmans, Green, and Co., 1902.

Johnson, Luke Timothy. *The Real Jesus: The Misguided Quest for the Historical Jesus and the Truth of the Traditional Gospels.* San Francisco: HarperCollins, 1996.

Johnson, Phillip. *Reason in the Balance.* Downers Grove: InterVarsity Press, 1995.

Jonas, Hans. *The Gnostic Religion.* Boston: Beacon Press, 1958.

Jones, Peter. *The Gnostic Empire Strikes Back.* Phillipsburg, NJ: Presbyterian and Reformed, 1992.

Kee, Howard Clark. *Jesus In History: An Approach to the Study of the Gospels.* New York: Harcourt Brace Jovanovich Publishers, 1977.

L'Engle, Madeleine. *A Stone for a Pillow.* Wheaton: Harold Shaw Publishing, 1986.

Lewis, C. S. *God In the Dock.* Grand Rapids: Eerdmans, 1972.

Lightner, Robert P. *Evangelical Theology: A Survey and Review.* Grand Rapids: Baker Book House, 1986.

Mack, Burton L. *The Gospel of Q and Christian Origins.* San Francisco: Harper, 1993.

MacLaine, Shirley. *Going Within.* New York: Bantam, 1989.

McDowell, Josh. *Evidence that Demands a Verdict.* San Bernardino: Campus Crusade for Christ, 1972.

Mollenkott, Virginia. *Sensuous Spirituality: Out from Fundamentalism.* New York: Crossroads, 1992.

Morris, Leon. *The Gospel According to John.* Grand Rapids: Eerdmans Publishing Co., 1971.

Morrison, Alan. *The Serpent and the Cross: Religious Corruption in an Evil Age.* Birmingham, UK: K&M Books, 1994.

Nakhleh, Issa. *Encyclopedia of the Palestine Problem,* 2 vols. New York: Intercontinental Books, 1991.

Oddie, William. *What Will Happen to God? Feminism and the Reconstruction of Christian Belief.* San Francisco: Ignatius Press, 1988.

Otis, George, Jr. *The Last of the Giants: Lifting the Veil on Islam and the End Times.* Tarrytown: Chosen Books, 1991.

Pache, Rene. *The Inspiration and Authority of Scripture.* Chicago: Moody Press, 1978.

Packer, J. I. *Knowing Christianity.* Wheaton: Harold Shaw Publishers, 1995.

Parrinder, Geoffry. *Jesus in the Qur'an.* New York: Oxford University Press, 1977.

Patterson, Stephen J. *The Gospel of Thomas and Jesus.* Sonoma: Polebridge Press, 1993.

Pollitt, Herbert J. *The Inter-Faith Movement: The New Age Enters the Church.* Edinburgh: Banner of Truth, 1996.

Reasoning from the Scriptures. Brooklyn: Watchtower Bible and Tract Society, 1989.

Reymond, Robert L. *Jesus, Divine Messiah: The New Testament Witness.* Phillipsburg, N.J: Presbyterian and Reformed, 1990.

Reymond, Robert L. *Jesus, Divine Messiah: The Old Testament Witness.* Scotland, Great Britain: Christian Focus Publications, 1990.

Rhodes, Ron. *Quick-Reference Guide to the Jehovah's Witnesses.* Eugene: Harvest House Publishers, 1997.

Rhodes, Ron. *Reasoning from the Scriptures with the Jehovah's Witnesses.* Eugene: Harvest House Publishers, 1993.

Rhodes, Ron. *The Counterfeit Christ of the New Age Movement.* Grand Rapids: Baker Book House, 1990.

Rhodes, Ron. *The New Age Movement.* Grand Rapids: Zondervan Publishing House, 1995.

Ruether, Rosemary Radford. *Liberation Theology: Human Hope Confronts Christian History and American Power.* New York: Paulist Press, 1972.

Ruether, Rosemary Radford. *Women-Church: Theology and Practice of Feminist Liturgical Communities.* San Francisco: Harper and Row, 1985.

Ryrie, Charles. *Basic Theology.* Wheaton: Victor Books, 1986.

Scott, Brad. *Embraced by the Darkness: Exposing New Age Theology from the Inside Out.* Wheaton: Crossway, 1996.

Shahak, Israel. *Jewish History, Jewish Religion: The Weight of Three Thousand Years.* London: Pluto Press, 1994.

Sjoo, M. S. and B. Mor. *The Ancient Religion of the Great Cosmic Mother of All.* United Kingdom: Rainbow Press, 1981.

Smith, David L. *A Handbook of Contemporary Theology: Tracing Trends and Discerning Directions in Today's Theological Landscape.* Wheaton: BridgePoint, 1992.

Starhawk, Miriam. *The Spiritual Dance.* San Francisco: Harper, 1979.

Steichen, Donna. *Ungodly Rage.* San Francisco: Ignatius Press, 1993.

Studies in the Scriptures. Brooklyn: Watchtower Bible and Tract Society, 1917.

Sugrue, Thomas. *There Is a River.* New York: Holt, Rinehart & Winston, 1942.

The Kingdom Is at Hand. Brooklyn: Watchtower Bible and Tract Society, 1944.

Things in Which It Is Impossible for God to Lie. Brooklyn: Watchtower Bible and Tract Society, 1965.

Tucker, Ruth. *Another Gospel: Alternative Religions and the New Age Movement.* Grand Rapids: Zondervan, 1989.

Veith, Gene Edward Jr. *Postmodern Times: A Christian Guide to Contemporary Thought and Culture.* Wheaton: Crossways Books, 1994.

Warfield, B. B. *The Inspiration and Authority of the Bible.* Phillipsburg, N.J: Presbyterian and Reformed, 1948.

Webb, James. *The Occult Establishment.* La Salle: Open Court, 1976.

Wilkins, Michael J. and J. P. Moreland, eds. *Jesus Under Fire.* Grand Rapids: Zondervan, 1995.

Wilson, Nancy. *A Lesbian Ecu-Terrorist Outs the Bible for the Queer Millennium.* San Francisco: Harper SanFrancisco, 1996.

Woychuk, N. A. *The Infallible Word.* St. Louis: Miracle Press, 1970.

You Can Live Forever in Paradise on Earth. Brooklyn: Watchtower Bible and Tract Society, 1982.

SPIRITUAL COUNTERFEITS PROJECT

Tal Brooke is president of Spiritual Counterfeits Project (SCP), a nationwide ministry. SCP's core staff is from top-ranked universities and have each traveled various spiritual paths before becoming Christians.

SCP's major publications is the *SCP Journal*, which has won three firstplace EPA awards. This in-depth publication explores the latest deceptive spiritual trends such as near-death experiences, deep ecology, UFOs, and the Jesus Seminar, and exposes their inside workings from a biblical perspective. SCP also publishes the *SCP Newsletter* four times a year with the latest news and developments on the spiritual frontlines.

The SCP Journal and *SCP Newsletter* are sent to those who contribute at least $25 annually ($35 outside the USA). The newsletter is available separately for a $10 annual donation (to offset publication, printing, and postage costs).

SCP, Inc.
Box 4308, Berkely, CA 94704
Business Office: (510) 540-0300
ACCESS Line: (510) 540-5767
Web Site: http://www. scp-inc.org

Enclosed is a gift of $25 or more—please send me the *SCP Journal* and *SCP Newsletter.*

Name _____

Phone _____

Address _____

City _____ State____ Zip_____

Other Good
Harvest House Reading

VIRTUAL GODS
by *Tal Brooke*

Computer experts explore the promises and threats of our growing dependence on global cyberspace. Topics include: the dangers of basing truth on personal experiences, the death of reasoning and the rise of data collecting, and the benefits and costs of instant communication.

OCCULT INVASION
by *Dave Hunt*

Occult influences march freely into America today, infiltrating schools, organizations, homes, and even some churches. Their rapid spread is successful because many of them don't seem dangerous. Often they appear innocent, sound reasonable, and seem to genuinely help people.

DARWIN'S LEAP OF FAITH
by *Ankerberg/Weldon*

In the face of magnificent mountains and oceans, an amazing abundance of plants and animals, and the spirit of mankind, which takes a bigger leap—believing in a creator or believing that the building blocks for life just happened to combine? As discoveries are made about our universe, some evolutionists now admit that much of the new evidence favors creation.

DECODING THE BIBLE CODE
by *Weldon/Wilson/Wilson*

The authors of the blockbuster book *The Bible Code* claim that God inserted hidden prophetic messages within the original Hebrew letters of the Old Testament. The authors show how simple it is to manipulate words to create almost any message, and how the core themes presented in *The Bible Code* are consistent with the teachings of most cults.

Dear Reader,

We would appreciate hearing from you regarding this Harvest House non-fiction book. It will enable us to continue to give you the best in Christian publishing.

1. What most influenced you to purchase *The Conspiracy to Silence The Son of God.*
   - ❑ Author
   - ❑ Subject matter
   - ❑ Backcover copy
   - ❑ Recommendations
   - ❑ Cover/Title
   - ❑ Other_____

2. Where did you purchase this book?
   - ❑ Christian bookstore
   - ❑ General bookstore
   - ❑ Department store
   - ❑ Grocery store
   - ❑ Other_____

3. Your overall rating of this book?
   - ❑ Excellent ❑ Very good ❑ Good ❑ Fair ❑ Poor

4. How likely would you be to purchase other books by this author?
   - ❑ Very likely ❑ Not very likely ❑ Somewhat likely ❑ Not at all

5. What types of books most interest you? (Check all that apply.)
   - ❑ Women's Books
   - ❑ Marriage Books
   - ❑ Current Issues
   - ❑ Christian Living
   - ❑ Bible Studies
   - ❑ Fiction
   - ❑ Biographies
   - ❑ Children's Books
   - ❑ Youth Books
   - ❑ Other_____

6. Please check the box next to your age group.
   - ❑ Under 18 ❑ 18-24 ❑ 25-34 ❑ 35-44 ❑ 45-54 ❑ 55 and over

Mail to: Editorial Director
Harvest House Publishers
1075 Arrowsmith
Eugene, OR 97402

Name_____

Address _____

State _____ Zip _____

Thank you for helping us to help you in future publications!